UNDER FIRE

UNDER FIRE

THE UNTOLD STORY
OF THE ATTACK IN
BENGHAZI

FRED BURTON
AND
SAMUEL M. KATZ

ST. MARTIN'S PRESS ≈ NEW YORK

www.stmartins.com

Design by Steven Seighman

The Library of Congress Cataloging-in-Publication Data is available upon request.

ISBN 978-1-250-04110-4 (hardcover)
ISBN 978-1-4668-3725-6 (e-book)

St. Martin's Press books may be purchased for educational, business, or promotional use. For information on bulk purchases, please contact Macmillan Corporate and Premium Sales Department at 1-800-221-7945, extension 5442, or write specialmarkets@macmillan.com.

First Edition: September 2013

10 9 8 7 6 5 4 3 2 1

To the four Americans killed by terrorists in Benghazi, Libya

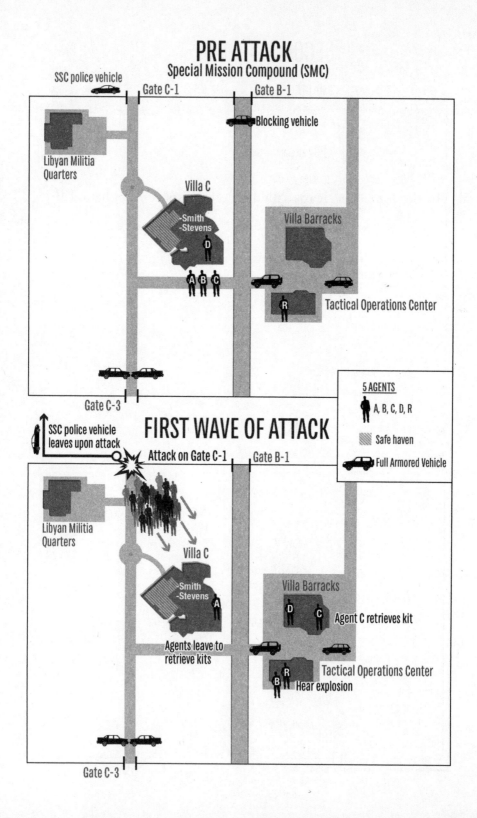

PRE ATTACK
Special Mission Compound (SMC)

SSC police vehicle

Gate C-1

Gate B-1

Blocking vehicle

Libyan Militia Quarters

Villa C

-Smith
-Stevens

D

A B C

Villa Barracks

R

Tactical Operations Center

Gate C-3

FIRST WAVE OF ATTACK

SSC police vehicle leaves upon attack

Attack on Gate C-1

Gate B-1

Libyan Militia Quarters

Villa C

-Smith
-Stevens

A

Agents leave to retrieve kits

Villa Barracks

D   C

Agent C retrieves kit

Tactical Operations Center

B   R

Hear explosion

Gate C-3

5 AGENTS
A, B, C, D, R

Safe haven

Full Armored Vehicle

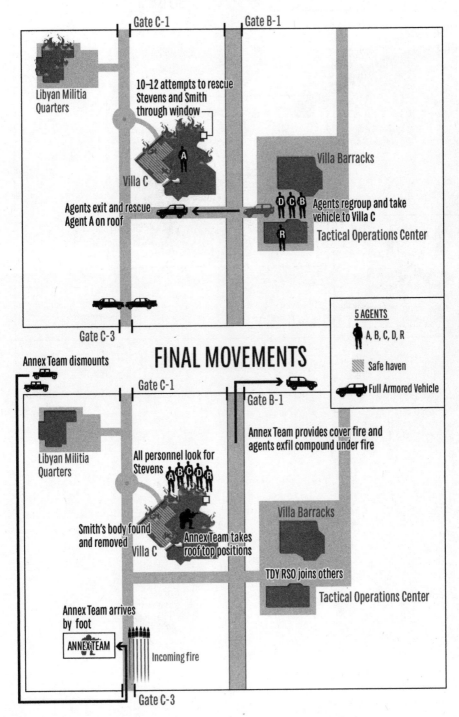

ANNEX ATTACK

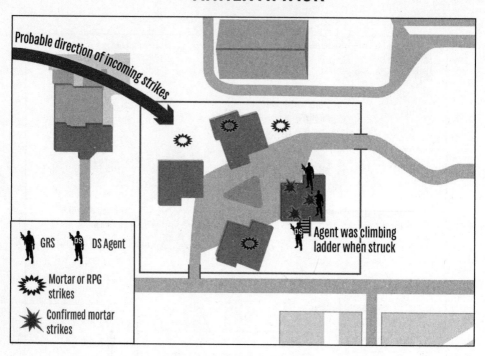

Probable direction of incoming strikes

Agent was climbing ladder when struck

GRS

DS Agent

Mortar or RPG strikes

Confirmed mortar strikes

CONTENTS

FROM THE DIRECTOR'S DESK

To the Diplomatic Security Service special agents who read this book: the courageous efforts of our brethren on 9/11 in Benghazi have in large part gone unheralded and unknown to the public. This has been the case for countless heroic acts by DSS and SY agents throughout our history. Regardless, I know you will remain as dedicated and selfless as always. Please be reassured that there are many of us, your colleagues past and present, who recognize and applaud your continuing sacrifices.

—Greg Bujac, former director, Diplomatic Security Service, and special agent

Long before the attack the Benghazi victims knew their lives were at risk, yet they never wavered from their commitment to advancing the cause of liberty in a land overrun with extremist elements. Even when they were outnumbered, outgunned, and under attack, they stood strong and defended our mission. Their sacrifice must not go unrecognized.

—Congressman Michael T. McCaul (R-Texas),
chairman of the House Committee on Homeland Security

Do what you can, with what you have, where you are.

—Theodore Roosevelt

AUTHORS' NOTE

The names, personal history, and backgrounds of the Diplomatic Security Service special agents who were in Benghazi on the night of September 11, 2012, are being concealed to protect them and their families from terrorist reprisals. As we have come to learn, some of the agents involved in the September 11, 2012, attack have already returned to duty in dangerous places overseas. Their involvement in such a high-profile incident can threaten their personal security while serving; it could threaten their wives and their children as well. One agent, severely injured in the Benghazi attack, has been publicly identified, but we don't intend to print his name for privacy purposes.

The special agents who were in Benghazi that fateful night were very young: all of them had less than ten years on the job, with most of them having been on the job less than five. Their careers will be forever marked by the terrorist attack that night in Libya, just as those special agents who came before them had their careers defined by the violent terrorist attacks they survived in places like Saigon, Beirut, Islamabad, Nairobi, Dar es Salaam, Baghdad, Kabul, Karachi, Jeddah, Damascus, and Cairo. The world for a Diplomatic Security Service special agent is one marked by landmarks of terror and scar tissue. But of all the posts that these brave men and women travel to in order for American diplomats to be safeguarded and American interests secured, Washington, D.C., can ultimately be the cruelest and most vindictive place on the planet to live and work.

Benghazi will haunt the five forever. Their names will come up behind closed doors in onward assignments, whispered in the hallways as they walk by, and their actions will be game-boarded and second-guessed forever. *Any* hint of blame is, of course, unfounded, but second-guessing is an element of the job and something all five will mull over for the rest of their lives, just like the Secret Service agents at Dealey Plaza in Dallas who also lost a protectee. One agent we know was in Beirut when the embassy was blown up by Hezbollah. His career was marked by that event—an event that was clearly out of his control. Street agents would shake his hand, but the armchair generals along the Potomac would shake their heads. Things are always simpler from behind a desk. It would be unfair on our part to cause any more personal self-doubting and anguish to those who have already endured enough.

As a former agent of the service and an author who has covered the Diplomatic Security Service since 1995, we understand that the world that these five must now live and work in is a dangerous place—inside the Beltway as well as the far reaches of the globe. The murders of Ambassador Chris Stevens and IMO Sean Smith were not the fault of the five Diplomatic Security Service agents in Benghazi that violence-filled night. They did everything humanly possible, and repeatedly risked themselves, to save the lives of the men they protected. They encountered a tide of absolute and overwhelming violence in a location void of law and order. These men, unequivocally, are heroes.

If the five agents want to publicly identify themselves, it will be their decision. The five agents, without question, exemplify valor and selfless dedication. These five men personify the all-too-often-untold story of the Diplomatic Security Service and its courageous and often unheralded contribution to safeguarding this nation and its interests around the world.

This is the story of these very special agents—men and women thrown into the fires of expeditionary diplomacy in a world that is turbulent and forever dangerous—as illustrated by one night of hell, inside the crosshairs, in the city of Benghazi.

CLARIFICATIONS

The Bureau of Diplomatic Security, sometimes known by the acronym DS, oversees all security-related matters for the U.S. Department of State, including but not restricted to security at embassies and consulates. Other responsibilities include dignitary protection of the secretary of state; dignitary protection for visiting non-head-of-state VIPs to the United States (ranging from foreign ministers to members of international royalty); international antiterrorism assistance training; protective intelligence and counterterrorism investigations, threats analysis; the Rewards for Justice program; and the criminal investigation of passport and visa fraud. The Diplomatic Security Service, sometimes referred to by the acronym DSS, is the law enforcement and security arm of the U.S. Department of State's Bureau of Diplomatic Security. Although DS and DSS are separate entities, they are often confused with each other.

In order to clarify matters, the authors have chosen to refer to the men and women who serve in the Diplomatic Security Service simply as DS agents. "DS" is the common term used for the service, and at a working level—domestically and internationally—the term "DS agents" is used throughout bureau materials and mailings.

Additionally, because of the sensitive nature of the events described, the dialogue, radio transmissions, and identifying details have been re-created to protect the DS agents, the CIA staff, and contract personnel attacked by terrorists in Benghazi, Libya, on the night of September 11–12, 2012. The authors have reconstructed the sequence of events at the Benghazi Special Mission Compound and Annex, based upon our subject matter expertise, countless interviews, discussions, analysis, and independent research of publicly available open source materials. As part of the final review process, a sincere and good faith effort has been made, to "black-out" and/or omit materials for operational security reasons. The analysis, views, opinions expressed in the narrative are solely those of the authors and not of any official government agency or department.

UNDER FIRE

PROLOGUE

The Oncoming Storm

Libya was the place where you needed to worry about the young men who ogled a woman in the street, and you had to worry about those who didn't!

—Dan Meehan, U.S. Diplomatic Security Service
special agent stationed to Libya[1]

The wine should have flowed freely at lunch, but this was Benghazi after all. A bottle of red or white was supposed to have been one of the trappings of civility handed to a city that had been colonized by Mussolini, but post-Qaddafi Libya would have none of the alcoholic pleasures of the West. There was very little law and order in the new Libya, bullets were still flying all over the country, and indeed much of the Arab world, but a glass of wine was forbidden by the clerics—pure and unadulterated *haram*—even though it would have been splendid with the meal.

The Venezia Café was one of the ritziest eateries in the western suburbs of Benghazi—a relic of those bygone days when a Qaddafi-crony elite class had disposable cash and an insatiable appetite. Establishments like the Venezia never disappeared in the smoldering debris of a revolution; they thrived. Once the smoke cleared, Venezia's tables, where despots—or their cousins—once sat and intimidated the Egyptian and Sudanese waitstaff, were cleared and set up with china and polished silverware for Benghazi's new movers and shakers. Diplomats, spies, businessmen, gunrunners, and oil industry magnates all competed for the best table. The Venezia was also a favorite of militia commanders, especially business-minded lieutenants who could combine the zealous passion of faith with the hard green cash of selling weapons, drugs, or women.

Located behind the sprawling estate of the unofficial U.S. diplomatic compound, the Venezia was blessed with a most convenient location. Most of the restaurant was nestled inside a plush green garden, with an impressive display of local cacti and flora. The Venezia provided pure serenity, and as a result it served as a safe haven—a no-man's-land—for all sides who had a stake or hand in determining Libya's future. Many considered it a Switzerland of sorts—completely neutral. Politics were left at the door, though the bodyguards never relinquished their sidearms. This was Libya after all.

The Venezia was, for Sir Dominic Asquith anyway, one of those cherished human reminders of what a world without the need for bodyguards was like, even though he was required to travel in a fully armored and fully armed cocoon of security. Her Majesty's special representative to the newly transitional democratic Libya, Asquith was a veteran Arab hand at the Foreign Office who, despite service in such pressure-cooker posts as Syria, Oman, Saudi Arabia, Egypt, Iraq, and now Libya, sported a youthful appearance that never betrayed his fifty-five years. As the great-grandson of a British prime minister, the ambassador was of noble stock and was considered a most capable diplomat who understood the complexities and realities of the Arab world and still reveled in its charm and wonder despite its bullet-strewn landscape. And Benghazi was indeed bullet strewn. The bodies were still being counted and scores still being settled as the port city recovered from the revolution that ended the forty-two-year reign of Colonel Muammar Qaddafi, but on this June noon, with an ever-so-wonderful ocean breeze bouncing off the palm trees nearby, the madness of the city and the sometimes drowning paperwork of top secret cables and e-mails made way for a meal outside the bunker of the British consulate. There were always eateries, even in war zones, that were known as safe havens. These restaurants were immaculately maintained bastions of fine food, generous bars, and discreet waitstaffs; they were neutral hangouts in locations where spies, soldiers, and those ever-present men in dark suits who played for both sides of any conflict felt at home. These establishments made sure that a favorite meal was always purely heartwarming and that there were always enough Cuban cigars at the ready.

The Italian restaurant was only a short ride from the ad hoc British consulate, located in the affluent Western Fwayhat neighborhood. The section of the city was a vast expanse of villas and estates, warehouses and buildings abandoned by war. Towering palm trees, as well as some slightly smaller, spread generous shade to the wide avenues and the gravel-strewn side streets. The neighborhood served as Benghazi's diplomatic enclave, home to missions and consulates, ambassadorial residences, and the city's much-envied International School. The food, the sun, and the sea breeze made it possible, even if for a brief moment, to forget that this luxurious oasis was inside the semi-lawless grasp of the Benghazi landscape, inside the epicenter of the Arab Spring and a just-relocated battlefield in the Global War on Terror. Ambassadors could dream, of course; close protection agents were paid to worry. Ambassador Asquith was always shadowed by a team of heavily armed security agents working for Her Majesty's Foreign and Commonwealth Office; the United Kingdom did not field a specialized security arm within its law enforcement and intelligence services and, as a result, relied on special operations units, or companies fielding retired special operations unit personnel. The contracting firm responsible for protecting British interests in Libya was GardaWorld.[2] GardaWorld, a global risk management and security services company, is the international division of Garda World Security Corporation, the largest privately owned security company in the world. Much of its corporate leadership was former British Special Forces; a member of its international advisory board was the retired U.S. Navy admiral Eric T. Olson, former head of U.S. Special Operations Command, who had been awarded a Silver Star for valor in the Battle of Mogadishu, Somalia, and who had played a critical role in planning the 2011 DevGru raid in Abbottabad, Pakistan, targeting Osama bin Laden.

Some members of Sir Dominic Asquith's security detail were undoubtedly veterans of 22 Special Air Service, or SAS, Great Britain's legendary commandos, whose motto is "Who Dares Wins." Others were members of the Royal Marines Special Boat Service, or SBS; a few were even experienced bobbies with a history of firearms use in units such as SO1, the London Metropolitan Police's Dignitary Protection Squad; SO6, the Diplomatic Protection Group; SO14, the Royal Family Protective Unit; and SCO19, the Specialist Firearms Command. Anyone accepted for such hazardous duty was considered top tier. All were veterans of Britain's terrorist wars—either overseas or at home, in London and beyond. The old-timers who had served in Northern Ireland, as well as those who had served in Iraq and Afghanistan, especially those from the SAS, never left home without their Browning Hi Power 9 mm automatic—the regiment's favorite and most reliable sidearm.

Ambassador Asquith's security detail moved out of the restaurant, some walking in front of and others walking behind the diplomat, toward the awaiting vehicles; the driver from each vehicle in the ambassador's package remained behind at the wheel in order to prevent any malicious elements from sabotaging the armored SUVs or in case the detail had to escape with no time to spare. When the ambassador finished his meal, the vehicles were summoned and pulled up in front of the main entrance.

The warm and soothing June sun had already baked everyone's face a shiny glow of reddish brown. With the sun and coastal breeze and the palms swaying ever so gently as they spread shade along the boulevard, Benghazi could have been a Club Med. It was even plausible, if just for a second, to forget that only five days earlier Abu Yahya al-Libi, the Libyan-born deputy commander of al-Qaeda, had been blown to bits by a CIA drone strike in Mir Ali, a rugged patch of hell in the northern part of Waziristan, Pakistan.

Ambassador Asquith could never enjoy the breeze of driving in a Benghazi June, because he rode in an armored SUV whose bullet-resistant windows were closed at all times. There were several cars to his motorcade—a lead, a follow, the principal's vehicle, and that of the armed specialists who escorted the ambassador everywhere. Traffic was frenetic that beautiful afternoon, Sunday, June 10, but maneuvering through any Arab city was always an exercise of honk, brake, curse, brake, honk. Protection specialists were always taught to never become a statistic in traffic, and Ambassador Asquith's motorcade swerved in and out of lanes as it moved along its short path toward the consulate. Two months earlier, on April 2, a U.K. consulate car found itself in between three warring militias—one of which was the local traffic police—and barely managed to escape from the melee. The warring militias weren't thugs or gangster groups, however; well, not officially at least. They were actually uniformed members of the local law enforcement community—the men sworn to protect and serve rather than rape and pillage—who were flexing their muscles and settling some scores.

The two assailants, masked persons unknown behind their camouflage fatigues and dishdashas, were waiting behind the neatly manicured trees and brush. The attack site was chosen very carefully. The terrorists had conducted advance surveillance of the area in order to pinpoint a specific choke point, known as the "X", where the motorcade would be at its most vulnerable and where the escape avenues would be easiest to access and they could disappear into the Benghazi landscape. Surveillance would have been intense, as the terrorists would have needed to know the travel patterns of the motorcade, as well as nearby traffic patterns; there could have been several RPG teams pre-positioned throughout the area, all connected by disposable mobile phones. The terrorists picked the X based on an extensive review of predictable patterns and, possibly, with the assistance of someone on their payroll who knew details of the ambassador's movements that day.

Reconnoitering the X was basic terrorist tradecraft. Their surveillance efforts illustrated that the assassination team was well trained and tactically proficient. And they also illustrated an inherent chink in the armored ring protecting the British ambassador. It is doubtful that Ambassador Asquith's security detail was large enough to field a countersurveillance force; without security controlling the geography, bad things could always happen.

The security detail could not have known that the assailants had taken weeks to reconnoiter the area in preparation for the attack, and they didn't know if an SMS from a member of the restaurant's kitchen staff had alerted them to the ambassador's departure back to the office. The details didn't matter the moment Ambassador Asquith's convoy crossed the parallel and horizontal lines of the RPG-7's optical sight and the cone-shaped antitank rocket was launched from the ubiquitous Soviet-era weapon. The RPG-7 was the perfect weapon system for en masse deployment. It was the perfect armor-punching tool for third-world revolutions and terrorists—cheap, easily produced, and designed for fighters who didn't have the time or the cerebral hard drive for in-depth training. The weapon was usually deployed by a two-man team. One operator inserts the projectile grenade into the tubelike launcher, and the second man takes aim and fires. The sound of an RPG being fired is unmistakable: a heavy whistling sound followed by the eardrum-pounding impact of a fiery thud.

The British security specialists did not see the two-man firing crew emerge from behind cover to take their shot. They did, however, hear a thud and then a swoosh and then saw a fireball when the penetrating punch of the warhead fell short of the target and erupted in a concussive wave of fire and shrapnel.

Traffic came to a complete standstill when the RPG was fired. Even the Benghazi natives who were so used to the sounds and sights of war were frozen by the sudden burst of bloodshed; instead of honking their horns and cursing out the window, they stared openmouthed in horror. A small cloud of black smoke began to cover the area. The warm summer sun disappeared into the spreading darkness.

The RPG-7 warhead fell short of the ambassador's vehicle yet still dangerously close. The bullet-resistant glass held up well, but when the cone-shaped high-explosive antitank projectile—capable of punching through nearly a foot of armored steel—detonated, chunks of the vehicle's armor protection splintered inside. Two protection specialists were seriously hurt by fragmentation when the blast and rocket punched out the windshield of the lead vehicle; their blood splattered throughout the vehicle's interior and then onto the street.

One of the specialists called for help on the police radio mounted below the SUV's dashboard, though his left hand was covered in blood and the pain was severe. The specialist found it hard to depress the talk button to transmit word that they had been attacked. The British agents, as per procedures rehearsed a thousand times in training, rushed Ambassador Asquith out of the targeted vehicle and into the follow car, which sped, against the flow of traffic in the other lanes, back to the consulate. A trusted local doctor would look at him and then let him know if he was medically sound enough to return to top secret cables and e-mails detailing the harrowing account of his close brush with death.

The security specialists had hoped to engage the attackers with their Glock 19 9mm semiautomatic pistols, drawn from holsters hidden inside their safari jackets, but the terrorists were not interested in a fight. The attackers, as many as five, according to eyewitnesses, fled into the invisible scenery of walls and brush.

A special operations team from the U.S. mission arrived on the scene first. The operators, looking every bit the part with their long hair and ratty beards, used their armored SUVs to create a perimeter, while the team's medic attended to the injured British agents. The Benghazi preventive security forces arrived a good wait later.[3] The Libyans knew little about crime scenes and wandered curiously across the pavement littered with debris and shiny glass spall. Transmission fluid and antifreeze flowed slowly out of one of the SUVs and mixed with the blood from the two specialists injured in the attack. Uniformed police officers scanned the destruction and used their AK-47s to wave off a throng of curious onlookers that was growing every minute; the policemen seemed angry that the terrorist attack required them to stand outside and keep the crowds at bay, rather than sit inside their American-supplied orange-and-white spanking-new— and always air-conditioned—Toyota Land Cruisers. The patrolmen trod carefully over the debris, though they crunched the specks of glass under the weight of their shiny black boots.

But an attack on an ambassador was not something that police commanders could treat nonchalantly, and the officers knew that the news cameras would be by shortly. Clearly there would be a live feed breaking the regularly scheduled broadcasts on the BBC and Sky News. Al Jazeera, the Doha-based regional super channel and network that was amenable to airing terrorist tapes, loved assassination attempts. Diplomats being killed were great for ratings.

The patrolmen read the pamphlets left behind around the scene, pamphlets from the Brigades of Sheikh Omar Abdel Rahman, with feigned curiosity. A greater concern was evident on the faces of the detectives and police commanders who left their safe havens in town and responded to the crime scene once they received word of the attack over their iPhones and Nokia smartphone devices. Senior commanders from the CID, the elite investigative branch of the Public Security Directorate, took deep drags on their Atlas cigarettes and sighed with a foreboding sense of dread. They were, of course, pleased—relieved!—that Ambassador Asquith had not been seriously hurt. Images of a dead Western ambassador would have been very bad for Libya's image had they gone viral on the Web, but they shuddered as to what was happening in the city. An attack, this brazen an attack, by jihadists fighting in the name of the Egyptian-born blind sheikh who was incarcerated in the United States, was not a promising sign for the new Libya.

Operationally, the terrorist attempt to assassinate the British ambassador that afternoon in Benghazi ended in failure. Strategically, the attack achieved its desired objectives. The British abandoned Benghazi days later.

It was summer in the Arab Spring. From North Africa's Atlantic coast to the oil-flush sands of Bahrain, the old world order was crumbling under the unstoppable force of democracy, Islam, iPhones, and Facebook. Some of the old guard evaporated into exile or prison with a muted bang. Tunisia's Zine El Abidine Ben Ali and Egypt's Hosni Mubarak, old-guard dinosaurs who had used an iron fist to enforce uncontested power and Just for Men to retain the eternal facade of youth, had been removed from power without the usual mass carnage of Middle Eastern foreplay. But nothing was ever easy in the Middle East. In Bahrain, where a Shiite version of the populist Arab Spring attempted to reroute the power of the emir, the calls for democracy ended with a brutal crackdown and scores of broken bones. And then, of course, there was Syria. Syria was the linchpin of Middle East madness where Sunnis and Shiites, Russians and Americans, Turks, Saudis, Qataris, and Iranians were all gambling with enormous stakes over who would own the winning hand in the struggle. By the summer of 2012 some thirty thousand combatants—men, women, and children—had been killed in the hell of the crumbling regime in Bashar al-Assad's Syria; the Lion Cub of Damascus was determined not to repeat the fate of Colonel Qaddafi and bow out pathetically in a suicidal escape rather than a Saladin-like last stand inside the Syrian capital.

The Arab Spring spark that lit the fuse to the Libyan civil war was rooted in the economics of Qaddafi's corrupt rule and not in the flames of militant Islam. Inspired by the popular uprisings in Tunisia and Egypt, housing riots erupted in Benghazi in January 2011; the rage soon spilled to other cities—primarily in eastern Libya. The rioting and repression that followed spread throughout the country. By the end of February, the protests had turned violent, and an armed opposition was challenging Qaddafi's forty-two years of rule. The country was in full-blown civil war.

Benghazi, the birthplace of the Libyan revolution, was the city where NATO—and the United States—drew their line in the sand. With a UN Security Council resolution providing the international mandate, U.S. aircraft launched a series of devastating air strikes against loyalist armored forces ordered to raze Benghazi to the ground. Qaddafi had labeled Benghazi's residents as "rats," and the U.S. air raids that eradicated Libyan air defenses and armor capabilities saved the city from certain destruction—the same kind of destruction that ultimately befell Homs and Aleppo during the Syrian civil war.

The NATO intervention—one of a small and deniable Special Forces and precision air strikes—decapitated the loyalists' command-and-control capabilities, as well as their control of the skies and roadways. Abandoned by defections and regional isolation, Qaddafi's forces waged a cruel campaign against the Libyan rebels and Libya's citizens. The mad colonel, interestingly enough, was prophetic in blaming al-Qaeda and bin Laden loyalists for the challenge to his rule, though his rambling seemed to inspire fundamentalist forces to play a role in the fighting. Unable to trust his own forces, Qaddafi hired mercenaries—inexpensive ones from Mali, Niger, and Ghana, as well as more costly dogs of war from the former Yugoslavia—whose thirst for cold-blooded killing was chilling.[4] But when the United Nations endorsed NATO military involvement, Operation Unified Protector, Qaddafi's fate was sealed. The bloody internecine fighting lasted another six months and resulted in the deaths of some thirty thousand Libyan civilians. Qaddafi's fate was an ugly one. Found hiding in a desert ditch, he was manhandled, sodomized, and then executed.

Democracy had come to Libya, though—as seen in the petri dishes of Iraq, Tunisia, and Egypt—the electorate's wishes often conflicted with Western hopes. The National Transitional Council, or NTC, the provisional government in Tripoli, officially declared Libya liberated on October 23, 2011. Freeing Libya from chaos would be another story.

The evaporation of the police state enabled an insidious reality to enter Libya. Weapons and MANPADs (man-portable air-defense systems) were everywhere. There were, of course, scores to be settled with the business end of the AK-47 and profits to be made trafficking in everything from cigarettes to narcotics. Criminal gangs flourished in the lawless chaos; the weapons, tools of conventional combat, fetched a high price in the arms bazaars of Mali, Niger, and Chad. Islamic gangs, also known on the street as militias, that had fought in the civil war now staked their claim on precincts of property. Like Beirut during the civil war and any other godforsaken war zone on the continent, checkpoints were everywhere. The situation was frighteningly evident to visiting members of the UN Support Mission in Libya. In an interview, Ian Martin, the secretary-general's special representative to Libya, stated, "The transition from the revolutionary brigades that were there at the end of the conflict, to state security forces having a monopoly on force, a national army and a proper police force—that can't be created overnight. The majority of the revolutionaries don't want to be in the security sector, they want civilian occupations—that's a big challenge. Libya has enormous borders—particularly its southern border is open to the trafficking of people, weapons, and drugs. Getting a grip on that is a huge challenge."[5]

The challenge, in fact, was insurmountable. And Benghazi was an ideal junction for the confluence of violence. Benghazi had been conquered by the Greeks, the Carthaginians, the Romans, the Ottomans, and the Italians and bombed heavily during World War II by both the Axis and the Allies, reducing its Mediterranean-style avenues and Italian-inspired architecture to rubble. The city was once again ravaged by Qaddafi loyalist forces during the bitter fighting of the Libyan revolution. In teeming Benghazi, a city of some one million inhabitants, grief, violence, and opportunity came together as one. It had always been a magnet for Africans, Berbers, and North African Arabs seeking work and safe havens for their varied and sometimes covert causes. With Qaddafi dead, arms smugglers from the Palestinian Authority, Bedouin narcotics traffickers from the Sinai, and Malian militants had flooded into its lawless confines. Libya, a global destabilizing force under Qaddafi, remained a source of regional mayhem.

Fundamentalist Islam was never a strong current in Benghazi, but the vacuum of authority allowed it to gain strength quickly in the shadows. The city's beach-and-bikini culture always seemed to be an antidote to medieval attempts to throw back the clock. But al-Qaeda in the Maghreb, a terrorist franchise that had escaped the wrath of the U.S. drone war in Pakistan and Yemen, was by mid-2012 still malignant and well entrenched, with new influence in all the countries impacted by the Arab Spring.

It should have then come as no surprise that the black flags of the al-Qaeda and fundamentalist movements would become so prominent in Benghazi. Qaddafi had been a secular dictator who jetted to the capitals of the Middle East with a harem of beautiful female bodyguards adorned in tight-fitting and cleavage-revealing fatigues. Qaddafi was the champion of left-wing and nationalist terrorist movements, but he was a fierce opponent of the Islamic fundamentalists. Qaddafi's secret police and intelligence services had used the iron hand of cruelty in dealing with the Muslim Brotherhood and other underground Islamic groups; bin Laden would not have found a safe haven inside Qaddafi's Libya. And once Qaddafi was dead, the fundamentalists embraced their newfound freedoms with religious zeal. Foreigners, especially Christians, were behind Libya's tragic years, preached clerics who emerged from the shadows to men who had previously avoided the mosques for years. "Libya was a weak nation, a lost nation," an Islamic militia member boasted in Benghazi to an amateur cameraman covering a fundamentalist demonstration that would be posted online, "because it had abandoned God's ways."

The telltale signs of a nation, or city at least, fueled by an Islamic awakening became obvious after Qaddafi's death. Men who once sported jet-black mustaches and wore polyester shirts and Western slacks now sported galabiya gowns and *thobes*. They grew long beards and dyed them bright orange with henna; these men, young and old, cropped their mustaches the way the Prophet did. Plain black kufi hats became unmistakably prevalent throughout the markets and at checkpoints, where armed men in camouflage chic now enforced neighborhood Sharia law in full Islamic regalia.

The new Islamic push in the city was spiced with violent militancy. On June 7, 2012, four days before Ambassador Dominic Asquith's armored convoy was targeted by Salafists, Ansar al-Sharia and other Islamic militias staged a show of force with a parade and rally. Ansar al-Sharia, or Supporters of Sharia, was a Salafist-jihadist militia headquartered in Benghazi; it was led by Sufian Ben Qumu, alleged to be a former driver for Osama bin Laden and, ultimately, a Guantánamo Bay detainee who was returned to Libya in 2007. Other Islamic militias, known as *katibas*, or battalions, raised their flags and fired magazine-emptying bursts of AK-47s into the air that day. The militia names were all insidiously telltale of violent intentions and, according to Western intelligence sources, constituted the bulk of al-Qaeda's power in Libya.*

The jihadist show of muscle and firepower was held near Liberation Square, along the main coastal road. Where Libyan women in

---

*According to the Tripoli-based daily newspaper *Libya al-Youm*, fifteen militias were represented at the gathering, including the Free Libya Martyrs, the Abu Salim Martyrs, Faruq, al-Sahati, Revolutionaries of Sirte, Ansar al-Hurriya, Ummar al-Khattab, Agency for Preventive Security, and Shahid Mohammed al-Hamma.

miniskirts once flirted with eager suitors, now thousands of *men* raising their AK-47s in defiant gestures rode in a parade of sedans and Toyotas sporting huge black al-Qaeda-like flags. The hypnotic cadence of vehicles blaring their horns turned the sunny seafront into an earsplitting storm of sound. The firepower on display was daunting. Dozens of Toyota pickups, rigged with twin-mounted 23 mm antiaircraft cannons, moved slowly along the boulevard, rotating their long barrels around in a celebratory challenge. Some of the super-tactical vehicles sported emblems belonging to one militia or another.

According to video footage, several vehicles bearing the emblem of a militia known as the February 17 Brigade were seen as well.

Men in Saudi robes, and those with Yemeni-looking features, sported RPGs and PKM machine guns; thousands had gathered, but many of the armed men with long hair and longer beards were definitely not Libyan. Egyptians, Tunisians, Palestinians, and southern Africans had all come to Benghazi in search of a war. Some men, perhaps indicating previous service in the campaigns of Kandahar and Helmand Province, wore the woolen *pakol* hat ubiquitous in Afghanistan. Still, there were remnants of a secular Libya on parade—some of the militants wore Lionel Messi Barcelona soccer jerseys underneath their robes, displaying more secular passions—but Benghazi that foreboding morning was an armed Islamic camp.

Fathers dressed their children in black headbands imprinted with slogans yearning for martyrdom. Men in fatigues concealed their faces from the eyes of curious intelligence services that might have been in the crowd by wearing ominous black balaclavas. The black al-Qaeda flags of the jihad were everywhere.

An older policeman, standing next to his white patrol cruiser, watched helplessly as he smoked a cigarette and listened to a long line of men vowing death to the foreigners. He didn't even attempt to coordinate traffic. Law and order—sanity—had fled Benghazi. Four days later, Ambassador Asquith barely escaped a military-style attempt on his life.

On June 14, Libyan authorities had identified the assailants responsible for the attempt on Ambassador Asquith's life as Salafists from the *Jamarat Islamiya Al-Moutashedida*. The attack was only the beginning for this self-professed al-Qaeda-linked gang. That same day gunmen from *Jamarat Islamiya Al-Moutashedida* shot up a beauty salon in Benghazi, because women were receiving Western hairstyles. On June 18, a swarm of heavily armed Salafists stormed the Tunisian consulate in Benghazi to express outrage over a display in the Tunis suburb of La Marsa, where artists had presented a naked woman being eyed by fundamentalists and the word "Allah" spelled out by a line of ants.[6]

The growing jihadist base in Benghazi was sparking both interest and fear. The British left the city after the attempt on the ambassador's life. The International Committee of the Red Cross, the ICRC, suspended operations in Benghazi and Misrata on August 5, 2012, after a series of terror strikes on its offices in both cities; the first attack, on May 22, was perpetrated by the Sheikh Omar Abdel Rahman Brigade, Red Cross officials stated, "because the group claimed that the ICRC was distributing Bibles and trying to convert Libyans to Christianity."[7]

The fundamentalist militias were growing more brazen in their attacks and in their assault on the new Libyan security apparatus. The public security directorate headquarters in Benghazi, the epicenter of all counterterrorism efforts in the city, was attacked in a dedicated strike by Salafist gunmen. The Libyan Military Intelligence headquarters was blown up in the city. Senior police and government security commanders were assassinated; some were killed as they left their homes, while others were shot in the back of the head as they prayed in city mosques.

Libya had become an al-Qaeda-inspired, if not al-Qaeda-led, training base and battleground. One of the terrorists, a Saudi national who was killed in a large-scale jihadist raid in Sinai on June 18, 2012, that resulted in the deaths of twenty Egyptian policemen, had trained with al-Qaeda in Libya. On June 21 the Tunisian Air Force engaged and destroyed three suspected al-Qaeda vehicles believed to be transferring arms from Libya to Algeria. Al-Qaeda had obtained advanced weapons—including MANPADs, antitank rockets, and heavy cannons—that the militias had pilfered from Qaddafi's military; more weapons and ammunition, some brand-new, had been supplied to all the anti-Qaddafi militias fighting for a new Libya by the intelligence services of the State of Qatar and the United Arab Emirates; these weapons were distributed generously, and with tacit U.S. approval; a good percentage of the hardware, though, ended up in jihadist hands.[8] Many of these advanced systems were finding their ways into the hands of Islamic extremists fighting in northern Mali.

Weapons, similar to those being used in the Syrian civil war, were being sold and traded openly. To the men of the intelligence agencies—Western and other—with an interest in toppling the Assad regime, Libya was a wholesale market for military surplus that the revolutionary fighters desperately needed, and Benghazi became a battlefield of those who were sellers, those who were buyers, and those determined to thwart both sides of the arms trade equation.

Wherever there were terrorists, there were bound to be spies, and Benghazi had become a den of spies. By the summer of 2012, those nations with the stomach to remain behind in Benghazi were represented by operatives, assets, and sources. Egyptians, Jordanians, Palestinians, possibly even the Israelis, all had an interest in what was transpiring inside the Benghazi arms bazaars, as did the secret police agencies of a dozen or so African states worried that the malignancy growing inside Libya would metastasize inside their own volatile countries. And, of course, wherever al-Qaeda ventured, especially an al-Qaeda thought to be in tatters and an al-Qaeda situating itself in a city with enough ordnance to start a large-scale African war, the Western and Arab intelligence agencies were never far behind. It would be safe to assume that there were spies loyal to several dozen nations wandering about Benghazi, meeting with sources and paying assets. Men in blazers and dark glasses wandered about the narrow streets of the medina, the old city, with briefcases full of cash and 9mm semiautomatics—the classic killing tool of the European spy. Rent-a-guns, militiamen with AK-47s and no qualms about killing, stood outside the cafés and restaurants where men with cash and those with missiles exchanged business terms. Benghazi was a cross between Chicago in the days of Prohibition and Sicily at the height of the Cosa Nostra's reign of crime and terror. The confluence of intelligence operatives, swindlers, and opportunists inside the Libyan city was akin to Humphrey Bogart's Casablanca.

Benghazi was a le Carré urban landscape where loyalties changed sides with every sunset; there were murders, betrayals, and triple-crossing profits to be made in the post-revolution reality. The police were only as honest as their next bribe. The floors of cafés in the notorious Assabri area near the old city were littered with disposable SIM cards that were destructively snapped in half—the telltale sign of a city populated by secrets and men with prices on their heads.

Most governments were eager to abandon the danger and intrigue of Benghazi. By September 2012 much of the international community had pulled chalks and escaped the inevitable cauldron of the city's violence. Other nations left Libya altogether. Even the Iranians, one of the world's most prominent state sponsors of global terror, who had seven members of its Red Crescent relief agency kidnapped in Benghazi by one of the government's primary militias, escaped the city.

Some countries remained. The Bulgarians, Egyptians, Moroccans, and Italians maintained consulates in the city. The European Union maintained a full-fledged consulate; the Germans staffed a small liaison office. The Turks and the Qataris stood fast, as well. Benghazi was very much a hub for their geopolitical interests and objectives.

Libya was a target-rich environment for American political, economic, and military interests, and the United States was determined to retain its diplomatic and intelligence presence in the country—including an embassy in Tripoli and a mission in Benghazi. Benghazi, rife with peril, was a linchpin of American concerns and opportunities in the summer following the Arab Spring. Tunisia had been swept by revolution, and so had Egypt. A Libya run by Qaddafi would have been a malignant growth inside the aspirations of both newly democratic nations. Qaddafi's time had come. "The United States was typically optimistic in its hope for Libya," an insider with boots on the ground commented, smiling. "The hope was that all would work out, even though the reality of an Islamic force in the strong revolutionary winds hinted otherwise."

Hope was fueling many fires. The United States no longer had the resources or the national will to commit massive military manpower to its outposts in the quagmire-strewn remnants of what was once defined as the new world order. This wasn't a political question but a boots-on-the-ground statement of reality. The fight against terrorism and Islamic fundamentalism, as well as the desire to quench the thirst of democracy in this part of the world, was a brand of warfare that would not be fought with brigades and Bradley armored fighting vehicles. This kinder and friendlier Global War on Terror would be fought by diplomats and spies and watched from above by drones and satellites. The footprint of the United States in this unsettled country and its ever-important but dangerous city would have to be small and agile.

Benghazi would be a test—one of many—for this new type of warfare on this new and untested battlefield. Washington knew of the dangers that existed in Benghazi; American diplomatic and intelligence representatives on the ground in Libya had sent precise reports detailing the threats in country. They had requested additional assets and protection to mitigate the uncertainty and violence that were rampant in the country.

Benghazi was considered too valuable a seismic sensor in the Middle East—and Arab Spring—for the United States to abandon, even though the security situation in the city was considered critical. The United States was staying put, even though the landscape was pure lawlessness.

"Benghazi was the kind of city," reflected a veteran Middle East war correspondent, "that once you left you never wanted to return to."[9] It was the city where American diplomats and the men sworn to protect them would wage the small-footprint, covert chess match of expeditionary diplomacy in the uncertain double-barreled fusillade of an angry Arab Spring.

Part One

THE DAWN BEFORE BENGHAZI

1.

The Libyan

*I proudly announce to the Muslim umma and to the mujahideen . . .
the news of the martyrdom of the lion of Libya Sheikh Hassan
Mohammed Qaed.*
> —al-Qaeda emir Ayman al-Zawahiri, in a videotape
> released on September 11, 2012, confirming the U.S.
> drone strike that killed the Libyan-born al-Qaeda deputy
> commander and commander of the Libyan Islamic Fighting
> Group, Abu Yahya al-Libi

The Hellfire missile arrived without warning and with little preamble.
They always did. At just after dawn's first glow on the morning of
June 4, 2012, in Pakistan's tribal Waziristan, a CIA Predator drone
hovering near its target at twenty thousand feet above the impassable
mountain terrain launched four AGM-114P Hellfire II antitank missiles at the turbid hovel where Abu Yahya al-Libi, the al-Qaeda deputy commander, and another fourteen low- and mid-level terrorists
were sleeping. The missiles, designed to punch a molten hole through
layers of armored steel, turned the mud-and-stone hut into a flaming
hole of destruction. The devastation was absolute. Even if the goat
farmers who had wandered toward the flaming ruins had years of

forensic training among them, scraping what was left of the terrorist leader and his minions off the mud and scorched earth would have required a deft touch. There was no doubt that the primary target had been terminated. The eighteen-pound shaped metal-augmented charge was a sure thing.[1]

Abu Yahya al-Libi was considered a CIA high-value target. There was a ghostlike mystique to him—especially after he had escaped from U.S. extrajudicial detention at Bagram Air Base in northeastern Afghanistan in July 2005, one of the most secured U.S.-run counter-terrorism facilities in the world; he was one of the U.S. Department of Defense's most wanted men. Although he was often videotaped in camouflage fatigues, firing his Russian-made AK-74 5.45 mm assault rifle as if he were a gangster with a tommy gun on Chicago's South Side, he was more a politician than a military field commander. Abu Yahya al-Libi was viewed as a visionary policy maker and, in his firebrand sermons, al-Qaeda's most capable salesman. When adorned in sparkling white robes that accentuated his dark eyes and North African features, he resembled a fierce warrior fighting his way across a desert battlefield. In an interview with *The New York Times*, Jarret Brachman, a former analyst for the CIA, claimed about al-Libi, "He's a warrior. He's a poet. He's a scholar. He's a pundit. He's a military commander. And he's a very charismatic, young, brash, rising star within A.Q., and I think he has become the heir apparent to Osama bin Laden in terms of taking over the entire global jihadist movement."[2]

The self-professed al-Qaeda global ambassador had been an in-strumental player in the spreading of the jihadist network to new venues and battlefields. He had achieved considerable success in his native North Africa in the Global War on Terror vacuum of the Arab Spring. In posting a $1 million reward for information leading to al-Libi's capture, the Web site of the U.S. State Department's Diplomatic Security Service Rewards for Justice Program claimed that "al-Libi was a key motivator in the global jihadist movement and his messages convey a clear threat to U.S. persons or property world-wide." When the CIA finally caught up with al-Libi, financially speaking the targeted killing was a frugal investment of taxpayer dollars: the four Hellfire missiles cost under $280,000.

There was always blowback when such a senior terrorist commander was targeted, and the question of retaliation wasn't as much an "if," as it was a "when" and a "where." Al-Libi's name, the translation meaning "the Libyan," should have provided intelligence specialists throughout the Beltway with some sort of inkling.

On the morning of September 11, 2012, the eleventh anniversary of the most destructive terrorist attack in history, the al-Qaeda commander Dr. Ayman al-Zawahiri formally confirmed the martyrdom of his Libyan-border deputy. The terrorist leader's footage was released early in the morning in Pakistan, just as Washington, D.C., was going to bed.

2.

The Global Protectors in a World at War

Midnight September 10–11, 2012, arrived with an exhausted dread at the Diplomatic Security Service Command Center, or DS/CC, on the ▊▊▊▊▊ floor in a nondescript building in the Virginia suburbs. As the agents in the evening tour packed up their gear and prepared to head out for the traffic-free drive back to their homes in northern Virginia, a few words were exchanged with the special agents coming in the late tour. For many years, the DS/CC was staffed 24/7 by ▊▊▊ agents. Now the day shift alone had grown to ▊▊▊ to meet the demands of an ever-changing, ever more violent world. The midnight shift was always a harsh one, as the garbage cans, filled to capacity with empty Starbucks coffee cups, would attest. Eyes were sometimes groggy, tempers short. Although the nation's capital was asleep, with the halls of power silent in a town never quite known for quiet, the world beyond was abuzz with activity. Midnight along the Beltway was midday in Jakarta and Kuala Lumpur; as CNN, Fox News, and MSNBC were winding down their nightly outgoing, exchanging distant views on the presidential election, a new workday was well under way in Kabul, Islamabad, and Doha. As American flags waved proudly in front of the White House and the Capitol under a dark autumn sky, they also flew stoically in front of the U.S. embassy in Cairo, Egypt.

The fluid and rapidly deteriorating situation in Libya was also monitored by the Diplomatic Security Service and State Department officials at the Operations Center, known as State Ops, located on the seventh floor inside Main State at Foggy Bottom. The center was purely antiseptic and looked like a thousand other government offices inside anonymous buildings that were either owned by or rented to the federal government. It was painted in a yellowish-taupe scheme and decorated with television monitors that covered major 24/7 news networks from around the world. A narrow rectangular digital clock spanned across a part of the room, pinpointing the times in capitals around the globe. Cubicles, with computer stations, provided special agents from the U.S. Department of State's Diplomatic Security Service and other Foreign Service professionals the means to react to any developing global crisis.

All over the world, and supported from Washington, D.C., the Diplomatic Security Service (DS) was at work protecting the 252 embassies and consulates. For the most part, even in a world at war, the command centers monitored day-to-day events without the need for a remarkable response. Certain days, however, always brought the staffers at these command centers to realize the importance and volatility of the world at large. The anniversary of the September 11 attacks was always one such day.

Ever since that horrific morning eleven years earlier, September 11 was a day of remembrance and foreboding for members of federal law enforcement. Agencies like the FBI geared up—with state and local law enforcement—to prevent an anniversary strike against the United States. Members of the intelligence community, the Department of Defense, and DS went on full alert to prevent terrorists hoping to seize on the anniversary to symbolically strike at U.S. interests overseas.

DS was not the most widely known of federal law enforcement agencies; few were familiar with its existence, and even fewer—including many in the State Department—understood what it did. It traces its roots to World War I, when the Office of Security for the

State Department was established in 1916 as a federal counterintelligence agency to deal with the activity of foreign espionage agents on American soil, but it soon expanded to become the security arm of the Department of State.

For many years, the Office of Security was known simply as SY. Agents began traveling overseas to safeguard embassies and coordinate their efforts with marine security contingents at diplomatic posts around the world. In Vietnam, SY faced enormous challenges as the beleaguered force of diplomatic security hunkered down inside a war zone. On January 30, 1968, the North Vietnamese launched the Tet Offensive, surprising the Americans and the People's Army of Vietnam with a massive multipronged invasion. The mission was to destroy the will of the South Vietnamese and American people, and diplomatic signals had hoodwinked the Americans into believing the North Vietnamese wanted peace. The Communists used the New Year's celebration as cover for action and mingled Vietcong (VC) operatives among the crowds. The size and scope of the Tet offensive was overwhelming. The city of Saigon was attacked along with thirty-six of the forty-four provincial capitals. Altogether, an estimated eighty-four thousand North Vietname Army (NVA) and VC guerrillas were used. In Saigon, the targets were the Presidential Palace, the Army of the Republic of Vietnam (ARVN) Joint Staff Command building, and the National Broadcasting Station, along with one more very special target.[1]

At 0245 hours, the U.S. embassy wall on Thong Nhat Boulevard was breached in an explosive charge by nineteen Vietcong commandos and sappers, dressed in civilian clothing. Ambassador Ellsworth Bunker was inside his residence at the time and secretly evacuated by SY agents and Marine Security guards (who worked under the command of SY agents); he was hidden in the SY regional security officer's house. Steve Bray, a U.S. Marine assigned to SY for protection duties on the ambassador, recalled the chaos of the night and the actions by SY to save the U.S. ambassador's life:

> *The VC placed a satchel charge against the exterior perimeter wall and blew a hole in it which they used to penetrate the Embassy compound. They killed the American MP's located on the inner perime-*

ter execution style. Intel sharing among U.S. Agencies was even worse than it is today. The VC Sapper Team went to the Deputy Ambassador's Residence by mistake. The Deputy Ambassador was Samuel D. Berger at that time. LBJ had called him (Berger) back to Texas for consultation and no one was at residence when the VC Sapper Team arrived at the wrong address. They had the wrong location but thought it was Ambassador Bunker's residence. SY Agent Bob Furey went through the hole blown in the Embassy perimeter wall by the VC with his Thompson submachine gun to help Leo Crampsey. Leo, Bob, along with a few MSGs on the Embassy grounds and some 716th BN MPs on the outer perimeter defended the Embassy, preventing the VC takeover of the Chancery. General Westmoreland did not send in supporting U.S. Military assistance until first light.* By that time, Leo, Bob and MSGs had secured the compound.²

Though this experience might have caused others to shy away from future missions, Bray went on to become an SY agent; that is the kind of person attracted to SY.

The last civilians evacuated by helicopter from the rooftop of the American embassy in Vietnam in 1975 were SY agents.³

The State Department's system of diplomatic security remained a small and fairly under-resourced, undervalued entity until terrorist attacks in Lebanon and other locations in the Middle and Near East. Attacks against American diplomats and diplomatic facilities during this period were widespread. On March 2, 1973, the U.S. ambassador to Sudan, Cleo A. Noel Jr., and the deputy chief of mission, George Curtis Moore, were killed in cold blood by Palestinian terrorists belonging to the Black September Organization. On February 14, 1979, Adolph Dubs, the U.S. ambassador to Afghanistan, was killed during a failed kidnapping attempt. On November 4, 1979, Iranian "students"

---

*For a full detailed account into the timeline of the Viet Cong attack against Saigon and the American embassy, see: Oberdorfer, Don, *Tet!: The Turning Point in the Vietnam War* (Baltimore: The Johns Hopkins University Press, 1971), p. 10; Major (U.S. Army) Robert J. O'Brien, *The Attack on the American Embassy During Tet, 1968: Factors That Turned a Tactical Victory into a Political Defeat*, U. S. Army Command and General Staff College Fort Leavenworth, Kansas; and, the history of the 716th MP Battalion, at: http://www.716mpvietnam.org/zz.716th%20MP%20History.pdf.

seized the U.S. embassy in Tehran, Iran; in the subsequent crisis fifty-two Americans were held captive for 444 days. On November 22, 1979, a mob set fire to the U.S. embassy in Islamabad, resulting in the death of a Marine Security guard. On April 18, 1983, Hezbollah terrorists launched a suicide truck bomber against the U.S. embassy in Beirut, Lebanon; the attack, believed to have targeted the U.S. intelligence community in country, resulted in the deaths of sixty-three people (fourteen Americans were killed, including the Near East Intelligence Officer, Robert Ames, and most of the CIA's assets in country) and the wounding of scores more (a year later, on September 20, 1984, twenty-three would be killed when the U.S. embassy annex across town in the Christian eastern half of the city was bombed). On December 3, 1983, a Hezbollah suicide truck bomber attempted to destroy the U.S. embassy in Kuwait City, Kuwait, killing five.

In 1985, Secretary of State George P. Shultz ordered the convening of the Advisory Panel on Overseas Security to respond to critical threats American diplomats and diplomatic facilities encountered around the world. The panel, chaired by the retired admiral Bobby Ray Inman, a former deputy director of the Central Intelligence Agency, reviewed the litany of tactics and tools that terrorists had employed in the past decade's attacks and what measures could be conceived to mitigate future threats. One of the primary findings of the Inman panel was the need for an expanded security force to protect American diplomatic posts overseas. On August 27, 1986, a new State Department security force and law enforcement agency, the Diplomatic Security Service, was formed to replace SY; DS was part of the Bureau of Diplomatic Security. According to the panel's findings, "the new Diplomatic Security Service must incorporate the best features and attributes of professional law enforcement in order that it will become capable of providing the level of competence that will be required in United States diplomatic and consular missions around the world in the face of the expected terrorist threat environment."

Another important finding to emerge from the Inman panel was its focus on physical security enhancements for embassies and consulates. As a result, the U.S. State Department was one of the first—

and remains one of the few—foreign diplomatic services to implement physical security protocols to prevent catastrophic attacks. These force protection specifications, unique in the world of diplomatic security, included blast-proofing breakthroughs in architecture to mitigate the devastating yield of an explosion or other methods of attack, including rocket and grenade fire. New embassies would be built with a minimum of a hundred feet of setback to prevent suicide truck bombers from ramming their explosive-laden vehicles into the actual buildings, as had been perpetrated in the West Beirut bombing. These new embassies, known as Inman buildings, incorporated anti-ram walls and fences, gates, vehicle barriers, and ballistic window film and supervised local guard forces to create impregnable fortresses that withstand massive explosions and coordinated attempts to breach an embassy's defenses.

Long before the term "global war on terror" entered the vernacular, DS was one of the sole U.S. law enforcement agencies fighting terrorists overseas in the effort to safeguard American embassies and consulates. Special Agents Daniel Emmett O'Connor and Ronald Albert Lariviere were killed on December 21, 1988, on board Pan Am Flight 103, bombed by Libyan intelligence agents and Palestinian terrorists; two special agents assigned to the U.S. embassy in Islamabad, Pakistan, captured Ramzi Yousef, mastermind of the 1993 World Trade Center bombing; and DS agents brought back the perpetrators of the August 1998 bombings of the U.S. embassies in Kenya and Dar es Salaam so that they could stand trial in a federal courthouse in Manhattan.

The September 11, 2001, attacks against the United States forever changed DS. The service, whose ranks had been understaffed in its domestic and global mission for years, nearly doubled its manpower after the 2001 terrorist attacks; today, the agency boasts two thousand special agents. DS personnel suddenly found themselves frontline warriors and counterterrorist operators; overseas, they found themselves outside their traditional comfort box of supervising the Marine Security Guard contingent and security programs and were now assisting and protecting covert aspirations of the intelligence community, fielding large contractor forces, and harnessing military support in nation-building endeavors. In the AfPak (Afghanistan and Pakistan) theater the Diplomatic Security Service fielded more agents than it did in most of its domestic U.S. field offices. There were more than ▮▮▮▮▮▮▮ special agents assigned to the behemoth fortress that became the U.S. embassy in Baghdad. Traditional protection tasks were dramatically redefined in the wake of Operation Enduring Freedom and Operation Iraqi Freedom. DS special agents hung up their Ralph Lauren suits and Rockport lace-ups for desert khakis, battle rattle, and an M4 ▮▮▮▮▮ carbine close at hand. The Diplomatic Security Service went to war after 9/11. Two special agents, Edward J. Seitz and Stephen Eric Sullivan, were killed in separate rocket attacks in Iraq, in 2004 and 2005.

For a decade, DS found itself with a broad global responsibility that was harnessed by a laser-sharp Near Eastern focus. The Global War on Terror meant that embassies already buttressed to above and beyond the Inman standards of security had to be reinforced and prepped for suicide truck bomb attacks and swarm assaults. Lessons were taken from al-Qaeda assaults in Kabul and Karachi and attacks against diplomatic facilities throughout the Arab world. DS special agents found themselves on the front lines of this borderless conflict and in the crosshairs of the terrorists' sights. Several DS agents, in fact, received top honors for their valor in the face of terrorist threats. Throughout the decade that immediately followed the 9/11 attacks, teams of operators from the hundred-man force known as MSD, or Mobile Security Deployment, the elite DS special operations and counterterrorist, counterassault unit, crisscrossed the globe, rushing to embassies where imminent threats were the currency of day-to-day life. U.S. embassies and consulates in Sana'a, Khartoum, Basra, Damascus, Beirut, and dozens more cities were reinforced by Kevlar-clad counterassault teams who took up positions inside America's most threatened diplomatic posts to augment the regional security officers, or RSOs (the DS agents assigned to an embassy), and Marine Security Guards. Unlike the U.S. Secret Service Counter Assault Teams, known as CATs, the DS Mobile Security Deployments do not have the luxury of operating on streets frozen by hordes of American police officers. As was so ominously observed by a former special agent, "In many locations abroad, especially in 'the Sandbox,' the cops are the enemy."[4]

Many MSDs were intelligence generated, and these tactical specialists were often flown to hot spots and targeted locations on emergency military flights, in order to provide vulnerable embassies with additional firepower support if needed.

When MSD wasn't hunkered down in preparation for some sort of terror strike, it assisted indigenous host-country security services with training. DS has always viewed capable host-country law enforcement as an invaluable tool to protect American embassies and diplomats. Embassy security was always layer based, and having a competently trained and counterterrorist-capable local law enforcement presence provided Diplomatic Security Service efforts inside the embassy grounds with an indispensable buffer. This policy was so important that DS trained thousands of international police officers and security service agents at locations throughout the United States in protecting national borders; protecting critical infrastructure; protecting national leadership; responding to and resolving terrorist incidents; and managing critical terrorist incidents having national-level implications. The program, known as Antiterrorism Assistance, or ATA, trained classes of police officers in the art of bomb disposal, SWAT tactics, countersurveillance, explosive detection dogs, K-9 equipment and awareness instruction, handlers, and even community policing. Over hundred thousand foreign police officers have been trained as a result of ATA courses: these men and women serve across the world in 164 countries.[5]

For over a decade following the 9/11 attacks, DS managed to contain the chaos of a world where fundamentalist fervor had the potential to inflict catastrophic damage on America's diplomatic interests around the world—especially in the Middle East. But the wave of civilian unrest that swept through the Arab world in the storm known as the Arab Spring took the region—and the United States—by surprise. Governments that had been traditional allies of the United States in the Global War on Terror and that had sent police officers to ATA training were overthrown in instantaneous and unexpected popular revolutions. In Tunisia, in Egypt, and in Yemen, traditionally reliably pro-American regimes were overthrown and replaced with new governments—some Islamic centered; in Bahrain the protests led to a brutal crackdown, while in Syria a popular demand for freedom resulted in one of the most violent civil wars ever seen in the region.

And then there was Libya, a nation emerging from the civil war that led to the death of Colonel Qaddafi and the dismantling of years of secret police rule. Militias, Islamists, and weapons proliferated throughout the country. As the special agents in the midnight tour settled into their shift and drank their lattes and Red Bulls in the Diplomatic Security Command Center, the focus of the employees on duty that night centered on America's embassies in the eye of the Arab Spring storm. When the clock on the wall hit 0000 hours, it marked the eleventh anniversary of the 9/11 attacks.

3.

9.11.12: A Fiery Morning in the Arab Spring

On the night separating September 10 from the eleventh anniversary of the 9/11 attacks, DS agents working the midnight tour at the Diplomatic Security Command Center watched the world from the "Big Blue Board," along with streaming live television feeds of CNN, Fox, Al Jazeera, and WTOP radio. The DS/CC was its usual organized chaos: a multiscreen command nerve center camouflaged inside the DS "world headquarters." On the eleventh anniversary of the 9/11 attacks, and over three months after the smoldering remnants of a terrorist safe house—and fifteen terrorists—were extinguished in Waziristan, the al-Qaeda leader Dr. Ayman al-Zawahiri released a forty-two-minute Web video eulogizing his deputy, the Libyan-born ambassador for the global jihad, Abu Yahya al-Libi. While CIA analysts and psychologists rushed to assess the video ramblings of Dr. Zawahiri, the tens of thousands of Arab protesters who had gathered for violent demonstrations outside American embassies throughout the Arab world had answered the call to arms over a different video.

On July 1, 2012, a fourteen-minute video titled "Innocence of Muslims" was first posted on YouTube. The amateurish film was produced by an Egyptian-born Coptic and U.S. resident known by the alias of Sam Bacile who financed the short movie that, according to a BBC review, "depicted Islam as a religion of violence and hate, and its Prophet Muhammad as a foolish and power-hungry man." Other reviews claimed that "'Innocence of Muslims' depicts Muhammad as a feckless philanderer who approved of child sexual abuse . . . and [who] is made to look like a murderer and adulterer as well."[1] The purposely insulting film was largely ignored until months later when, on September 8, it was picked up by various Arab television networks, and Islamic networks and video sites in particular. Realizing how combustible the video was, multiple Middle Eastern and Islamic nations blocked it from the airwaves and the Web; Indonesia, India, Saudi Arabia, and Afghanistan did all they could to prevent their citizens from viewing the inflammatory film. In Egypt, Sheikh Khalad Abdalla, a presenter on the religiously themed Al-Nas television station, began broadcasting scenes from the movie that were dubbed into Arabic. The following day, throughout the Arabian Peninsula and North Africa, American embassies became lightning rods of violent protests.

The largest protests—and certainly the most violently symbolic—were in Egypt. The sprawling U.S. embassy in Cairo at 5 Tawfik Diab Street in the Garden City section of the thriving metropolis—until the Iraqi war, the largest American diplomatic post overseas—found itself surrounded by thousands of violent protesters chanting, "Death to America" and "Death to Israel." The wrath emanating from the Egyptian street was expected. As the noted Middle East scholar Professor Fouad Ajami stated in a forum for the Hoover Institution, "The Egyptians, who viewed themselves as the center of the Arab world, provided the Arab Spring with a theater worthy of its ambitions. Cairo, after all," he noted, "was long considered the center of the Arab world. It was known as *Um al-Dunya* in Arabic, the Mother of the World."

With former president Mubarak in prison and the newly elected Muslim Brotherhood president flexing muscle for his base, Egyptian security forces, once positioned in front of the fortresslike embassy as an integral part of the landscape, had neither the mandate nor the desire to disperse the riots. Many police officers left their stations for an elongated falafel break or simply watched as the crowds burned flags, declared their support for a jihad, and demanded that the United States release Omar Abdel Rahman; known as "the Blind Sheikh" (or "Santa Claus," as per the not so affectionate NYPD vernacular), Rahman was the inspiration behind the first World Trade Center attack in 1993. Convicted for his role in that attack, as well as a planned "Day of Terror" in New York City to destroy the United Nations and several federal buildings and assassinate ambassadors and government officials, Rahman is serving a life sentence in North Carolina, at the Federal Medical Center at Butner Federal Correctional Complex.

Years earlier, at the slightest suggestion of a demonstration in front of the U.S. embassy, Mubarak would have dispatched his riot squads to blind the mob with tear gas and to break their bones with truncheons; secret agents in plain clothes from the hated *Mukhabarat* would snatch those worthy of snatching for some specialized attention in the dungeons beneath their headquarters.

For P.,* the RSO in Cairo, the protests and lack of host-nation intervention were troubling, especially when protesters scaled the walls surrounding the grounds and began to penetrate the embassy perimeter. The protesters spray painted anti-American and fundamentalist Islamic slogans along the embassy walls and even tore down the large American flag that was flown pronouncedly at the entrance to the sprawling facility, replacing it with an ominous black jihadist one.

The fear, of course, was that the U.S. embassy would be overrun and set ablaze. The protests in front of the U.S. embassy were eerily foreboding. Nearly a year to the day earlier, on September 9, 2011, hundreds of Egyptian protesters had descended upon the Israeli embassy in Giza, on the outskirts of Cairo, armed with battering rams and sledgehammers. Within hours, the mob had grown to several thousand men. They burned American and Israeli flags, scribbled on bedsheets with red and blue markers, and chanted "God is great" and "Death to the Jews." By midnight the mob had broken through a wall

---

*Identity withheld for security considerations.

that Egyptian security forces had hastily erected and it infiltrated the skyscraper that was home to the Israeli post; the actual Israeli embassy consisted of only two floors in the sprawling building. Egyptian riot police did little to stop the rabble. As the night's chaos attracted more rioters and a swelling army of opportunistic looters who by now were coming in from all over the city, the security situation became dire. The mob had broken through the main lobby and rushed to the twentieth and twenty-first floors toward the chancery. It ransacked much of the embassy and tossed sensitive documents out the windows; many of these documents were seized and scanned and quickly found themselves translated and featured on jihadist Web sites. Fires were ignited. The embassy staffers retreated behind an armored steel door inside a safe haven. They hurriedly destroyed classified material and waited for the mob to break through and rip them to shreds. As the cadence of the outer security doors being pounded by fists and hammers reached a deafening crescendo, security agents from *Bat'Mah*, the Hebrew acronym for *Bitachon Misrad Ha'Hutz*, or Foreign Ministry Security, unholstered their specially modified Glock 17 9mm semiautomatic pistols and prepared to take out as many of the mob as they could before ultimately and fatally being overrun. The agents feared that they would be burned alive or beaten to death.* They thought of the images of the American helicopter pilots shot down in Mogadishu and dragged naked through the streets after a mob had beaten them. They thought of the Blackwater contractors in Fallujah whose torched bodies were strung up for the world to see. They wondered if their wives, children, and parents would be spared seeing the images of the fate that would soon befall them.

In Jerusalem, Prime Minister Benjamin Netanyahu, Defense Minister Ehud Barak, and other high-ranking members of Israel's security echelon watched the events unfold in real time, on news reports

---

* See Evelyn Gordon, "Cairo Encouraged Embassy Attack by Letting Previous Attackers Walk," *Commentary*, September 12, 2012; Mostafa Ali, "The storming of Cairo's Israeli embassy: an eyewitness account (part 1)," September 10, 2011; and Barak Ravid, "*Shagrir Yisrael B'Mitzraim, Ha'Ovdim U'bnei Mishpachotai'hem Punu Ha'Layla Be 'Tisa Meyuchedet,*" *Haaretz*, September 10, 2011.

on Al Jazeera and Egyptian state-run television; this was a story that the Arab media outlets enjoyed covering. It was unthinkable for Israel to dispatch troops to Egypt; it could not send additional security agents. Reportedly, Minister of Defense Barak personally requested that President Barack Obama call the newly elected Egyptian president and demand intervention. Egyptian commandos ultimately intervened, but the incident could have become a true spark to the eruption of a Middle Eastern war. The incident was so severe that the foreign minister of Bahrain, Sheikh Khalid bin Ahmad bin Muhammad al-Khalifa, stated on his Twitter page, "The failure to defend the embassy building is a blatant violation of the 1961 Vienna Convention on Diplomatic Relations."[2]

Back at the American embassy in Cairo, P. did not want to have to retreat to an inner sanctum with sidearm at hand. He remembered the stories of how an angry mob materialized in a flash in front of the U.S. embassy in Islamabad, Pakistan, on November 21, 1979, after local radio stations broadcast completely erroneous reports that American soldiers had attacked the Masjid al-Haram, Islam's holiest site in Mecca.* Shouting "Kill the American dogs,"[3] the protesters broke through the main gate of the sprawling compound and proceeded to set the chancery ablaze. More than a hundred members of the embassy staff hunkered down inside a protected safe haven and cooked in suffocating smoke as flames engulfed the majestic structure; a Marine Security guard, Corporal Steven Crowley from Long Island, New York, was shot in the head as he gauged the situation from the embassy rooftop. The embassy staffers were eventually saved by Pakistani forces, but not before six were killed in the attack.

---

*Saudi Wahabi fanatics seeking to instate the Mahdi, or redeemer of Islam, in the kingdom, seized the Grand Mosque in Mecca, along with hundreds of pilgrims who had traveled to the holy city for the hajj. The Saudi National Guard and military were incapable of ending the takeover by hundreds of militants seeking to martyr themselves. According to reports, French counterterrorist commandos from the GIGN (the *Groupe d'Intervention de la Gendarmerie Nationale*) were temporarily converted to Islam so that they could enter the holy city and handle the hostage-taking ordeal; once the French operators were done with their mission, they simply converted back to Christianity. After two weeks and nearly two hundred dead, the Saudis pacified the uprising.

Applying tactics and protocols learned after Islamabad and embassy bombings and attacks in Beirut and East Africa, the RSO and the gunnery sergeant, the commander of the MSG contingent, set in motion the emergency tactics to safeguard the embassy. At Post One, the primary checkpoint in the lobby of an embassy, the MSGs behind the blast-resistant transparent armor donned helmets and body armor—the proverbial "battle rattle"—over their service uniforms; access controls for the entire compound were checked for any intrusion; the scene was repeated at Post Two and Post Three. Reportedly, a REACT alert was ordered for the rest of the Marine Security Guard contingent and their RSO supervisors as well. This force would assemble in the embassy's REACT room and don battle rattle and weapons (an M4 5.56mm carbine rifle or the ever-trustworthy Remington 870 12-gauge pump-action shotgun) to respond to any intrusion into the chancery. The MSGs also raced to the roof to secure the high ground and to provide countersniper cover, as well as to monitor the growing crowds.

There was an absolute need for the tactical concern. The protest outside the embassy wasn't solely a spontaneous expression of Islamic rage. It was a highly organized eruption orchestrated by the next generation of jihad leaders. Sheikh Abu-Yahya al-Masri, the spokesman for the Voice of Wisdom Coalition, a Salafist group with links to alleged fundamentalist elements, and Sheikh Gamal Saber, coordinator of the Hazimoun movement and cofounder of the radical Egyptian Umma Party, orchestrated the demonstrations. Mohammed al-Zawahiri, the al-Qaeda leader Ayman al-Zawahiri's brother, and several sons of the jailed cleric Omar Abdel Rahman were honored guests at the event; they were filmed chanting "Death to America" outside the embassy gates.

By midday, as dawn was breaking over Washington, D.C., and the midnight tour was ending its shift at the DS Command Center, the Middle East was ablaze. The situation in Cairo was critical. The DS/CC would have spent the night sending NIACT (Night Action) precedence situational reports, or SITREPs, of the events in Cairo to embassies and consulates across the globe, in an effort to keep the agents in the field in the loop with the most accurate and timely intelligence available.[4] In a giant game of Twister, the agents multi-tasked with open and secure lines crisscrossing the command center, stopping to watch and listen to breaking-news media updates on the television and radio. Egyptian security forces were impotently allowing the protesters to run amok in a furious frenzy. State Department officials, especially those in the Near Eastern Affairs Bureau, closely monitored events from Foggy Bottom as they attempted to reach out to their political liaisons in Egypt and plead for police—even military—intervention. Egypt, even in the post-Mubarak abyss, maintained a strong security infrastructure, and embassy officials were cautiously confident that the rule of law would prevail and a repeat of an Islamabad-like horror would be prevented.

Libya, Egypt's neighbor to the west, was another story altogether.

4.

Libya

The United States has had a violent history with the North African nation of Libya—a history of conflict, warfare, and bloodshed that has dated back to the campaign against the Barbary pirates and the deployment of the fledgling U.S. Marine Corps against Yousef, the pasha of Tripoli. In June 1967, the U.S. embassy in Benghazi was attacked by a violent mob that destroyed much of the facility; at the onset of the June 1967 war, Libyan radio had reported that American warplanes, flying with Israeli aircraft, had bombed Cairo. Benghazi was the launching pad of Muammar Qaddafi's overthrow of King Idris and his monarchy. The United States had not had a formal embassy in Libya since 1972; the abandoned embassy building was torched and burned to the ground on December 2, 1979, during protests that charged U.S. involvement in the Grand Mosque seizure in Mecca.

Libya under Colonel Muammar Qaddafi had provided the United States with what appeared to be an endless list of reasons why diplomatic relations could not exist between the two nations. The flamboyant and unpredictable Qaddafi had led a Champions League of international terrorist movements, ranging from the Provisional IRA to most of the Palestinian liberation movements; in June 1976, when Palestinian terrorists hijacked an Air France aircraft in Athens, their first stop was Benghazi and a welcome from Qaddafi's forces (that incident would end in Entebbe, Uganda, days later when Israeli commandos rescued the hostages in an awe-inspiring raid). Qaddafi had dispatched his army to take over neighboring Chad, and he was believed to have ordered hit teams to the United States to assassinate President Ronald Reagan. Libyan-backed terrorists and agents were also responsible for attacks on U.S. diplomats in Khartoum and Sana'a in 1986. The Libyan dictator Muammar Qaddafi had branded himself as the most dangerous terrorist in the world.[1] President Reagan ordered the U.S. military to carry out Operation El Dorado Canyon, the April 15, 1986, bombing of targets (including Qaddafi's lair in Tripoli) in response to the Libyan bombing of the La Belle discotheque in Berlin frequented by U.S. servicemen; two American soldiers had been killed in the attack. Libyan agents were responsible for the bombing of Pan Am Flight 103 over Lockerbie, Scotland, on December 21, 1988, that resulted in the deaths of 270 people, including the two DS agents on board the aircraft.[2]

Qaddafi's Libya was a pariah: an insane (though oil-blessed) state led by a crazy megalomaniac who traveled the world in flamboyant costumes with an entourage of AK-47-toting beauties. Following the 9/11 attacks, Qaddafi was determined to distance himself from the President Bush–dubbed axis of evil. He came clean on an extensively advanced nuclear weapons program—one that had embarrassingly evaded both the CIA and Israel's Mossad—and provided the U.S. intelligence community with invaluable assistance in the Global War on Terror; Qaddafi's intelligence services prevented al-Qaeda operatives from establishing nodes inside Libya and provided information on known cells and operatives plotting attacks in North Africa.

Relations between Libya and the United States were restored on February 8, 2004, with the arrival of diplomatic and security personnel at the U.S. Interests Section in Tripoli; the mission was upgraded to a liaison office on June 24, 2004. After Qaddafi paid reparations for his past sins in order to return to the fold of friendly nations, the United States reestablished formal diplomatic ties with Libya. On May 31, 2006, the United States and Libya exchanged diplomatic notes confirming the upgrade of the U.S. Liaison Office in Tripoli to an embassy.

The DS special agent Dan Meehan was the first official RSO to serve in Libya in twenty-five years and responsible for making sure the liaison office was safe for the mission at hand. His two years in Tripoli would be rife with the typical challenges that would haunt an RSO opening up a mission inside new, uncharted territory in a nation where spies outnumbered civilians. When Meehan arrived in Tripoli, the Interests Section was opened at the same time that embassy operations in Kabul and, ultimately, Baghdad would occupy much of the already limited DS human and financial capital. The diplomatic post was nestled inside four floors of the Corinthia Bab Africa Hotel located near the seafront; the hotel, the only five-star facility in town at the time, was woefully inadequate by the comprehensive Inman security requirements. There was no physical setback, no defensive hard line, and no marines. There was no secure area for reviewing classified materials, and there were no methods to receive classified documents.

In the normal world, and Libya was anything but normal, the outgoing RSO would hand the baton to his replacement: the transition would include introducing the new DS agent in charge to the local police and counterterrorist commanders and acclimating him to the lay of the land. The personal relationship that would—have to—develop between the embassy security chief and his local counterparts was a critical component in securing the American presence; in case of terrorist attack, the RSO could always call on a favor and request additional host-government resources. Some RSOs would call upon their local counterparts when they didn't need anything at all. They would provide gifts and American staples such as M&M's and scotch to grease the wheels and cement long-standing working relationships. When they did have to call the locals for help, the local security counterpart knew it was dire.

Meehan's counterpart was the notorious Mousa Kousa, a Michigan State University alumnus and confidant of Colonel Qaddafi's who commanded the *Mukhabarat al-Jamahiriya*, Libya's external security organization that spied on political thought at home, political dissidents overseas, and operations against the West; the service was responsible for the Berlin disco bombing, Pan Am Flight 103, and the September 19, 1989, bombing of French UTA Airlines Flight 772. But, Libya being Libya and the Interests Section embroiled in its territorial struggles, Meehan never met Mousa alone—they always met together with the embassy's principal officer (the de facto ambassador). Arranging a meeting with Kousa was never easy, and embassy personnel—with diplomatic, security, and intelligence requirements—had to maximize the opportunities when meeting with this close Qaddafi aide. Even later, when Meehan met with Kousa's executive officer, he did not meet him alone. This difficult situation was only exacerbated by the fact that Meehan was alone for much of his time in country; he only received an assistant agent six months into his two-year tour. After all, as it was always said, DS agents always do more with less—especially so considering that the local police that protected the hotel were unarmed and wore torn sandals, even though the terrorist threat to the hotel, from the Libyan Islamic Fighting Group, or LIGF, was very real.

Undeterred by the challenges and the turf wars so common among the different agencies who work together at U.S. embassies overseas, Dan Meehan and the DS agents who followed him to the shores of Tripoli made sure that American diplomacy proceeded unimpaired by violence and threat; the United States, after all, has shared a long and tumultuous security relationship with Libya. John Christopher Stevens was the Foreign Service officer who made sure that American diplomacy in Libya flourished. Chris, as he was known, was a true Arabist; he was known to sign his name on personal e-mails as Krees to mimic the way Arabs articulated his name.[3] Born in Grass Valley, California, in 1960, Chris Stevens had developed a passionate love for the Arab world while working for the Peace Corps in Morocco in the early 1980s; ironically, and perhaps fittingly, he learned the intricacies and magic of the Arabic language and of the Arabic people while teaching them English. Stevens was ideally equipped for work at the State Department and a career with the Foreign Service. A graduate of Berkeley, he earned his law degree and practiced trade law before joining the Foreign Service in 1991. Virtually all of Stevens's posts were in the Middle East and in locations that can best be described as dicey. Early assignments included serving as a junior political officer at the U.S. consulate in Jerusalem, where he dealt with the Palestinian populations in the West Bank and Gaza; he later worked in Damascus, as well as in the Kingdom of Saudi Arabia, at the U.S. embassy in Riyadh. He was ideally prepped in crisis management and conflict response, having been posted in D.C. on the Iran desk.

It would, however, be North Africa where Stevens would excel as a diplomat and as a reliable face of American reach. When the United States reemerged as a political player in Libya, Stevens jumped at the opportunity to work in an emerging new arena for American diplomacy.

Stevens served as the Deputy Chief of Mission in Qaddafi's Libya from 2007 to 2009. In that position he helped advance Washington's visions for the region while seeking opportunities for American multinational corporations and other interests in the über-rich oil state. The American political push, which coincided with a concerted effort to sanitize Libya's inescapable past and leadership peculiarities, was determined to advance the needs of the United States to field allies in the Arab world in the War on Terror. In that role, Stevens met and developed relationships with key figures in the Qaddafi regime, and he served as a conduit for visiting politicians—ranging from junior members of Congress to powerful members of the House and Senate such as Peter Hoekstra, a Republican congressman from Michigan, and the Republican congressman John Boehner, at the time of this book's writing the Speaker of the House.

Stevens was a greatly admired diplomat—respected by men and women on both sides of the political divide. Personable and self-effacing, he was described, in absolutely complimentary terms, as a relic: a practitioner of diplomacy from days past. He displayed street smarts and an affinity for what has been categorized as low-key negotiations. He achieved agreements and cooperation courtesy of interpersonal relationships;[4] he was known to have achieved more over cups of rocket-fuel coffee in a market gathering spot than could ever have been achieved in reams of paperwork or gigabytes' worth of e-mails.

Stevens was considered *the* State Department's subject matter expert (SME) on Libya; as the most respected and energetic SME in its ranks, in March 2011 he was dispatched to Libya for a second tour by Secretary of State Hillary Rodham Clinton to be America's man on the ground in the Arab Spring conflict to oust Qaddafi. Stevens was a natural for this sensitive assignment. His fluency in Arabic and his fluency in spreading the American message of freedom to people who have never known liberty were reported as infectiously convincing; his experience, in Libya, of working closely with the CIA made him an essential and highly effective bridge builder. Establishing a rapport with the many militias that battled Qaddafi loyalists required a deft hand and a talent for breaking bread with men in camouflage fatigues who talked about long-standing relationships while a walkie-talkie stood on the table next to their plate of hummus and an AK-47 was nestled by their feet. The uprising erupted in Benghazi, and that's where Stevens needed to be.

He arrived in country on April 5, 2011. There were no commercial air connections into Benghazi, so Ambassador Stevens and a gutsy crew of support diplomatic and security staff arrived in the port city by boat, a Greek freighter, the SS *Maria Dolores*, which made a run from the ancient harbor in Valletta, Malta, to Benghazi. Stevens's DS entourage was small, though the agents packed a powerful punch. The *Maria Dolores* carried, in its cargo hold, several armored bullet-resistant SUVs and numerous pallets of communications gear, computers, and, of course, weapons and ammunition. "My mandate was to go out and meet as many members of the leadership as I could in the Transitional National Council," Stevens said. "I've gone around with our small team and tried to get to know other people in the society there."[5] The Libyans were so grateful upon Stevens's arrival—and America's role in the liberation of the country from the yoke of dictatorship—that they hoisted British, Qatari, French, and American flags in Freedom Square, in front of the central hall of justice.

When the fighting stopped and Qaddafi's humiliating end had been completed, Chris Stevens was an obvious choice to be President Barack Obama's personal representative to the new Libya. In May 2012 he presented his credentials to Ashour Bin Khayal, the Libyan National Transitional Council's foreign minister, as the American ambassador.

Stevens's office in the U.S. embassy in Tripoli was one of the newest facilities to emerge out of the chaos, fury, and joyous hope of the Arab Spring. Situated on a sprawling patch of sunbaked acreage in the posh Sidi Slim neighborhood, along the Walie al-Ahed Road, in Tripoli, the embassy was a heavily fortified facility.

Tripoli wasn't the sole U.S. diplomatic outpost in Libya. Special Mission Benghazi, an ad hoc consulate not meeting the security requirements of the Inman standards, had been hastily set up in the eastern city of Benghazi in the fluid reality of the Libyan civil war. The city, a hub in the murky waters of the Arab Spring and transition in Egypt and conflict in the Horn of Africa, was a dangerous and despicably lawless place and, as a result, vital to American interests. The consulate wasn't really a consulate but a temporary facility bypassing security standards; "expeditionary diplomacy" dictated that DS do the best it could without the protections afforded official consulates.

5.

Special Mission Benghazi

Ambassador Stevens's first night in Benghazi was spent sleeping on the ship that brought him to Libya; there was no other safe haven for him in the city. He bunked with his DS contingent, consisting of Special Agents Brian Haggerty, Kent Anderson, Josh Vincent, Chris Deedy, James Mcanelly, Jason Bierly, Ken Davis, and Keith Carter, the SAC, or special agent in charge of the detail. The DS agents were wearing U.S. government desert mufti: 5.11 trousers and a one-size-too-large button-down 5.11 tactical shirt; the larger than necessary blouse not only enabled the agents to conceal their holstered SIGs but also provided them with easy-to-reach access in case they found themselves in a firefight. It was hard to mistake Ambassador Stevens's detail for anything other than a group of American agents. Their khaki-green U.S. State Department baseball caps and shiny new armored SUVs were typical Uncle Sam calling cards in the Sandbox. The DS agents, armed with a street map of Benghazi and the service of a few reliable local Libyans, were tasked with one very important mission: locate a safe venue where Ambassador Stevens could set up shop.

The U.S. Special Mission Benghazi, as the ad hoc facility was known in the hallways of the seventh floor of Main State, also known as Foggy Bottom, was a temporary facility that bucked the Inman standards for security recommendations.

Benghazi was important to U.S. interests in Libya and, indeed, the entire Arab world. NATO nations had seized the risky yet necessary initiative in assisting the fledgling Libyan democracy and influencing its policies and its very future. Nongovernmental organizations, or NGOs, followed close behind to assist in the humanitarian and nation-building needs of the Libyan people. Multinational corporations would follow as well. After all, there was a new political leadership to befriend, minds to win, and dollars to be made.

Special Mission Benghazi was temporary and ad hoc; the U.S. future permanent *diplomatic* presence was planned to be a fortress in a fluid city percolating with the molten fires of fundamentalist Islam. To quickly get a diplomatic location up and running for "the needs of the Foreign Service," security exemptions and waivers were obtained, bypassing the physical security requirements established after Beirut and East Africa. Building a brand-new diplomatic facility inside a nation still at war with itself was a lengthy process that could take years to accomplish. In order to get Benghazi up and running, the Bureau of Diplomatic Security was saddled to do the best it could as quickly as possible.

The first post-revolution U.S. special mission in the city was set up inside the penthouse suites of the Tibesty Hotel in the Assabri section of the city overlooking the sea along the Al Madinah Ar Riyadiyya. According to its official brochures, "In the heart of the magnificent Benghazi city, with its wonderful weather, clear skies and friendly people, rises the fifteen-story Tibesty hotel. The hotel welcomes its guests and comfortable stay in its warm and friendly atmosphere through Tibesty hotel, 220 rooms, twenty-two luxury suites, nine presidential suites and several restaurant and coffee shops, as well as a number of shops and places of leisure." And, as a wartime hotel, it was truly an oasis, even though it resembled a Soviet-era guesthouse more than a palatial center of diplomatic activity; its mauve hallways and seedy check-in area looked as if they needed a coating of superstrength deodorant. The Tibesty did boast a marvelous indoor swimming pool and buffet, however.

During Qaddafi's time, the hotel lobby was always crowded with intelligence and counterintelligence operatives, all in civilian dress, chain-smoking cigarettes as they sipped supersweet tea and observed the comings and goings of Western businessmen and local military commanders, along with the female—or male—company they kept. Little changed in the post-Qaddafi era, though the volume of smugglers, weapons merchants, and prostitutes increased. The fifteen-story hotel had little setback, or the distance, separating it from the street. As a result, a vehicle-borne improvised explosive device (VBIED), like the ones used in the 1998 bombings of the U.S. embassies in Nairobi and Dar es Salaam, deployed against the Tibesty Hotel would have had catastrophic results. The Tibesty Hotel did not meet even the most basic of the Inman mandates concerning physical security for the U.S. diplomatic presence in the city. On June 1, 2011, a powerful car bomb exploded outside the hotel—an attempt by terrorists to bring the building down.[1] On December 20, 2011, Libyan protective security agents foiled a plot, a large-scale terrorist strike that was dubbed Operation Papa Noel. Qaddafi loyalists were behind the planned attacks that were to simultaneously strike American and Western embassies and consulates with RPGs and suicide squads of gunmen. Libya was rife with violent intent and fanatical resolve—a terrible combination when the country was awash in the weapons of war.

As one of the MSD operators pointed out, in reflecting on those early days of the State Department and the DS presence in Benghazi, "The crackle of gunfire in the dark is not the sound a Bureau of Diplomatic Security agent longs to hear, but during the past six months in Benghazi, Libya, it was all too common as exuberant fighters celebrated the day's revolutionary successes with rounds dispatched randomly into the night's sky."[2]

But there needed to be a secure and reliable office where U.S. diplomats could carry out their assignments when in Benghazi. On June 21, 2011, the State Department located a place.

Special Mission Benghazi was a lavish sprawl of villa and manicured grounds. Trees and flowers bloomed on the compound, making it resemble a lord's estate (or one belonging to a drug lord) more than just another palatial home inside a well-to-do neighborhood in Libya's second city. Guava trees were heavy with fruits; purple grapes were swelling on rows of vines.

Its vast expanse provided setback, and its upper-scale surroundings would satisfy the need for anonymity. Security enhancements would be ad hoc and piecemeal.[3] Security engineering officers, known as SEOs, inside DS were masters of LEGO-block building. Engineers by trade, with a laser-focus expertise on physical and technical security, the SEOs were true unsung heroes inside the service, nimble as a Leatherman multi-tool.

The compound was in the Western Fwayhat section of the city, north of the Fourth Ring Road, and sandwiched in between Shari al-Andalus and Shari al-Qayrawan Streets south of the Third Ring Road. The sprawling eight-acre estate included a main gate that had been reinforced by seven concrete inverted T-shaped Jersey barriers; the obstacles, which consisted of a flat base and a three-foot-high barrier, were primitive yet effective measures to impede the plans of a suicide car or truck bomber hoping to rev up his engines at full speed and crash into the compound. An orange metal swing gate completed the outer ring of vehicular hindrance.

There were two halves to the compound—the eastern half, which was the primary diplomatic office and residence, and the western half, where the DS personnel were housed; a wall and access points connected the two pieces of this puzzle.

At the entrance to the diplomatic section, a black metal gate secured the main entrance—past the Jersey barriers and orange-and-black metal swing crash beam gate. The agents had mounted a single surveillance camera with digital-video-recording capabilities that could pan only in and around the northern edge of the property at the main gate, providing some standoff visual capabilities to the DS contingent on the estate. A nine-foot-high concrete wall surrounded the compound; some portions of this wall, but not all, were augmented by thick and deterring rows of concertina razor wire. The wall was decorative, often entangled with the thick green bushes and trees that surrounded the compound, and could easily be compromised.

Security was tenuous even on the best of days, however, no matter how high the perimeter walls were. On March 22, 2012, at 0227 hours, seven heavily armed Ministry of Defense personnel driving armed Toyota Hilux trucks began kicking the rear Charlie-3 gate to the compound in an attempt to gain entry. The militiamen began screaming "God is great!" and firing their AK-47s into the air; the gunfire caused the local guard to flee in panic, though he alerted the contracted militiamen to respond and force the brigade members to apologize to DS personnel.

There were two "IED events" that targeted the main security wall. At 2300 hours on April 6, 2012, a crude IED was thrown over the wall. The device was a primitive yet effective "fish bomb" made of "gelateena." Damage was not significant, but it would be a harbinger of worse to come.

Shortly after midnight on June 6, 2012, a terrorist placed an IED along the north gate. The blast, which many have considered a probing action, blew a large hole through the concrete wall—a hole high and wide enough to permit the entry of swarms of attackers. The suspect in both facility bombings was a disgruntled former guard force member who was fired by the RSO for gross misconduct. His white pickup truck was observed in proximity to both attacks by surveillance videotape, according to a source familiar with the case. DS agents in Benghazi were successful in persuading the Libyan government to arrest the suspect and hold him for two months. However, there was no judicial system in place to oversee his prosecution.[4] Therefore, he was released by the Libyans shortly after the last bombing.

The section of the wall blown open in the June IED attack was directly in front of the headquarters for the mercurial February 17 militia, the local and seemingly friendly armed force that had been contracted by the State Department to augment security at the facility. Cooperation with such a ragtag force was incredibly rare but deemed necessary to survive the absolute mayhem of Benghazi. The militiamen slung AK-47s over their shoulders and sported an odd mosaic of attire that combined camouflage fatigues, Adidas tracksuits, and North African gowns, robes, and headdresses; during the civil war, they played a significant role in the defeat of Qaddafi loyalists and showed little restraint in flashes of unforgiving brutality when in control of prisoners or suspected traitors. At the compound, the militiamen prayed a lot and chain-smoked smuggled Western cigarettes as they milled about their Toyota pickup trucks that sported 14.5 mm and 23 mm heavy machine guns and cannons. The militia's small corner at the northwest section of the main gate boasted a meticulously cared-for grass lawn.

Reportedly, the February 17 militia was owned by the Gulf states and other commercial and religious interests that helped make it one of the largest militias operating in the city. The U.S. government considered them to be somewhat trustworthy—especially in comparison to some of the other armed groups that controlled patches of other vital interests of the city. "Benghazi," a security head for a European government consortium operating inside Libya and a veteran of several Middle Eastern civil wars, commented, "is the kind of typical lawless latrine where everyone pisses into the hole in order to claim ownership and participation in possible positive outcomes, or claim that the stink was too bad and that they ultimately had to walk away." Reportedly, members of the militia had traveled across the Mediterranean to fight alongside Syrian rebels in the bloody civil war to remove Bashar al-Assad and his Alawite regime from power.

The head of the February 17 militia was a mysterious figure named Fawzi Abu Kataf, a Libyan of Palestinian descent and someone whom intelligence sources on the ground in Benghazi referred to as opportunistic to the point of being suspicious. "He was known as someone with a long list of divergent business interests that he used for maximum opportunity often playing one against the other," stated a Libyan security insider who for the security considerations of his family will remain anonymous, "and he also had close operational links to the Muslim Brotherhood."[5] It was assumed that he also had close links to Hamas as well as other groups designated by the U.S. government as terrorist.

In a perfect world, the Libyan intelligence services and the Libyan police would have been responsible for the integrity and safety of America's diplomats in country. But because of the absence of a strong centralized Libyan government to faithfully execute its responsibilities as a host nation, under the Vienna Convention,* the State Department had no choice but to rely on militias for protection. When Secretary of State Hillary Clinton traveled to Libya in October 2011, she was met at the airport by armed men from the Zintan militia. The military council of the Zintan area is best known for detaining Saif al-Islam Qaddafi after his capture in November 2011.

Great efforts were made to ensure that the February 17 Brigade was reliable and properly trained, however. The brigade's loyalty—or competency—might have been suspect, but DS agents, especially those on Ambassador Stevens's first detail, instituted a crash-course training program for this first layer of protection of America's expeditionary diplomats in Benghazi. The agents procured surplus British Disruptive Pattern Material, or DPM, camouflage uniforms for the militiamen, as well as surplus body armor, load-bearing vests, and other staples of personal security detail, or PSD, work in an environment like the one that existed in Libya. The training program included internal defense planning, weapons safety, and basic marksmanship. Dry drills, conducted with loaded weapons, were held on the plush green grass of the

---

*Under the 1961 Vienna Convention on Diplomatic Relations and the 1963 Vienna Convention on Consular Relations, nearly all the countries around the world abide by reciprocal responsibilities and obligations regarding the diplomatic facilities and personnel dispatched overseas. Section 3 of Article 31 of the 1963 Vienna Convention states that "the receiving State is under a special duty to take all appropriate steps to protect the consular premises against any intrusion or damage and to prevent any disturbance of the peace of the consular post or impairment of its dignity." Additionally, Article 40 of the same treaty specifically states that "the receiving State shall treat consular officers with due respect and shall take all appropriate steps to prevent any attack on their person, freedom, or dignity." An attack against an ambassador is also covered under Article 29 of the 1961 convention, which states, "The person of a diplomatic agent shall be inviolable. He shall not be liable to any form of arrest or detention. The receiving State shall treat him with due respect and shall take all appropriate steps to prevent any attack on his person, freedom or dignity." The grounds of a diplomatic post are also protected under the 1961 Vienna Convention, which states, "The receiving State is under a special duty to take all appropriate steps to protect the premises of the mission against any intrusion or damage and to prevent any disturbance of the peace of the mission or impairment of its dignity." See Alex Tiersky and Susan B. Epstein, *Securing U.S. Diplomatic Facilities and Personnel Abroad: Background and Policy Issues*, Congressional Research Service, November 26, 2012.

Special Mission Compound. MSD medics provided combat casualty care training, to prepare them for stabilizing a wounded comrade with burns, lacerations, or sucking chest wounds.

The MSD detail, fulfilling a foreign internal defense mandate usually reserved for U.S. Army Special Forces, realized that the February 17 militia would eventually be tested in battle. To shore up their defensive and counterattack capabilities, should they lead the defense of the Special Mission Compound, MSD operators helped the militiamen set up sandbag fortifications in front of their barracks; the barracks also fielded high-power perimeter lights that faced toward the main structure on the compound—the ambassador's residence and office.

To augment the DS contingent situated at the compound, the State Department had contracted a Wales-based security firm named Blue Mountain that fielded a local Libyan affiliate to provide unarmed uniformed guards at the perimeter entrances to the facility. On paper, and in the mind-numbing world of government contracts in war zones, Blue Mountain appeared impressive. David Nigel Thomas, the company's director, was a former member of 22 SAS, the storied British commando and counterterrorist force legendary in special operations circles; the firm's name, in fact, was derived from a poem inscribed on the clock tower at the headquarters of the regiment in Hereford: "We are the pilgrims, master; we shall go. Always a little further; it may be. Beyond that last blue mountain barred with snow. Across that angry or that glimmering sea." In reality, however, Blue Mountain was one of an endless list of have-gun-for-hire security firms that emerged overnight in the wake of the international coalition involvements in Afghanistan, Iraq, and other battlefields in the Global War on Terror. Blue Mountain, according to its corporate profile, provided clients with close protection services; penetration testing (veteran British military and law enforcement special operations personnel would probe existing security protocols in embassies and other high-threat locations to expose critical weaknesses); surveillance and investigations; maritime security; and high-risk static guard personnel. Blue Mountain claimed an esteemed list of past performance operations in countries around the world, including

Afghanistan, Iraq, various locations in Europe, and even the Caribbean; some of its reported corporate clients included BAT, BG Group, Cadbury, Canon, Capgemini, DHL, Excel, Google, Jaguar Land Rover, Lufthansa, Orange, Sony, and Viacom.[6]

Blue Mountain promoted SAS-like professionalism and quality in its corporate ethos, but its business pedigree was, in fact, reportedly suspect. Like many other American and European security companies that employed special operations veterans, Blue Mountain sought business by bouncing around Arab capitals seeking projects—as either prime contractors, subs, or those working at bottom dollar for the subs. These executives stayed at mid-level hotels (or more luxurious digs if their businesses were fluid); they wore 5.11 tactical khaki trousers and Under Armour tight-fitting polo shirts to highlight gym-generated muscles and mosaics of martial tattoos. They were the proverbial blonds in a sea of brunets, and it was common to see these former operators turned salesmen promising top-tier services to governments—Western and other—with bottom-feeding budgets. Blue Mountain was one of the too-many-to-count companies employing special operations veterans in hopes of getting a piece, even a crumb, of one of the high-risk and high-reward government contracts being doled out without too much scrutiny.

The new Libyan government was very sensitive to the notion of mercenaries operating on its soil, and it severely curtailed the freedom of private military companies to operate inside the country. Libya had a long history of armed foreigners inside its boundaries—Italians, Germans, British, and Russians—and the fear was that the country would soon be awash in Blackwater-like personnel with Blackwater-like collateral damage, such as the incident that occurred on September 16, 2007, at Nisour Square in Baghdad, when seventeen civilians were killed and over twenty wounded by Blackwater personnel operating in a personal security detail, or PSD, convoy as part of a U.S. State Department contract. In order to bid for the State Department contract in Benghazi, Blue Mountain had to set up a local office in Libya, known as Blue Mountain Libya. Blue Mountain Libya eventually won a $387,000 contract to provide unarmed guards at the Special Mission Compound. According to records, many were shocked over the award. Blue Mountain faced serious questions concerning its practices and its integrity. Although its pedigree was 22 SAS, its personnel were minimum-wage and subpar. A security professional was quoted as saying that the level of service Blue Mountain provided did not appear adequate to the risks presented by a lawless city; another insider claimed that the Libyan Ministry of Interior was not happy with Blue Mountain and had the company on its close observation/target list.[7]

Blue Mountain's guards were paid 5.21 Libyan dinars per hour (roughly $4.15) and they were guaranteed eight-hour shifts. Their training and their capabilities appeared to matter little. What was imperative, as per the outlines of the employment contract, was that the guard force did not show up to work high or drunk; they did not fight or perpetrate physical abuse on one another; they didn't lie, steal, bully, sabotage, and defy basic personal hygiene requirements. The guards couldn't, of course, download pornography on facility computers, and accepting bribes was not allowed. Reportedly, Blue Mountain's program manager traveled to Benghazi only once to review the status of his guard force. The guards' loyalties—and indeed capabilities—were highly suspect.

Armed with the most minimal of training and equipped with an identifying blue vest, a Taser, and a pair of handcuffs, the guard force and a handful of members from the February 17 Brigade presided around the perimeter at the Special Mission Compound.

The residence was a palatial mansion that, on the exterior, was painted in a typical, though ornately opulent, desert-yellow scheme. The mansion consisted of a main entrance, a master bedroom, two rooms—reportedly, a study and a communications room—a bathroom, and a common area large enough to amply entertain a sultan's harem. A yellowish marble floor was shiny and polished. A square chestnut table held two ornate candles on it; a gaudy vase, the kind often found in southern mansions or Donald Trump casinos, was positioned squarely on the table. A short climb of stairs led to the living room. It, too, was decorated for a wealthy noble, complete with a chandelier, a ruby-red sofa, and a plasma TV; an air conditioner hung over the TV and controlled the climate in the room by a remote control console. Several other sitting corners were adorned with upholstered armchairs and love seats and small oak tables covered in glass. The dining room was spartan. Eight cushioned chairs spanned a rectangular table; there were no paintings on the dining room walls, just a neatly painted yellow that blended with the Persian-style rug and the dark marble floor. The kitchen was modern and magnificent— black wood cabinets and all the appliances that would make a new homeowner envious. Fresh fruits from a nearby Benghazi market filled a large glass fishbowl.

Half the house, in keeping with the most rudimentary of security requirements, was outfitted with a safe haven that could provide temporary protection in case the facility came under attack. In Inman-era embassies, FE/BR, or forced-entry and blast-resistant, doors and windows were to enable the safety of personnel inside a post that was under assault and provide them with the time to wait for rescue and to destroy classified materials; SY had learned its lessons about the destruction of classified materials during the 1979 seizure of the U.S. embassy in Tehran, after Iranian operatives had pieced together single-cut shredded cables line by line.

The FE/BR concept was time based; the doors and the transparent armor, depending on their classified thicknesses and properties, were designed to delay attackers, even those armed with sledgehammers and battering rams, by fifteen, thirty, or sixty minutes. There was no classified material inside the residence, however: just the ambassador. Security, therefore, was enhanced by safe rooms and emergency egress windows—both a primary and a secondary—that were designed to keep attackers out. The safe haven was not fireproof, however. There was no emergency high-volume air system to remove suffocating smoke in case the building was set ablaze; there were no smoke hoods stored inside the safe haven, as such emergency gear was not part of such a standardized specification. An iron gate with a lock sealed off the safe haven from possible outsiders who breached the residence's sculptured wooden doors. Ground-floor windows were reinforced with security bars; primary and secondary egress windows in the safe haven were fitted with metal bars and security shutters.

The residence was situated some 150 feet behind the main security fence. The standoff was just enough to protect someone inside the building should a sedan crammed with explosives be detonated right at the main gate. Sandbags were hastily positioned to the right of the main entrance as a means to safeguard the security force from ordnance should it be involved in a battle to prevent a takeover of the residence. A flak vest was pre-positioned in the safe haven just in case. To enhance security at the Special Mission Compound, drop bars were added to the main gates to control vehicular access and to provide anti-ram capabilities. The State Department classifies such physical security items depending on the type of threat they can mitigate; a K12 rated drop gate, for example, must be able to stop a fifteen-thousand-pound vehicle traveling at fifty miles per hour at a ninety-degree point-of-impact angle, and not penetrate more than thirty-six inches from the point of impact.

Special Mission Benghazi's grounds were roughly six hundred feet long by six hundred feet wide. A redbrick driveway split the grounds in two and ran all the way from the main Charlie-1 gate south, approximately two hundred meters toward the rear wall that bordered the Fourth Ring Road to the south. The northern half of the compound consisted of immaculately groomed grounds and Libyan shrubs and trees; the greenery would have made a sultan proud. The southern half of the diplomatic portion was more spartan, with rows of olive trees planted recently into the rich reddish earth.

A small swimming pool enabled the ambassador and possible guests to enjoy some cooling waters to defeat the relentless Libyan sun. A water tower, perhaps a remnant of the Italian occupation, stood idly along the northeast corner of the diplomatic half of the compound.

A smaller gate, code-named Charlie-3, provided special access—and emergency egress—toward the Fourth Ring Road. The gate was small and could only accommodate one direction of traffic. It was not meant to be a security gate.

Adjacent to the residence was the area where the DS contingent ate and slept; the building, in fact, looked like a miniaturized copy of the diplomatic residence and resembled servant quarters. The gardens and grass around the diplomatic security quarters were well-groomed and typical of Libya's upper class; gardeners from the nations below the Sahara Desert, the migrant green thumbs of the Qaddafi regime, were the regulars who crouched on their knees to make the desert—or at least the grounds of lavish estates of Qaddafi loyalists and those who thrived economically under the dictator—bloom. A carpet of gray bricks covered much of this half of the modest grounds.

Access to this part of the overall landscape was made through Bravo-1 gate, which faced the main road on the northern envelope of the grounds. A man gate, a smaller cast-iron doorway that could be dead bolted from inside, positioned adjacent to Bravo-1 gate, enabled access for visitors without having to open the main vehicular entrance.

The windows on the main floor of the DS residence were all reinforced by steel gates. In case it came down to a firefight, chest-high rows of white burlap sandbags were tactically positioned outside the building near where the special agents occasionally parked their vehicles.

The agents' residence had bedrooms, a recreation room, and a small cantina. The kitchen was equipped with the spartan trappings one would find in a corporate office. There was a sink, a stove, a communal table, a coffee machine, and, of course, a fridge. The kitchen had all the trappings of Americans abroad—especially armed Americans on a tactical protective assignment. The fridge was stocked with bottled water and Gatorade. A Price Club's worth of PowerBars and soft drinks were warehoused in a corner; there were also enough Meals Ready to Eat, or MREs, to feed a hungry army. And, of course, where there were cigars, there was television: a dish made sure that the comforts of American security personnel abroad—Fox News and ESPN—could be followed.

A carport adjacent to the building was covered by a white-and-gray awning that kept the armored SUVs—Toyota Land Cruisers—protected from the harsh Benghazi sun. The vehicles were outfitted with run-flat tires—special "tactical" tires that are designed to perform while deflated; they enable a vehicle to drive at a top speed of fifty miles per hour for up to fifty miles. They were also equipped with tow straps, fire extinguisher, binoculars, sledgehammer, medical kit, bottled water, MREs, spare tourniquets, and ballistic soft-armor vests with plates. The vehicles were always fully gassed and ready to deploy immediately; they were equipped with Motorola radios for communications with the U.S. residence and the TOC—the tactical operations center.

The TOC was the security nerve center and common hub of the facility and was always manned by one or two DS agents. Situated south of the residence, the TOC was a small and constricting structure of gray cement and small windows sealed in by iron bars. An agent's battle rattle, on such an assignment, was not a Jos A. Bank suit, but rather a ballistic helmet, body armor, Colt assault rifle, spare magazines, a tourniquet, pressure bandage, pen flares with a launcher, SureFire flashlight, whistle, compass, Leatherman multi-tool, and Spyderco folding knife. An open radio link existed between the TOC and the Regional Security Office at the U.S. embassy in Tripoli.

An alleyway, a ten-foot-wide and four-hundred-foot-long walkway between the two nine-foot-high walls that separated the residence and the DS half of the compound, enabled access between the two halves of the sprawling estate. The alley, however, in case of attack, was a kill zone. If enemy forces scaled the outer wall and gained the high ground, if they managed to zero in on the complex with a mortar or an overhand weapon such as the Soviet-era RKG-3 antitank grenade, anyone in the alleyway link would be decimated. The RKG-3 was a handheld shaped-charge grenade that became the most prolific and successful weapon in the insurgent campaigns in Iraq. When its pin was pulled and it was thrown overhead, a parachute emerged, forcing the grenade to land at a ninety-degree angle, maximizing the impact of the shaped charge. Tens of thousands of RKG-3s were in the hands of militiamen and jihadists in Libya.

It appears, though, that the DS contingent was poised for worst-case eventualities and swarm attacks from all angles. Sandbag emplacements dotted the rooftop of the agent barracks. They had been tactically placed by MSD agents on previous trips into Benghazi, to provide cover for anticipated fields of fire.

The sandbags would soon prove invaluable.

6.

The Special Agents

Benghazi wasn't that long-coveted temporary assignment position that DS agents compete for. The temporary slots that opened for Benghazi every three months were not equivalent to a stint in Rome or Paris; wives would not go on the pilgrimage to Neiman Marcus to prepare for the few months inside the bosom of fashion and cuisine. Wives and children couldn't even go. Benghazi was a hardship post—no spouses or children permitted. It was a spartan post inside the hell of a raging inferno. There was a bright side, though. Unlike a stretch in Baghdad, Sana'a, Peshawar, or Kabul—to name a few—a trip to Benghazi promised to be a short one. Still, the agents assigned to the Special Mission Compound had to persevere. They had to survive.

There was a revolving-door churn of TDY, or temporary duty, agents coming in and out of the post. "They [the DS agents] served on average less than forty days, many for thirty days or less, with similar rotations at the U.S. embassy in Tripoli," the former U.S. ambassador Thomas Pickering indicated in an interview with Reuters. "Into a very dicey environment," he added, "came security officers who had high-threat training, no State Department overseas experience, and there was no continuity. Getting on top of your job in a difficult situation obviously takes more than thirty days. And so these really good officers were disadvantaged by the fact they had no memory beyond thirty days of what was going on and what happened except what their predecessors left them."[1]

Many of the men—and women—in this churn could shoot like top-tier commandos and drive like NASCAR champions, but they lacked even the most basic of Arabic and Islamic cultural awareness skills. Most agents, upon being assigned to an embassy or consulate as an RSO or ARSO, would embark on intensive language instruction to prepare them for their particular country; sometimes, in fact, language school could take as long as a year to complete, and agents, after many years in the field, could boast three or four languages, as diverse as Russian, Japanese, and Spanish, in their repertoire. The investment that the DS would make in these special agents would be reflected in the lengths of their tours in a particular country. But in the reality of the new world of critical-threat posts that DS had to safeguard, there was no continuity of agent personnel in Benghazi. The RSO and ARSO were so understaffed and temporary that they didn't have time to get to know the local security chiefs; they didn't have the opportunity to host parties, visit these men and their families in their homes, and create human bonds of friendship that could one day be crucial. Benghazi even lacked an interpreter, or an experienced Foreign Service National Investigator. The FSNIs, as they are known, are often retired local police or military men who are subject matter experts (SMEs) on their country's inner workings; they have a Rolodex of contacts, and they are a buffer between the security needs of a U.S. diplomatic post and the day-to-day limitations of the host nation. RSOs consider their FSNIs to be an inseparable piece of the security package they are responsible for maintaining.

On August 15, the temporary security staff at Special Mission Benghazi convened an emergency meeting to address the deteriorating security reality in the city. The exchanges at the meeting were direct and ominously honest. The TDY RSO expressed his concerns that the DS contingent would be unable to defend the post if it was subjected to a coordinated and serious terrorist attack. They cited a lack of manpower, insufficient physical security infrastructure, limited weapon systems at their disposal, and the lack of *any* reliable host-nation support.

The meeting, held inside the small cantina at the agents' residence on the compound, was conducted without anger—just genuine foreboding. The next day, in a cable marked "SECRET," the RSO in Tripoli dispatched the conclusions of the Benghazi sit-down to his superiors in Washington, D.C. The TDY RSO emphatically stated that he did not believe the mission could be adequately defended. The cable struck a resonant chord with Ambassador Stevens, who, along with other elements of the U.S. intelligence and defense community, agreed with the DS in-country assessment that the security for the Benghazi Special Mission Compound was tenuous.

It wasn't the first time that such a stark statement of security was transmitted to the State Department.

In 1976, a young special agent named Al Golacinski, working for the old SY, sent a similar cable to headquarters, after being temporarily assigned to the U.S. embassy in Beirut as a replacement for the then RSO Sid Telford. Telford was allowed a brief home leave in order to get a much-needed break from dealing with the rapidly deteriorating security environment in Beirut; Telford performed tirelessly and heroically on an almost daily basis, rescuing American citizens from the chaos that was then Beirut. Civil war had broken out in Lebanon pitting Christian and Muslim forces against each other; heavily armed Palestinian groups were in the center of most of the violence. Adding to the chaos were the intra-religious rivalries that, taken together, made Beirut one of the most dangerous cities on earth. This was a civil war of massacres and random deadly violence. Young Christian militia women kept the ears of the people they killed in designer handbags they wore off their shoulders. Telford and Golacinski made almost daily visits to the morgue in an attempt to identify missing American citizens. Unfortunately, the U.S. embassy was located on the very dividing line between Muslim and Christian fighters; this became known as the Green Line. Incoming sniper and artillery fire from the Christian side regularly impacted the embassy building. Embassy personnel were forced to come and leave work in surprise high-speed, serpentine rushes in lightly armored vehicles. Outgoing tank and mortar rounds launched from just in front and behind the embassy building by Muslim forces drew additional fire and sometimes resulted in airbursts impacting the building. This was by no means a safe environment for embassy personnel. Golacinski and the marines joked that they slept under their mattresses, not on them.

During one particularly heavy artillery exchange one night, the embassy building took numerous hits. Golacinski was on the phone with the State Ops Center and repeated that "our position is untenable." He was duly advised that the embassy must remain open in spite of the clear dangers faced by the personnel. Secretary Henry Kissinger stated that the continuing presence of the United States in Lebanon served a higher purpose, so the embassy remained open. Unfortunately, a short time later, the newly appointed U.S. ambassador to Lebanon, Francis E. Meloy Jr., was abducted by Palestinian terrorists as he traveled to the presidential palace, along with the U.S. economic counselor Robert O. Waring, to present their credentials to the new Lebanese president. Both men were shot dead; their bodies were later dumped on a nearby beach.

Golacinski had no illusions that working for SY was akin to working for the FBI or the Secret Service, organized as separate agencies but under the supervision of Justice and Treasury. In spite of its law enforcement mandate and high-stakes responsibilities for protection of life and U.S. interests abroad, the SY mission was viewed by the State Department as anathema to the conduct of diplomacy, and the department was therefore committed to not granting the authorities and resources necessary for SY to carry out its responsibilities. SY agents quickly recognized this and learned to do the best they could with the limited resources available. The job attracted a certain type of individual who thrived on dealing with these kinds of challenges. "At the end of the day we [the agents] signed up for the risks associated with our positions with our eyes open."[2]

Three years later, while serving as the RSO in Tehran, Golacinski would send cables to the State Department warning of the dangers to U.S. personnel; these cables, of course, were similar in language and concern to the messages sent from Benghazi to Foggy Bottom in August 2012. The decision to grant the Shah of Iran entry to the United States prompted a cable and numerous phone conversations warning that the situation would be untenable if the embassy were attacked; months earlier, in February 1979, the embassy had already withstood an attack. Even before the admission of the Shah, the embassy faced a progression of dangerous attacks on its compound ranging from frequent automatic gunfire directed at the compound to grenade attacks and an RPG attack on the newly completed consulate building (located on the compound). Incursions by armed intruders occurred on various occasions, including once when two marine guards and the chargé d'affaires were held at gunpoint in the ambassador's residence. Large-scale demonstrations took place in front of the embassy common; embassy personnel were evacuated to other locations when there was advance warning of trouble. These circumstances were the norm, and it was left to the RSO and his limited staff to deal with them. Washington was aware of these occurrences, but, not unlike Beirut earlier and Benghazi much later, the State Department failed to accept the possibility that tragedy would follow.

On November 4, 1979, the embassy was stormed by radical elements of the Iranian regime. Efforts to negotiate a way out of the attack, as Golacinski had done previously, were to no avail, and Washington finally ordered the embassy to surrender. "Our personnel were held hostage and subjected to unspeakable horrors for 444 days," Golacinski reflected, "and eight U.S. military personnel lost their lives at Desert One during the course of an aborted rescue attempt."[3]

In considering the similarities—the warning signs—between attacks against America's diplomatic posts in Beirut, Tehran, and Benghazi and Washington's tendency to turn a blind eye to the inconvenient realities on the ground, Golacinski simply quoted the French author Jean-Baptiste Alphonse Karr: *"Plus Ça change, plus c'est la même chose."* The more things change, the more they stay the same.[4]

To the State Department, Beirut and Tehran were ancient history. The perils of abiding by Dr. Kissinger's "higher purpose" in spite of all warnings and at the likely expense of U.S. personnel were quite clearly ignored. In an action memo for Undersecretary of State for Management Patrick Kennedy from the Near Eastern Division head, Jeffrey Feltman, titled "Future of Operations in Benghazi, Libya," the importance of a continued U.S. presence is requested and defined as a small State-run presence. "A continued presence in Benghazi will emphasize U.S. interests in the eastern part of Libya," the memo states. "Many Libyans have said the U.S. presence in Benghazi has a salutary, calming effort on the easterners who are fearful that the new focus on Tripoli could once again lead to their neglect and exclusion from reconstruction and wealth distribution."[5]

As a result of the higher purpose even in light of the security threats, the Benghazi protection model—as insufficient as it was—was accepted; after all, it had become the norm in this new world disorder.

Headquarters assembled temporary duty lists like a jigsaw puzzle, juggling global personnel needs. The agents all began their journeys to the hot spots of America's pressure points around the world in the business-class lounges at Dulles International Airport. The younger agents gravitated to the hot spots; it had always been that way. Danger pay, especially for newlyweds and those with newborns, helped cover the bills, and doing your time in the barrel of some hellhole was viewed favorably by the star chamber that etched permanent assignments into stone. Even the old-timers felt compelled to sign up for the endless list of hardship posts that came up for consideration. Men with twenty years on who had already served in places like Beirut and Monrovia now found themselves competing for assignments in Baghdad, Peshawar, and Khartoum. The agents would sometimes laugh about this twist of fate at a point in their careers when they were thinking more about retirement than high-threat tactical training and looking forward to some quiet time at home, in the northern Virginia enclaves, now that their children were in college. "I am getting too old for this shit," these graying men in their late forties would joke to one another, paraphrasing the Danny Glover character's famous expression from the film *Lethal Weapon*, as they crossed paths in the business-class lounges at Dulles, Dubai, or Amman's Queen Alia International Airport, heading to Iraq, Pakistan, or Yemen.

Special agents serving in DS, even those who had migrated to federal work from municipal, county, and state law enforcement agencies, knew that it was pointless to complain about their lack of support from the Foreign Service lifers at Main State, or "Bow Ties," as they were known. DS agents, by the fibers of their DNA, were stoic. After all, the legacy of the agency was that the DS special agent was a jack-of-all-trades and a master of doing a great many things with few resources. But in this particular case, stoicism made way for a reality check: in 2012, in the upside-down world of endless threats, the intelligence indicated the security posture was spiraling out of control.

Five agents found themselves in Benghazi during Ambassador Chris Stevens's week in the city. They became a team, and like many details that DS has thrown together for protective assignments, the agents at the Special Mission Compound represented different backgrounds and experiences—both in their lives before DS and while carrying the badge.

They were, as coined so aptly in the field office, known as "hump agents." These were bodies, inexperienced yet willing to do what they were told and to work the worst shifts, who were the nuts and bolts of the protection backbone. Protective details couldn't function without them. To headquarters and management, these men and women were names and numbers on assignment boards.

The five men in Benghazi were the new DS, a mixed bag of overachievers: former street cops, U.S. Marines, a U.S. Army Iraqi war veteran, and academics; one was a class valedictorian at his small, faith-based college in the Southwest. Some were battle trained and had seen war. All had ten years or less on the job; most had carried a DS badge for less than five years. All joined the service after 9/11.

They will be identified as: R.,* the TDY RSO who was the senior man among the group and the person who was on long-term post in Libya, borrowed from the RSO's office in Tripoli. A. and B. were the two junior agents assigned TDY to serve in Benghazi. C. and D. were the two young agents who constituted Ambassador Stevens's ad hoc protective detail and had flown with him from Tripoli.

The detail assigned to Benghazi, especially the younger agents, reflected an ethos that was always viewed as one of the most valuable aspects of the job—learning by doing. DS had always thrown young agents with little or no experience into the mix of multidimensional

---

*Identities withheld for security and privacy considerations.

protection assignments; agents based in the United States who had not previously served abroad did not have the opportunity to receive overseas RSO training before serving in Benghazi.[6] At a UN General Assembly in New York City, DS was responsible for over 150 protective details, a seemingly impossible feat to pull off considering that before 9/11 the agency fielded only twelve hundred agents. Some of the details were small and routine: a European foreign minister, or the secretary of state from some South American nation that had few enemies. But other details, like the Iranian or Cuban foreign minister, or for Yasir Arafat during his time as head of the Palestinian Authority, were monstrous and high-threat endeavors. Veteran agents, some with years of experience overseas, would head these details, and junior agents would be thrown unmercifully into the mix conducting advances and preventive intelligence gathering and countersurveillance and negotiating traffic in midtown Manhattan in a shiny Suburban full of Uzi-wielding agents. It was here, learning by doing and dealing with different agencies and personalities, that young agents would learn that on a detail a smile always won friends and an upbeat attitude always enlisted the help of others. But these learning-by-doing assignments were domestic details—not international TDYs and not to locations like Benghazi.

The dichotomy of life inside this *new* DS was that new men and women on the job no longer learned by doing by being hump agents in a field office and flying from one city to another inside the United States to help out protecting the Dalai Lama on a Monday and a NATO foreign minister taking his family to Disneyland on a Friday. The new DS sent its newest agents into the eye of the storm, in Afghanistan and Kurdistan, where they could learn under fire. As remarkable as this trial-by-fire reality was, the retention rate for agents remained high; the selection process, which picks approximately two hundred candidates from a sea of ten thousand hopefuls, has been remarkably successful. These new agents are evaluated and judged by their ability to sink or swim inside the war zones of the world. The same standards don't hold true for the top tier of management. While new agents are judged and advance onward and upward based on flying by the seat of their pants, this new phenomenon has rewarded bosses who play it safe politically. Safe decisions, safe choices, and safe outcomes are what have guaranteed careers. Most of the DS directors who have been appointed to their posts over the past twenty-five years have *not* served in critical-threat posts. A director must be able to navigate through high-level bureaucracy and to deal with and negotiate with the "suits" and "dresses" at the highest levels of government. Those traits are best honed in Washington, D.C., and in places like London and Paris. "These skill sets aren't perfected in Baghdad or Beirut," said one retired RSO.

In DS, even in the old SY days, there were always those special characters, the thrill seekers, who volunteered to venture where others were unwilling. They traveled to places the FBI would never dream of sending an agent to. There was Jack Herse, murdered in 1974 under suspicious circumstances in Rosslyn, Virginia, steps away from the current DS headquarters; Herse, old-school SY and a decorated U.S. Marine at Inchon, had single-handedly arrested Dr. Timothy Leary in Kabul after Leary was broken out of jail by the Weather Underground. Known as the "Troubleshooter," Jack was sent to hot spots—alone!—whenever embassies were attacked or ambassadors kidnapped in the 1970s. His backup was a five-shot Smith & Wesson Model 60 revolver and a Beretta submachine gun.

Herse's legacy continued with the creation of DS. In the years preceding the 9/11 attacks—indeed, in the beginning of America's war against fundamentalist terror—a good many Benghazi-like assignments fell to MSD and especially a small cadre within the special response force who were known as the "gunslingers" or the "go-to guys." Many were military veterans, some with combat experience, who brought with them specialized skills—and a specialized psychological package—that made them uniquely qualified for the most dangerous of assignments. This cadre was made up of some of the agency's most experienced operatives and, in many cases, the most undisciplined. They were able to thrive because, as the retired DS agent Scot Folensbee, one of the go-to guys, would reflect, "DS at the time gave agents in the field, especially in dangerous locations, a lot of latitude."[7]

Folensbee, a highly decorated paratrooper and medic in Vietnam, and men like Tony Deibler, a decorated marine, were all type G personalities—thrill seekers! These guys rode BMW motorcycles, scuba dived, skydived, and drove fast cars. The workload during their tenure—they traveled the world to hot spots and under-threat embassies 250 days a year—still enabled them to attend top-tier training courses with the best of the best of America's spec ops and intelligence communities. From "Wally World," the Delta Force compound in Fort Bragg, to explosive and explosive-ordnance-disposal instruction with elements of America's covert community, these State Department agents broadened their horizons and prepared themselves for what no other federal agent ever has to contend with—the madness of this world's regional and tribal conflicts.

Folensbee and his fellow Dirty Harrys ("every rotten assignment in the book") found themselves in shoot-outs in Bosnia, in El Salvador, in Lebanon, and in Africa. In one TDY to a Liberia covered in the blood of a civil war, a deployment that both Folensbee and Deibler volunteered for, the two State Department agents found themselves at an embassy surrounded by a city of madness and slaughter. Guerrillas and gang members slaughtered one another in front of the embassy gates, sometimes cutting out the hearts of the men they had killed and eating the still-pumping organs for the embassy staffers to see. Folensbee and Deibler didn't drive through checkpoints; they shot their way through. And in acts of great courage, they rescued trapped American civilians and journalists with weapons ablaze. "Many people back home, on the Hill or at headquarters, couldn't understand what happened in places where violence was out of control," Folensbee said. "There were no right decisions or wrong decisions in such places; only individual decisions."[8]

Benghazi, too, was an assignment where there were no wrong and right decisions—only issues of reaction and survival. The ancient town was simmering with passions and preclusions of peace and in the power vacuum of a civil war had become a nerve center for the

North African jihad. DS, even with two thousand agents, was stretched thin; a significant percentage of the agents overseas were in Baghdad or Kabul; Pakistan and the Arabian Peninsula required vast human capital. MSD teams were crisscrossing the globe on emergency tactical assignments. With the Global War on Terror placing virtually every U.S. embassy and consulate inside the crosshairs, the tactical specialists of MSD had, in many ways, become the new DS.

RSOs at embassies often have a hundred tasks and responsibilities in the course of their day-to-day duties. Benghazi was about safety and survival. It was an assignment that would require each man assigned to the post to utilize the resourcefulness and think-on-your-feet instincts that DS was so good, during "normal times," at fostering in its young agents.

The five men hunkered down in Benghazi were modern-day Crocketts, Bowies, and Travises at an Alamo outpost very far from home. Although trained for every worst-case scenario imaginable, no agent ever expects it to happen, but knows that when things start to go bad, they go bad very quickly. Time stands still for those engaged in the fight, but how quickly things go south is only known to those who have been there and done that. Who lives and dies depends a great deal on training, teamwork, and fate.

The agents at the compound knew that they were on their own.

7.

Life in Critical Threat

From 1998 to 2008—in fact, from the true emergence of al-Qaeda as a potent global terrorist force to the height of the bitter battles waged against Osama bin Laden's army around the world—there were thirty-nine attacks against U.S. embassies and consulates, as well as against U.S. diplomatic personnel, excluding regular attacks against the U.S. embassy in Baghdad, Iraq.[1] Many of the posts that were attacked were locations that are defined as under "critical threat." According to its protocols and mandate, DS, along with other federal law enforcement and intelligence communities, classifies the threat level at a particular embassy or consulate in order to determine what resources are needed to adequately provide security support. Six threat categories are reviewed, including terrorist activity (from both international groups and domestic organizations) in the host country, political violence, crime, ████████████, and ████████████. A rating is then assigned for each category on a four-level scale: critical threat; high threat; medium threat; and low threat.

Libya was just another of the many critical-threat posts that dotted the world map at DS headquarters. But the violence and uncertainty of a Libya in a post–Arab Spring vacuum, with Islamic militants looking to establish new global outposts, made the country uniquely dangerous for American diplomacy.

September 2012 promised to be bloody in Libya. A "state of maximum alert" had been declared for Benghazi and other parts of the country on August 29, 2012. There was an intense fear among Libyan officials that pro-Qaddafi loyalists would use the September 1 anniversary of Qaddafi's rise to power as a springboard for a bloody attempt to retake control of the country. September also had started on a troubling note for Ambassador Stevens and the security staff at the U.S. embassy in Tripoli. On September 4, a local guard, one of the 125 local bodyguards hired by the RSO's office, had been killed in a tragic accident when he was crushed to death by a roll steel gate controlling the entrance of the compound. The gate was mechanically operated, but because it had been battered and abused in the course of day-to-day operations, it had to be manually slid open and shut; the Libyan guard was killed when the gate dislodged and fell off its frame.[2] The tragic incident happened in front of several embassy employees as well as Ambassador Stevens.*

Diplomats *do* operate from the safety of bunkers and fortresses, and the systems required to create a secure environment are cumbersome and heavy; mass and might are required to absorb the destructive shock and awe of modern terrorism's VBIEDs. The gates, and the guard force, were one of the many security enhancements made to the sprawling embassy facility to cement a long-standing and safe American presence inside Libya.[3] Security, of course, was a primary concern and difficult to provide in the fluid reality of a nation that had just been through the hell of civil war and the onset of sectarian and Islamic scores being settled. Ambassador Stevens's work in Tripoli was the iconic emblem of America's mission to maintain influence and support for the democratic aspirations of the Libyan people inside the tumult of the Arab Spring. Benghazi was the out-of-sight and out-of-mind meat grinder where that influence would be challenged. As special envoy, Stevens visited Benghazi frequently; he would do so less often after he became ambassador. He had scheduled a trip to the

---

*The DS Foundation, a charitable nonprofit, provided $1,500 to the surviving family of the guard killed.

city for the week of September 10–14. It would be his first trip to Benghazi in nearly a year.

An ambassador's movements in a city like Paris, let alone a war zone like Libya, do not occur in a vacuum. There were itineraries to be prepared, commercial flights to book, liaisons to forewarn, security provisions to put in play, and contingency planning to envision and execute. That was the big-picture end of the equation. On the ground, in Benghazi, the five DS agents assigned to the Special Mission Compound were no strangers to such requirements of the protective security world; it was, after all, a significant part of the special agent's job description. The art of protective work was something learned at the basic agent level and bequeathed by senior agents to rookies in the field. Much of the work required doggedness and instinct, as well as luck and the knowledge that if and when a threat materialized, reaction time would be preventively instantaneous.

Part of the DS special agents' job description is preparing for the worst and reviewing a mental checklist to make sure they are ready to respond to any and all eventualities. "An agent on a detail always goes through a lengthy mental checklist to make sure he's ready for anything," reflected Special Agent T.,* a former DS agent with tours in Jerusalem, Sana'a, and Karachi, to name but a few. "This list is very introspective and personal. How will I respond to the first sight of the man in the crowd who could be an assassin or a suicide bomber? Will I trust the hairs that stand up on the back of my neck when I see what I think are the telltale signs of an IED? Will the sun be in my eyes when we are under attack and I have to respond with my SIG and M4? Will I ever see my wife and kids again? And that's on an assignment inside the real world. Your senses and your concerns sharpen significantly when you find yourself on a hardship tour to some far-flung outpost somewhere in between hell and a firefight."[4]

The wars in Iraq and Afghanistan blurred the lines between what had traditionally been the domain of DS and that belonging to the military. DS found itself in the crosshairs of two major international

---

*Name withheld for security considerations due to the special agent's current work for another federal agency.

conflicts, and RSOs and their staffs pivoted from traditional diplomatic security tasks to such endeavors as nation building, hostage affairs, and long-range convoy security. The embassy in Baghdad had, at any given point, nearly two hundred special agents. Their tasks were endless, their numbers relatively small, and the risks enormous. Agents summoned to deploy to these high-threat zones lacked high-threat training; not all the agents were young and veterans of the armed forces (though many were); some of the men and women on short lists for posts in Iraq and Afghanistan were salty veterans and had had careers in academics and business before joining the ranks of DS and did not have combat pedigrees. Preparing these men and women for the realities of warfare was an absolute necessity.

Originally, the High-Threat Training, or HTT, as it was known, was a prerequisite for agents en route to Baghdad and Kabul and ultimately grew into mandatory instruction for all DS personnel heading to critical-threat posts around the world. The thirty-two days of instruction are pressure filled and intense—much like the hot spots the agents will soon find themselves operating in. The curriculum, a speed/low-drag mixture of tactical, medical, survival, navigational, and driving, includes advanced tactical protection skills (which include how to shoot from a well of a follow car to how to conduct a twelve-man advance, using four-point ███████████████ and shooting ███████); small-team room clearing (which came in handy in 2008 when DS agents helped to clear the Serena Hotel in Kabul after it had been seized by Taliban terrorists); enhanced combat medicine (the ███████████████); field navigations (including use of GPS); tactical and covert communications; escape and evacuation training (similar to the SERE, or Survival, Evasion, Resistance, and Escape, training offered to U.S. military Special Forces); and advanced driving skills (agents had to know how to change a run-flat tire, are tossed around in a mechanical spindle to experience disorientation in a vehicle rollover, and learn to drive Humvees in soft sand). Agents destined for the Middle East also receive intelligence briefings on the terrorist threat awaiting them. The instruction culminates with an intensive three-day practical exercise. The DS instructors are all veterans of extended tours of critical-threat posts or subject matter experts like

former 18-Delta medics and doctors from the Johns Hopkins Hospital. In advanced MSD training, agents are taught how to be Dedicated Defensive Marksmen, better known ████████████████████
████████████████████

One of the primary objectives of the training focuses on driving; indeed, much of the training is carried out at the Bill Scott Raceway, a facility in West Virginia, about seventy miles from Washington, D.C. The facility, one of the most unique driving training tracks in the world, enables students in the course to focus on practical, hands-on driving skills in realistic settings at the hands of some of the most experienced evasive and counterassault driving instructors in the world.

By 2012, though, the instruction had morphed into a training regimen with a much higher level of octane. Known as the Tactical Combat Casualty Care training, or TCCC, the instruction was intended to keep personnel alive in the field—alive after they had encountered a suicide bombing or IED event; alive after they had been involved in a catastrophic event; and alive if they found themselves, and their protectee, in the center of a swarm attack. Great emphasis was placed on providing the special agents with advanced tactical trauma instruction so that they could keep others alive, even after the most horrific of casualties, until help would come and evacuate them out of the danger zone.*

The training is absolutely dynamic and designed to leave a permanent imprint. "We have a number of individuals that serve overseas and around the world in some of the most hostile environments, and it's incumbent on us to give them the training to increase their chances of being a successful tour overseas in a safe fashion," commented the DS Assistant Director for Training Mark Hipp.[5] Hipp, who had spent a good portion of his career in MSD crisscrossing the globe from danger zone to danger zone, and members of his staff with similar backgrounds were able to impart their knowledge and experience to new generations of DS agents.

---

*A full description of the TCCC course guidelines can be found at: http://www.health.mil/Libraries/120917_TCCC_Course_Materials/TCCC-Guideliness-120917.pdf.

TCCC was designed for preparing DS agents—young and old alike—with the tools for dealing tactically with the worst locations on the planet. DS agents were never intended to be full-time operators like members of the U.S. Navy SEALs. "Not that we are incapable of such a task," a former agent with years of overseas assignments in crosshair capitals like Beirut and Baghdad reflected, "but it's not our primary mission. We don't have the in-depth training of armament. And if we do, it's a small portion of our careers. If need be, we must sit down with an ambassador, a personal representative of the president of the United States, and tell him 'NO! NO! NO!' when the ambassador is pushing an issue. WE can. We have. I have. I did it many, many times! Fighting terrorists and negotiating with ambassadors, shows the breadth of our duties and abilities."[6]

That ability—to make the switch from Colt M4 vests and ceramic inserts to Ralph Lauren suits and SIG-███ and ███ semiautomatic pistols, to change gears from a warlord sit-down in Anbar Province to working a NATO summit in Brussels—was a fiber in the DNA of these agents that made DS truly unique. So, too, was the fact that their mission was multifaceted and their precinct truly global. They traveled to the most amazing cities in the world and to the very worst.

The Department of Defense, realizing that DS was stretched thinly throughout the world and especially at diplomatic posts inside the new and emerging realities of the Arab Spring, created, through the National Security Council, regional and nation-specific site security teams, or SSTs. Dubbed a traveling circus, twenty such teams crisscrossed the world visiting some of the most dangerous capitals and regions.

The Libyan SST was commanded by the Utah National Guard lieutenant colonel Andrew Wood, a veteran and well-respected Special Forces soldier, and consisted of sixteen spec ops personnel; these operators came from various units inside the conventional Special Forces community (Green Berets and SEALs) and the covert end of the spectrum (Delta and DevGru). The SST worked for the RSO and was answerable to the deputy chief of mission, or DCM. The SST split its time between the embassy in Tripoli and the Special Mission Compound in Benghazi.

Tripoli was the primary recipient of the SST focus. When, in February 2012, the SST first arrived in country, the situation in the Libyan capital was tense but easing slowly toward normalcy—Arab Spring normalcy. The sounds of gunfire that resonated at night as part of the revolutionary soundtrack soon reverted to the vibrancy of other North African cities: car horns blaring, eateries blasting the latest techno-Arab tunes, police sirens wailing, and the calls to prayer coming from the muezzin five times a day. Still, the security situation in the capital was volatile. At given times there were three eight-man MSD teams posted to the embassy. The SST operators greatly enhanced the embassy's deterrence and counterattack capabilities. But the threats were inescapable. Jihadist groups, conducting surveillance of the embassy grounds, knew that Ambassador Stevens was an avid runner, and they expressed their desires to kill him while he jogged. Stevens never ran alone again.

The SST also traveled to Benghazi. Lieutenant Colonel Wood was, in fact, in the city in June when the British ambassador Asquith's motorcade was targeted in an RPG attack; with its combat medics, or 18-Deltas, in tow, the SST provided emergency medical care and security support to the wounded British security agents; it also assisted the British, and the local authorities, with their investigation into the attack. Special Mission Benghazi, the lesser post, inexplicably usually staffed with only one agent, always needed more hands and more guns to stand at the ready. RSO Tripoli, Eric Nordstrom, regularly struggled with headquarters, often with the help of Ambassador Stevens, to get additional agents to bolster the garrison.

DS headquarters ultimately assigned three agents to Benghazi in August 2012. Benghazi was clearly a unique post, and considered a frontline outpost, more than the standard fixture of a critical-threat facility—such as the consulates in Pakistan (Karachi, Lahore, Peshawar) and Iraq (Basra, Kirkuk, and Erbil). Because Benghazi was ad hoc, there was a temporariness to the Special Mission Compound that impacted staffing and physical security measures. More significantly, the three agents assigned to Benghazi were TDY—dispatched to the post on temporary duty. Benghazi wasn't a city on the official bid list for postings overseas, and even if it was, it is doubtful that many in DS, if any at all, would volunteer for such an isolated and critical-threat assignment. Because of the Special Mission Compound's unmistakably temporary footprint, the RSOs assigned to it were never able to establish long-standing personal relationships with the local security heads; not only were the DS agents in charge never on the ground long enough to schmooze and win over a local police commander or a responsible militia leader, but, thanks to the internecine violence, there were no police commanders or local militia leaders who were around long enough to schmooze. When Ambassador Stevens's plans for Benghazi were revealed—from a particularly DS perspective—the challenge the agents on the ground faced was greatly amplified.

The agents were therefore forced to rely on their wits and training. They had to reconnoiter all the venues the ambassador planned to visit and prepare contingency plans just in case. No matter where any of the agents were in the city, no matter what time of day, they had to know the driving distance and the shortest possible route between their location and the closest medical trauma center; it didn't matter if their protectee was choking on a pretzel or suffering from a gaping chest wound, the agents involved in the detail had to have every worst-case scenario painted in their minds and responses preplanned. Agents were always hopeful to be on the right side of Murphy's Law on a detail—especially one that was high threat. There was never complacency on a detail. No lapses of judgment or focus were permitted. Even the smallest of items contained the explosive potential to become catastrophic; the assassinations of presidents, prime ministers, and kings defined preventable moments in time that forever scorched the logbooks of history.

There were two additional components laid out in advance of Ambassador Stevens's arrival. The first involved the February 17 Brigade. On September 9, 2012, the militia had solidified an agreement with the State Department concerning the establishment of a special force from within its ranks, called the Quick Reaction Force, or QRF, that would respond to any worst-case scenarios at any of the two American outposts in Benghazi but especially when Ambassador Stevens, or the "principal officer," was in the city. The QRF was to be on call 24/7 with at least three armed members. QRF members were to man the main Charlie-1 gate from 0800 to 0000 daily and conduct roving patrols throughout the compound from 0000 to 0800. There was one stipulation to these preset hours of operation: the QRF was to make personnel available at "all hours of the day and night" to prepare for any movements or operations outside normal business hours.*

At least one QRF member was to accompany DS agents on their trips to and from the Benina International Airport for their meet and greets with Ambassador Stevens or other notable diplomats or military and intelligence officials coming or going to Benghazi. DS demanded that the QRF hone their tactical skills and required that the force train at least once a week; the regimen had to be approved by the RSO, though it was a far cry from the standards of most third-world forces. The militia was responsible for providing the QRF members with their uniforms, though there was no standardization expected or supplied; the militia wore what can best be described as guerrilla chic: soccer jerseys and camouflage trousers. The QRF had to supply its own weapons and ammunition, but in post-civil-war Benghazi an AK-47 and a truckload of 7.62 mm ammo were as easy to come by as a Starbucks coffee in midtown Manhattan.

For the all-important task of security at the Special Mission Compound, QRF members earned 35 Libyan dinars a day—roughly $27.

The DS crew in Benghazi had to be ready to react and respond to any and all contingencies, ranging from suicide truck bombs to even CBRNE (chemical, biological, radiological, nuclear, and high-yield explosives) events; protocols, in such an event, included the compound's staff hunkering down in sealed rooms and donning pre-positioned chem-bio suits.

In case of an immediate emergency, such as full-scale war or

---

*Numerous documents, including sensitive ones that were ultimately redacted, were found in the smoldering debris of the Special Mission Compound Benghazi, and published by the *Washington Post* on October 3, 2012, in an article/feature titled "Sensitive documents left with little security at U.S. mission in Benghazi." Details concerning the QRF and local guard force were found in these published documents.

massive civil unrest, the Special Mission Compound security team was to evacuate the country by any and all means possible. The plan, known as E&E, or escape and evacuation, involved the initiation of a REACT plan that warranted the destruction of any classified or sensitive documents or material with the exception of the DS personal weapons, or ███, for special-purpose equipment, as the SIG ██ and ██████mm semiautomatic pistols were referred to. The preferable evacuation route from Benghazi for fleeing diplomats was by air. If the airports were closed, though, the consulate staff was to try to escape via the Mediterranean and notify the National Security Agency, the NSA, and the RSO's office in Athens, Greece. An overland escape, to the Egyptian frontier, was the last resort. At the Egyptian border crossing, the evacuees were to present their diplomatic passports and request consular notification; they were also supposed to dispose of their SPE prior to reaching the frontier. The RSO at the U.S. embassy in Cairo was to be notified immediately.

The State Department and the Department of Defense had a long-standing agreement to provide support for evacuation and security at diplomatic facilities. For Libya, primary responsibility rested with AFRICOM, based in Stuttgart, Germany. AFRICOM is one of DOD's six global geographic commands and maintains a single base on the continent in Djibouti. In a perfect world, DOD would have had noncombatant evacuation operation plans in place to evacuate the post. A myriad of bureaucratic reasons, logistics, distance, and balls dropped caused neither government agency to have emergency evacuation plans in place for Benghazi. AFRICOM had no visibility into the number of total U.S. government personnel stationed in Benghazi during the week of September 10. It lacked a dedicated Commander's In-extremis Force: a specially trained force capable of performing no-notice missions. There was also no marine expeditionary unit, carrier group, or smaller group of U.S. battleships closely located in "the Med" that could have provided aerial or ground support. The leash stopped with DS.[7]

Even the briefest of visits by the ambassador required weeks of tireless work. Communications were critical for Stevens's diplomatic missions from Benghazi, which also required the presence of an information management officer. The position, mysteriously known as a "communicator" in the Foreign Service vernacular, was responsible for facilitating the transmission and receipt of encrypted communications—primarily e-mails—through a system known as the Secure Internet Protocol Router Network, or SIPRNet. SIPRNet, a closed system that connected computer networks used by the Department of State—as well as the Department of Defense—was the primary mover of all information and items marked as "Secret"; top secret information was relayed by JWICS, or Joint Worldwide Intelligence Communications System, pronounced, in that special world of U.S. government acronyms, "JayWicks." Sean Smith was the man selected to assist Ambassador Stevens in Benghazi with communications.

Smith, an always-smiling thirty-four-year-old U.S. Air Force veteran and radioman, was ideally suited for the sensitive task of communicator. The married father of two girls had served in The Hague, Pretoria, and Baghdad. Smith was one of those many go-to guys in the Foreign Service who would be summoned for such assignments because of talent and past performance. Benghazi wasn't Smith's regular post; it was a brief TDY assignment so that he could serve as Ambassador Stevens's lifeline back to civilization—the embassy in Tripoli and Washington, D.C. Benghazi was probably an odd and frightening reality for Smith, who was suddenly shipped to a war zone and thrown together with a group of armed men, strangers, whose schedule was dictated by the movements of a highly energetic ambassador who was running around performing a mixture of diplomatic and intelligence-related activities. Such, however, was the reality of American diplomacy in a post-9/11—as well as post–Iraq and Afghanistan and post–Arab Spring—world. It was clearly the reality of America's diplomatic pursuits in a Libya trying to survive its post-revolutionary convulsions.

8.

From Wheels Down to Lights-Out

Ambassador Chris Stevens arrived in Benghazi at about noon on September 10; his protective detail, Special Agents A. and B., was with him at all times. It was bright and hot in Benghazi—it always was—and he was quickly ushered from the gate to his awaiting dark gray armored Toyota Land Cruiser by A. and B. and driven straight to the Special Mission Compound by one of the ARSOs; the motorcade was led by a team of February 17 militiamen cutting through the vehicular and pedestrian traffic with their heavily armed Toyota pickup truck. Stevens was accompanied by another individual, identified only as a "principal officer" from the U.S. embassy in Tripoli, who was supposed to remain in Benghazi for only one night; the principal officer could have been a member of the intelligence community from the CIA or he could have been a commercial officer. His identity remains unknown.

The convoy moved as fast as the traffic would allow, twisting and turning in and out of the Benghazi gridlock through junctions, traffic lights, and traffic circles. The convoy used an unannounced route—a quick and unobstructed route—that potential threats couldn't anticipate that would bring Ambassador Stevens to the mission without incident. The ride took twenty minutes.

Ambassador Stevens had prepared an intensively busy dawn-to-dark itinerary for his week in Benghazi. His meetings ranged from sit-downs with the local council to top secret briefings. He had meetings set with local political leaders, civic organizers, and top executives from the Al-Marfa Shipping and Maritime Services Company and the Arabian Gulf Oil Company, a former subsidiary of the state-owned National Oil Corporation, involved in crude oil and natural gas exploration. AGOCO, as it was known, had roots dating back to 1971, following the implementation of Law No. 115, issued by the Libyan Revolutionary Command Council nationalizing shares held by British Petroleum.

Ambassador Stevens had meetings scheduled with NGOs and educators to talk about Fulbright scholarships. September 13 was to be the only media appearance of the week: a thirty-minute meet and greet, a photo op, and a five-minute speech for the opening of an American Corner in the city (an American Corner is a "public diplomacy" outpost—a library, discussion forum, program venue, and place with Internet access—available for the use of the local population in a host country). And of course, Benghazi being Benghazi, and the city's nest of spies always up to something, Stevens had a scheduled priority meeting with the CIA research administration officer. The intelligence meet, in fact, was his first meeting of the afternoon.

They met behind closed doors in a quiet room at the compound; the details of their discussions remain open to speculation. The meeting lasted close to two hours.

Later that day, Ambassador Stevens was rushed to the Fadeel Hotel, where he was to meet with the ten members of the local chapter of the National Transitional Council. The Fadeel Hotel, located approximately two miles from the mission, was listed as a four-star Benghazi luxury hotel, but it was more like a spruced-up youth hostel. Much of the building faced the sea, which provided some peace of mind for the DS agents worried about snipers and access for VBIEDs. The meeting, held behind closed doors and in Arabic, was cordial and was a chance for the ten men responsible for transitional government in the war-torn city to provide the American ambassador with a state of the union of sorts. The picture must have been gloomy.

After a dinner, hosted at an off-site location,* Ambassador Stevens was ushered back through the darkened streets and avenues toward Charlie-1 gate in a fully armored Toyota Land Cruiser that bore no registration plates or tags. In cities like London and Paris, diplomatic plates get you out of speeding tickets, but in Benghazi special tags constituted a huge red bull's-eye. In hot spots like Iraq, agents even carry throw-down plates, to quickly mask the vehicle's identity. The Blue Mountain Libya guards opened the gate the moment the ambassador's motorcade neared, and by the time the dust on the road outside the compound had settled from the high-speed entrance, Stevens was already inside his residence preparing for a well-deserved good night's sleep. D. said good night to the ambassador at 2030 hours. Another long hard day had ended. It was time for lights-out.

Dawn broke brilliantly over Benghazi at precisely 0638 hours on September 11, 2012; it was Patriot Day and National Day of Service and Remembrance, marking the eleventh anniversary of the 9/11 attacks against the United States. The meaning of the day was not lost on Ambassador Stevens or the five DS agents assigned to his detail and the Benghazi Special Mission Compound who stood stoically at dawn's first light to lower the flag to half-staff. The organism that ultimately metastasized into al-Qaeda originated thousands of miles away from Libya, inside the mosques of Arabia and beneath mountains in Afghanistan, but the reverberations of that malignant jihad were now felt in North Africa and inside Benghazi. Benghazi was a new outpost in the attempt to once and for all excise this presence from the Arab and Muslim worlds. The war that began in Arabia and whose battles were waged in East Africa, at the World Trade Center and the Pentagon, inside Afghanistan and Pakistan, and throughout the Arab world was now being waged inside the epicenters of hope that were the Arab Spring—in Tahrir Square in Cairo and in the blood-soaked streets of Aleppo. In this new phase of the war, shock and awe would have to be replaced by finesse and bridge building. It

---

*Location withheld for security considerations.

was a different war where diplomacy would guide the required covert forces who used guile and muscle in pursuit of American security and America's interests.

There were no countersurveillance agents on the perimeter of the facility due to the limited resources and a lack of MSD assets on the ground; this was a critical handicap in observing those who might be watching the compound. Just as dawn broke, Sean Smith reportedly noticed someone in a police officer's uniform photographing the Special Mission Compound from an observation perch in a building across the street. The security staff was concerned that the compound was being observed as part of a preoperational surveillance sortie. This sort of surveillance, classic terrorist tradecraft, was usually conducted before the launch of an attack.

The man in law enforcement tactical kit was taking pictures of the compound with a smartphone. He belonged to the Libyan Supreme Security Committee, or SSC. The SSC was to provide a routine presence in front of the Special Mission Compound as a show of deterrent force, but it was just one of many militia organizations whose motives were suspect and intentions possibly hostile. Numerous police organizations within the Benghazi security apparatus were nothing more than neighborhood militias that used a mosque as their center of power and spent their days settling age-old scores and chasing their small percentage of Libya's riches that were long reserved for those inside the Qaddafi sycophant circle whose loyalty was absolute and family and political connections certain.

The SSC was known as the Libyan militia that battled militias—a semiofficial force to measure and restrain the influence and armed presence of the lawless. They were anything but. The SSC was accused of numerous crimes and abuses of human rights. One such instance involved Salem Forjani, a heart surgeon working for the Ministry of Health. He was kidnapped on May 17, 2012, when he went to the Tripoli Medical Center on orders of the health minister to remove the director, who was accused of links with the Qaddafi regime. He was kidnapped, beaten without mercy. The SSC had also been admonished for its role in the extrajudicial killings of former Qaddafi regime security officers, and even the kidnapping of Iranian Red Crescent humanitarian workers. "The SSC were gangsters," an intelligence source in Libya proclaimed. "They were definitely not in tune with the interests of the United States in Benghazi."[1]

Dauntingly, there were eighteen thousand heavily armed and unsupervised members of the SSC wandering about in Libya. The SSC was far more organized than most militias. It had its own logo, a black shield with the new Libyan flag inside its crest, and its fighters were issued black baseball caps, black T-shirts with the logo above the left breast, and black military surplus trousers. Its fighters were, perhaps, the only fashionably correct semiofficial instrument of violence meandering through Libya.

Two Blue Mountain Libya guards tried to question the photographer, but he claimed no wrongdoing and drove off with several others without offering much further elaboration. In a country with an organized security apparatus, such an instance would have sparked diplomatic outrage. Benghazi wasn't the precinct for law enforcement accountability.

Ambassador Stevens's schedule that bright Tuesday was low-key; it was the most easily managed of the entire week's itinerary. There was a meeting with the commanders of the February 17 Brigade and some commercial interests to discuss with the Arabian Gulf Oil Company and the head of the Al-Marfa Shipping and Maritime Services Company. One of the directors from Al-Marfa, in keeping with the all-important gestures of Arab hospitality, invited Chris Stevens to his home for dinner. The offer was respectfully declined. Stevens had a previous engagement. He was scheduled to sit down with the Turkish consul general, His Excellency Ali Sait Akin, at the Special Mission Compound for a behind-closed-doors meeting.

Their meeting had no time limit to it in the itinerary—scheduling slang for there was a lot to discuss.

Part Two

ATTACK

9

The Cool of Night

There is a soothing relief that overruns a desert landscape once darkness falls. The moment the unforgiving sun retreats for the brief respite of night, the cruel heat dissipates with a welcome anticipation. Visitors to the desert, the dreaded *salibiyeen*, or crusaders, never respected the preciousness of night. They raced about, perspiring madly in their blue blazers and khaki trousers, loosening their ties as they tried to show their hosts that the stifling heat didn't matter to them. The masquerade was foolish. Those who dwell in the desert, people who have endured the skin-searing scorch of the sun, awaken once darkness falls. Throughout the Middle East, daytime is for shelter and incubation. Darkness is when life begins. The sun set at 1851 hours on the evening of September 11, 2012.

Benghazi's Western Fwayhat neighborhood was eerily quiet on the night of September 11. Most of the homes in Western Fwayhat were villas, and neighborhood residents were still behind their walls and gates once darkness fell; the sun had to stay hidden for several hours before the neighborhood awoke and people emerged to their lemon-tree-covered patios to grill meats and entertain or visit friends and family. Dusk was the time to enjoy one of the several dozen cups of eye-squinting diabetic sweet tea that was a staple for Libyans, or, for the less pious, some black-market vodka; Libya, officially, is a dry country, though spirits from all over the world are plentiful in the markets of Tripoli, Benghazi, and the border regions. The main roads, both the Third and the Fourth Ring arteries, saw the usual Tuesday evening traffic. The odd SUV or Mercedes sedan raced along the dimly lit roadways, ignoring any semblances of speed laws, but that didn't matter; few of the drivers had licenses, and virtually none had insurance. Many of the drivers, expressing an absolute disdain in the face of both the Qaddafi loyalists and the Salafists, shouted out their sense of liberation by raising the volume on the car sound systems to window-shattering levels, so that the heavy bass beats of Lebanese songstresses singing the usual fare of ten-minute-long ballads with the words *habibi* (my dear) and *ya-albi* (my heart, or "apple of my eye" for a truly romantic Arabic colloquial) were heard coming and going throughout the darkened landscape. The smaller roads, some that were paved and others that just connected the main roads to the villas and the square lots of barren real estate, were quiet.

Pedestrians were few and far between in Western Fwayhat—one of the trappings of an affluent area where Mercedes sedans and satellite dishes outnumbered residents. Many of the homes were abandoned, and many residents were absentees; wealth had afforded those with means and with links overseas to flee the city when the civil war began. Occasionally, though, people did use the side and back streets to walk to the homes of friends and relatives, or for a stroll to work off the gut-busting breakfasts of hummus, eggs, and fava beans that were the Libyan staples that usually parked themselves inside one's belly for most of the day. Sometimes two or three men, cigarettes in one hand and prayer beads in the other, walked slowly in their flip-flops and gowns as they discussed their affairs. People also sometimes walked to the Venezia Café for an escape.

Darkness brought a beguiling eeriness to the neighborhood. The thick rows of foliage and beautiful desert flowers—some manicured in meticulous shapes and heights just outside the walled barriers separating homes—became blackened shapes that twisted in the shadows. The local streetlights cast a flickering fluorescent whitish glow to parts of the street and provided a diffused haze to others. There was the sound of the odd car engine zooming away and, of course, the nerve-punctuating shrill of feral cats at play in the dark. The quiet was occasionally interrupted by the unmistakable clank of a security gate opening or closing; this meant someone was leaving his grounds for a night out inside the medina, the dangerous old city, or that he was returning home for the evening and putting his property on lockdown.

The security crew at the Special Mission Compound was pleased when, at 1940 hours, Ambassador Stevens escorted his Turkish guest outside the residence, on foot, to the Charlie-1 gate. Chris Stevens was the central-casting Californian—full of energy and great enthusiasm. Ali Sait Akin possessed a bookish aspect. He had a narrow face and wire-rimmed headmaster glasses and could have, a hundred years earlier, played the part of a stern Ottoman governor. Both men seemed truly out of place under a calm night's sky inside the most dangerous city in North Africa. Stevens, the gracious host, walked his Turkish guest out the front door and down the marble steps and then slowly toward the front gate. The two men spoke in a deep and flowing conversation as they made their way toward Charlie-1. Two members of Stevens's detail, and the lead agent of the consul general's protective detail, followed faithfully one step behind; the two DS agents scanned the surroundings, and the local guard force, suspiciously as they walked to the main gate. As the two diplomats reached the gate, Stevens offered his hand to Ali Sait Akin in a warm and friendly embrace. "Good night," Stevens said to his guest. "*Iyi geceler,*" the Turkish diplomat replied with a smile.

Stevens, the gregarious person who never shied away from a chance to meet and greet and make new friends, engaged the Blue Mountain Libya guards at the gate in flawless colloquial Libyan Arabic. The conversation was brief yet very respectful and made it clear that Ambassador Stevens appreciated the work of the men, wearing their light blue uniforms, who helped protect the compound.

D. walked back to the residence with Stevens as the Turkish consul general's bullet-resistant sedan sped off into the darkness. A Blue Mountain Libya guard watched as a February 17 militiaman shut the main gate. A lone dog was heard barking in the distance. The grounds looked majestic at night as the well-placed night lights illuminated the garden to its full glory. It was time to call it a night. D. walked step in step with Ambassador Stevens inside the majestic home and retreated to his room to watch a video. Sean Smith was in his room, immersed in his online gaming forum, and Ambassador Stevens wrapped up some paperwork and checked in with his staffers at the embassy in Tripoli. He had been trying to keep up with developments in Cairo, Tunis, and at his own post in Tripoli concerning the rioting and the breach of the perimeter in Egypt, but the news in North Africa was fluid and violent. Stevens was sending out e-mails and trying to assemble a clear picture of what had happened and what the next day might bring. It had been a long day, and even though the cooling breeze was ideal for a blissful night of sleep, there was still work to be done. It had been a tremendously busy day for Stevens. Earlier, in fact, he had cabled Main State over his growing concern with the problem of security in Benghazi and his sense of absolute frustration with the local militias and the so-called Libyan police. According to reports, the cable specifically addressed Stevens's worry that these forces were too weak to keep the country secure.

At the outer gate, there was still some activity at Charlie-1, though. Members of a British specialist protective detail arrived at Charlie-1 to drop off their vehicles, Heckler and Koch MP5 9 mm submachine guns, M4s, and their personal sidearms at the Special Mission Compound. The British, in the wake of their immediate pullout from the city following the attempt on the life of their ambassador in June, had called upon their American allies to assist them with special security considerations and arrangements when they had personnel moving about through Benghazi; they also had left behind one of their armored SUVs following the assassination attempt. Such arrangements were common in critical-threat locations and, as explained by a former DS agent who spent time at the U.S. consulate in Karachi, Pakistan, critical to emergency contingency planning. "One of the jobs of an RSO is to get to know the local police commanders and internal security heads, as well as the security staffs at friendly posts. We knew our counterparts at the British, Australian, New Zealand, French, and other consulates, and we all knew if and when the shit would hit the fan that we would have one another's backs."[1]

There were friendly consulates in town—the Turks, the Italians, the European Union representation, and the Qataris—but no mutual aid agreement existed between the Special Mission Compound and any other government. The Brits were in town for just the day, and they departed Charlie-1 at precisely 2030.

With no more visitors scheduled that night, the last security protocols were attended to. One agent was responsible for securing the grounds one last time the night of September 11. He suited up for his patrol on foot, harnessing himself inside the standard DS critical-threat uniform—oversized blouse concealing his holstered SIG. The security walkabout was never carried out alone; an armed member of the February 17 Brigade always walked shotgun next to the watch commander. The militia member was brought along for tactical support, as well as to serve as translator if an intruder was found inside the wire or milling about the outer perimeter in a suspicious manner. R. checked in via radio with the Blue Mountain Libya guard at Charlie-1, as well as with the personnel at Bravo-1. It was, seemingly, just another night. There was nothing suspicious to report. The four guards on duty that night, identified as Nasser, Ubayd, Abdullah, and Anwar,[2] thought that they were in for a routinely boring midnight shift.

The militiaman retreated to his headquarters on the compound near the northwest corner of the perimeter wall for his evening prayers; they would be operating on a skeleton crew that night, as one of the February 17 troopers had called in sick, leaving only three armed Libyans on the compound for that shift. R. removed his tactical kit when he returned to the TOC and quickly hydrated himself with bottled water. It had been a stress-filled, danger-strewn day on the ambassador's detail, and the time had come to unwind.

High-threat tours drained an agent of his strength and lowered his alert levels; the Benghazi heat didn't help much, either. It was impossible to live off the adrenaline of threat for more than a few days. "Sleep was a welcome respite from the exhaustion of dignitary protection work," the retired agent Scot Folensbee reflected, referring to his countless danger tours to Africa, the Middle East, and South America. "Sleep was a tool by which an agent could deal with the

mind-numbing exhaustion, the fear, and the sense of being so isolated, so very alone, in the heart of such danger. Sometimes, though,
it was just impossible to let down your guard to properly rest. You always slept when you could, but in reality you weren't really sleeping.
Some places are just too dangerous to sleep."[3]

But there was also a therapeutic quality to downtime. Downtime
was also known as "smokin' and jokin'" among the working humps—
the semi-affectionate and completely accurate term for agents in the
field. The DS slang originated from the New York Field Office, known
as NYFO. Inside their temporary command posts in New York hotels,
inside their rooms or sometimes in the lobby, agents read, played
cards, watched TV, or rested their eyes while on the couch. In Benghazi, agents sat around at night waiting and watching, never in a
truly restful state. Protection TDYs placed agents on constant edge,
like coiled snakes. Some agents on critical-threat details exercised
until their brains reveled in endorphin overload. Others, in posts
where there were women, applied the "five thousand miles from
home rule" and found comfort in the sexual pleasures of convenience
that they hoped would remain secret forever. Some agents simply immersed themselves in music or books; iPods and Kindles made a library full of tunes and learning available for agents crisscrossing
time zones, and they fit neatly in the Maxpedition hard-use gear bags
that many carried their extra necessities in. For the ARSOs in Benghazi downtime meant cards.

With the day done and the night still young, A., B., and C. retreated to the pool deck behind the villa. They hadn't had the time
on the job to truly get into the game of "I remember when" and talk
about the wild and crazy experiences that older agents usually played
when in the company of their contemporaries—each side trying to
outdo the other with stories, extravagance, and laughs. Most had not
been through RSO training, which prepared agents for one- to three-
year tours in embassies and consulates, due to the endless demands of
protection work around the world or assignments to task forces and
overworked domestic field offices inside the United States. The agents
had, though, all been through the cutting-edge high-threat tactical
course that prepared them for places like Libya, including the intense

tactical medicine instruction. The agents in Benghazi were a new breed of DS agent—one rushed into the fire to stand guard for an American world that was spread thin.

The blue light from the pool glistened in the floodlights of the compound. From inside the walls, the special agents could have been at a resort in the Bahamas or enjoying some free time in the Caribbean on the secretary of state's detail. Of course, paradise was nowhere near the reality that existed outside the walls, and State Department agents were still on 24/7 duty. The agents never went anywhere without their SIG ███ SIG ███, or Glock ███mm semiautomatics and two additional magazines. Still, the night was blissful. On the eleventh anniversary of the September 11 attacks against the United States, under a North African sky, three State Department agents enjoyed the relaxing pleasures of a Montecristo and played a hand of cards. Aces were high.

D. had put Ambassador Stevens and Sean Smith to bed and checked the residence one last time before turning in. Tomorrow, after all, was going to be another hectic day. Following breakfast, the ambassador had a meeting scheduled with executives from the Arabian Gulf Oil Company, AGOCO, at their corporate headquarters in the Dar al Kish area of downtown Benghazi; such moves, inside the twisting and narrow streets of the city, warranted advance trips and route suggestions. Even with the assistance of the February 17 militia and their Toyota pickup and the 14.5 mm heavy machine gun it towed, motorcades inside town were fast-moving targets, but targets nonetheless. And that was just getting to the meeting.

AGOCO's corporate headquarters consisted of several multistory office buildings spread throughout a complex of smaller buildings. There was a common area near the two main parking lots with trees and heavy underbrush. There were at least a dozen ideal sniper positions available to anyone interested in taking out the American ambassador, as well as choke points where suicide bombers or VBIEDs could deploy. There were militia checkpoints all along the route; some belonged to gangs of armed thugs who sought a toll in order to

enter and whose sole goal was money and watching the neighborhood, while other checkpoints were manned by militias espousing
fundamentalist militancy.

To safeguard Ambassador Stevens during his meeting at AGOCO,
the DS agents conducted advance route checks, as well as a thorough
review of the building where the meeting would be held. The agents
had to examine all emergency exits, stairwells, and other physical
features of the blueprints in order to prepare evacuation plans should
someone make an attempt on the ambassador's life during his time
at the location and they had to get Stevens out in a hurry. The agents
would also coordinate their movements—arrival and departure—
with the corporate security force. In most countries large corporations fielded suit-wearing retired secret service agents or police
officers to protect their premises. But in Libya, these security officers, whose backgrounds could be very suspect, carried AK-47s and
would be close to the ambassador. The resulting security challenge
was daunting.

D. shut the lights around the lavish mansion and then retreated
to his bedroom to unwind with a video and then, shortly thereafter,
some well-deserved shut-eye. He took off his shoes and his pants and
then went to lie down. He was exhausted. He closed his eyes and saw
flashbacks of the route the detail had taken earlier in the day into
town. He saw the faces, the hundreds of nameless faces that he passed
as the motorcade raced across junctions toward the ambassador's des-
tinations. As D. closed his eyes, he could hear the small talk and
laughter of the agents near his window as they relaxed at poolside.

R. monitored the cameras from his fortified command-and-control
center inside the TOC. He was the senior man on post, and his mind
was wandering and thinking about the surveillance report earlier in
the day on the perimeter. "Why was the so-called cop taking a picture? Why was the threat level severe? What in the hell does that
mean?" He knew that previous TDY agents had identified vulnera-
bilities, but those were always there. Risk can never be eliminated,
only mitigated. There was no countersurveillance support, or "watch-
ers," on the perimeter. In a perfect high-threat world, MSD operators lurked as shadows on the outside, watching for surveillance

indicators, fixated on a mental matrix of time and distance variables. These highly experienced hunters, eyes searching for the same car, truck, vendor, or person seen earlier in the day or last week, were able to provide invaluable proactively tactical and defensive eyes-outside-target intelligence. The Special Mission Compound had no observation perch, or safe house, across from the main gate manned by agents, with eyes and cameras trained 24/7 on the main gate, looking for assassins or suicide bombers. The agents were inside behind protective walls, much like prisoners, on foreign soil.

In many ways, without the outside eyes and ears, the Special Mission Compound was blind and deaf. The computer monitors showed no activity outside the gate, but of course the camera monitor in the local guard force booth for Charlie-1 gate was inoperable; additional surveillance cameras that were supposed to be set up throughout the compound were still in their boxes, unopened and uninstalled.

Still, those cameras that were up and running enabled DVR surveillance coverage of much of the inner perimeter. The radio on the Blue Mountain Libya frequency was silent. There was no chatter on the February 17 frequency, either.

There was, for the most part, silence. And then, like a wind from the east, there were the sounds of slow-moving tires rolling on a road strewn with sand and gravel. It was 2130 hours in Benghazi—1500 hours in Washington, D.C.

10.

Attack! Attack!

2140 hours: Benghazi, Libya.

The Blue Mountain Libya security guard at Charlie-1 sat inside his booth happily earning his 40 Libyan dinars for the shift. It wasn't great money, clearly not as much as could be earned in the gun markets catering to the Egyptians and Malians hoping to start a revolution with coins in their pockets, but it was a salary, and it was a good job to keep in a city where unemployment was plague-like. The guards working for the Special Mission Compound tried to stay alert throughout the night, but it was easier said than done. Some of the guards chain-smoked the cheap counterfeit cigarettes from China that made their way to North Africa via Ghana, Benin, and Togo in order to stay awake; the smuggled cigarettes are a billion-dollar industry in the northern Arab rim of the continent and have become a major revenue source for al-Qaeda.[1] The nicotine helped, but it was so easy to occasionally doze off and sleep inside their booths and posts. Sleeping on duty was risky. The DS agents routinely made spot checks on the guard force in the middle of the night. In a perfect world, concentric rings of security are used to protect a diplomatic post. Special Mission Benghazi had Blue Mountain Libya. This unarmed force was the compound's first line of defense; the Blue Mountain force was a trip wire.

All appeared quiet, though, as well as safe. The feeling of security—or complacent foreboding—was enhanced a half hour or so earlier, at

2104 hours, when an SSC patrol vehicle arrived. Pulling off the side of the road and onto the gravel curb, the tan Toyota Hilux pickup with an extended cargo hold, decorated in the colors and emblem of the SSC, stopped in front of Charlie-1. The driver then shut the engine. He wasn't alone; the darkened silhouette of a man was seen to his right. The pickup sported twin Soviet-produced 23 mm antiaircraft guns; the twin-barreled cannons were lethal against Mach 2.0 fighter aircraft and devastating beyond belief against buildings, vehicles, or humans. The Blue Mountain Libya guards watched curiously as the darkened cab of the truck situated itself directly across the street. The two men inside didn't come out in an attempt to engage the militiamen in obligatory small talk; they didn't get out of their vehicle to bum some cigarettes from the guards or even to rob them. The Blue Mountain Libya guards, after all, were not armed. They were equipped with a Taser and a pair of handcuffs and would never be able to persevere in a fight with men towing rapid-fire artillery. The RSO in Tripoli already had efforts under way to properly train the Blue Mountain Libya force, but there were critical performance issues with the local Libyans who had been hired for the security work. The two SSC militiamen just sat quietly inside their vehicle; the flickering light from cigarettes being lit and chain-smoked was seen behind the glass of the cab's darkened windows.

Then, in a departure as sudden as his arrival, the SSC militiaman behind the steering wheel of the mobile heavy-artillery piece simply fired up his engine and then headed west, crunching the gravel with the weight of his vehicle's tires.* It was 2140 hours.

There was no trip wire pulled to provide the guard at Bravo-1 with the time needed to sound an alarm. There was no loud rumble to forewarn the guards at Charlie-1 that danger was slinking its way onto the street in front of the Special Mission Compound. There was

---

*Following the attack, according to the official (unclassified) Accountability Review Board that investigated all details pertaining to the attack, an SSC official was quoted as saying that "he had ordered the removal of the car to prevent civilian casualties." The statement hints that the SSC was aware that an attack was imminent; of course, if they knew that an attack was imminent and did not warn the security assets in the Special Mission Compound, the implication is that the SSC, and elements of the new Libyan government, were complicit in the events that transpired.

no loud roar of chants or gunfire. There was no demonstration. The attack was announced suddenly, with a rifle-butt knock on the guard booth glass.

"*Iftah el bawwaba, ya sharmout,*" the gunman ordered with his AK-47 pointed straight at the forehead of the Blue Mountain Libya guard at Charlie-1. "Open the gate, you fucker!" The hapless guard, working the thankless job that was clearly not worth losing his life over, acquiesced and did exactly as he was told. Once the gate was unhinged from its locking mechanism, armed men appeared out of nowhere and began to filter into what, if there had been a formal agreement with the Libyan government, would have been official U.S. territory. The silence of the night had been shattered by the thumping cadence of shoes and leather sandals rushing onto the ground and the clanking sound of slung AK-47s and RPG-7s banging against the backs of the men swarming into the compound.

The armed invaders first punched their way through the perimeter at Charlie-1. Once inside, they raced across the compound, to open Bravo-1 and enable others to stream in. Once Bravo-1 was open, four vehicles screeched in front of the Special Mission Compound and unloaded more than a dozen fighters. Some of the vehicles were Mitsubishi Pajeros—fast, rugged, and ever so reliable, even when shot at. They were a warlord's dream mode of transportation, the favorite of Benghazi's criminal underworld and militia commanders. The Pajeros that pulled up to the target were completely anonymous; there were no license plates or any other identifying emblems adorning them, and they appeared to blend invisibly into the darkened landscape, especially when the attackers disabled the light in front of Bravo-1.

Other vehicles were Toyota and Nissan pickups, each sporting single- and even quad-barreled 12.7 mm and 14.5 mm heavy machine guns. They took up strategic firing positions on the east and west portions of the road to fend off any unwelcomed interference.

Each vehicle flew the black flag of the jihad.

Some of the attackers removed mobile phones from their pockets and ammunition pouches and began to videotape and photograph the choreography of the assault. One of the leaders, motioning his men forward with his AK-47, stopped to chide his fighters. "We have no time for that now," he ordered, careful not to speak in anything louder than a coarse whisper. "There'll be time for that later."

Sean Smith was in his room at the residence, interfacing with members of his gaming community, when Charlie-1 was breached. The small reading light on his desk provided some illumination for his gaming laptop. Earlier in the day, Smith had ended a message to the director of his online gaming guild with the words "Assuming we don't die tonight. We saw one of our 'police' that guard the compound taking pictures." He was online when the enemy was at the gate, chatting with his partners and his opponents. Then, suddenly he typed, "Fuck" and "Gunfire." The connection ended abruptly.

One of the gunmen had removed his AK-47 assault rifle from his shoulder and raised the weapon into the air to fire a round. Another had tossed a grenade; others fired rounds into the air from their AK-47 assault rifles. The Special Mission Compound was officially under attack.

11.

The Annex

Street names are rare in many cities in the Arab world. While main thoroughfares are usually named after some king or warrior, it is quite common in Benghazi, and indeed in many cities throughout the Arab Middle East, to have nameless roads that are simply known by nearby landmarks. A mosque, a market, a roundabout, a geographic landmark, are all pins on a mental map that direct people to where they want to go. There is no need for house numbers, either. The compound southeast of the Fourth Ring Road was such a landmark in Benghazi.

Neighborhood residents called the complex the CIA base. That the Annex was, in fact, a secret CIA outpost was, perhaps, the worst-kept secret in Benghazi. This was common wherever the CIA or intelligence community pitched its tent. "At the onset of Operation Iraqi Freedom," a former RSO in the Persian Gulf recalled, "the U.S. military's Central Command, or CENTCOM, had opened a 'forward' intelligence outpost in the desert. I was brought in to investigate a 'security leak' because a TDY soldier had landed at the international airport and had lost his travel orders. He was trying to explain to his cabdriver where to go when the driver said, 'Oh, the secret base . . .' [And he took him where he needed to go.] Needless to say, I was *not* seen at the taxi stand the next day interviewing the drivers."[1]

In a neighborhood of abandoned villas and the odd shop here and there, a sprawling complex kept behind closed gates that saw a constant coming and going of armored Mercedes G-Wagon SUVs with very tinted windows was bound to spark suspicion. "Americans don't do subtle very well," a retired Middle Eastern intelligence colonel stated quite bluntly. "They tend to leave a loud footprint."[2] Throughout the Arab world's frontline cities in the Global War on Terror, such not-so-secret secret locations were plentiful. They were walled-off mini forts meant to fit benignly inside neighborhoods where the residents knew the comings and goings of all their neighbors. In Libya it was even harder to maintain a covert cover to the Annex. The country had been a secret police state for forty-two years; if for nothing other than their personal survival, Libyans under Qaddafi had been schooled in surveillance and countersurveillance skills. "Everyone knew about the existence of the *secret* CIA base," a resident of Western Fwayhat commented. "Even the baker down the road knew what this place was all about."[3] It was, after all, hard to hide lily-white men with warrior physiques who sported tattoos and Wild West beards.

The Annex was, indeed, the secret satellite CIA Benghazi station; the base was subordinate to the agency's main station in country, at the U.S. embassy in Tripoli. The Annex was located on a nameless side road running east to west inside a vast three-hundred-by-four-hundred-foot plot of land near a slew of homes and businesses; it was southwest of the Al-Misrati farm and adjacent to several large and often neglected plots of land. A thick wall surrounded the complex; much of the wall was covered by growing clumps of flora that helped to obscure details of what went on behind the foreboding walls. The complex consisted of four large warehouse-like buildings that cornered a green roundabout traffic circle in the center; several smaller buildings dotted the grounds. Money did not appear to be an issue of any sort at the Annex: a small fleet of brand-new armored Mercedes G-Wagon SUVs, all of which had local license plates, dotted the parking spots. These vehicles were mini mobile fortresses and armories; they were equipped with navigation gear, extra ballistic vests, smoke, flares, trauma kits, an ax, a crowbar, and extra ammo rounds and magazines. The Global Response Staff, or GRS, teams used the M4-family assault rifle as their primary weapon of choice; each operator, depending on what branch of the military special operations community he grew up in, favored one manufacturer or another and was given the latitude to carry into battle the precise weapon he felt comfortable with. Most—members of the SEAL teams, operators inside the CIA's elite and covert special operations forces—considered the Heckler and Koch 416 5.56 mm carbine to be the Rolls-Royce of the assault rifle options. Conceived as an improvement to the Colt M4 base, the HK416 was viewed as an incredibly accurate and rock-solidly robust weapon. Reportedly, the weapon was inspired and partly designed as a result of an initiative from the U.S. Army's elite counterterrorist and hostage-rescue force, the First Special Forces Operational Detachment–Delta, or SFOD-D, or its more colloquial designation, "Delta Force." The HK416 was considered the "operator's weapon."

The GRS teams also carried heavier firepower, including the Mk 46 Mod 0 5.56 mm squad-support weapon. The Mk 46 Mod 0 was the U.S. Special Operations Command variant of the M249 Minimi. With an effective range of eight hundred meters and a rate of fire that hovered near a hundred rounds per minute, the Mk 46 was a potent tool that, interestingly enough, had also been adopted by DS/MSD. As a result of the seemingly endless supply of former Soviet-bloc ammunition available in Libya, the GRS operators also fielded one of the most lethal tools ever placed in the hands of the mujahideen, the Soviet-era PKM squad-support weapons.

The Annex was also a banking institution of sorts. Intelligence work in Libya was not a credit-card-driven industry. The spies paid cash, a lot of cash, and most of the cash paid out to informants, assets, and sources was stored at the Annex.

There was one way into the Annex—a twisting narrow roadway that fed off the main road that was met by a security checkpoint and barriers. A small gate, large enough to accommodate a vehicle, was carved out of the perimeter's eastern wall. The Annex's rear wall pointed north and was, on a map at least, less than a kilometer from the Special Mission Compound. The real path connecting the two

The DS shield.

A long history of attacks against U.S. embassies and diplomatic posts is evident in this photo, taken from the inside of the third floor at the embassy in Saigon, showing the damage inflicted by a Viet Cong B-40 rocket to the sunscreen (designed as a blast barrier) during the 1968 Tet Offensive. *(Courtesy of Steve Bray)*

eirut—April 18, 1983: Marines and ebanese security personnel seen here front of the U.S. embassy, which as destroyed by a suicide truck bomb. *Courtesy of U.S. Department of Defense)*

Special Agent Al Golacinski (in blazer) mixes with locals at an arms bazaar in Afghanistan, while investigating the assassination of U.S. Ambassador Adolph Dubs. *(Courtesy of Al Golacinski)*

Special Agent Scot "Doc" Folensbee, one of the DS "Dirty Harrys," seen here in El Salvador during the height of the civil war. *(Courtesy of Scot Folensbee)*

August 1998: The U.S. embassy in Dar es Salaam, Tanzania, in the aftermath of the August 7, 1998, al-Qaeda suicide bombing. Eleven Tanzanians, including seven Foreign Service Nationals, died in the blast, and seventy-two others were wounded. The same day, al-Qaeda suicide bombers launched another near-simultaneous attack on the U.S. embassy in Nairobi, Kenya, which killed 218 and wounded nearly 5,000 others. *(Courtesy of DS Records)*

A DS agent sits behind the wheel of his follow car—communications gear and 12-gauge shotgun at the ready—during a dignitary protection detail in New York City in 1999. *(Courtesy of Samuel M. Katz)*

DS Special Agent Todd Keil, at right with lapel button, watches protectively over U.S. Secretary of State Madeleine Albright after she confers with Palestinian Authority President Yasser Arafat in Gaza. Protecting the secretary of state, as well as non–head-of-state foreign dignitaries, is one of the many domestic and global missions of the Diplomatic Security Service. *(Courtesy of U.S. Department of State)*

Prior to the September 11, 2001, attacks against the United States, MSD provided unique training to embassy security staff and Marine Security Guards at embassies around the world. MSD's size and scope increased dramatically in the years following the attack and the U.S. lead in the Global War on Terror. *(Courtesy of Samuel M. Katz)*

Global Responsibilities: A DS special agent (second from right) leads the U.S. Embassy Baghdad Helicopter Insertion Rapid Response Team on a training mission in Baghdad's International Zone. The team's medics, marksman, and protective security specialists work with ground tactical support teams to respond to critical incidents, such as a motorcade in trouble in the Red Zone. *(Courtesy of U.S. Department of State)*

Two Diplomatic Security special agents preparing for a dynamic-entry exercise during a training course for Mobile Security Deployments teams. *(Courtesy of U.S. Department of State)*

The U.S. embassy in Tripoli, Libya, that was abandoned in 1980. *(Courtesy of Dan Meehan)*

Long before the Arab Spring the complexion of security in Libya was dictated by a secular dictator, cutthroat intelligence services, and Qaddafi's own presidential guard—female security guards, as seen here in Sharm el-Sheikh, Egypt, protecting the Libyan strongman, during an African Union Summit in July 2008. *(Courtesy of U.S. Air Force / Tech. Sgt. Jeremy T. Lock)*

The Libyan Strongman, seen here at the 12th African Union Summit in Addis Ababa, Ethiopia, February 2, 2009, Col. Muammar Qaddafi. Qaddafi had been a champion of international terrorism but had battled fundamentalist Islamic forces inside his own country. *(Courtesy of U.S. Navy / Mass Communication Specialist 2nd Class Jesse B. Awalt/Released)*

Jamie Smith (right) stands with a local guide during the effort to oust Qaddafi. *(Courtesy of Jamie Smith)*

Rami el-Obeidi, responsible for foreign intelligence for the National Transitional Council of Libya, photographed during the fight to oust Qaddafi. *(Courtesy of Rami el-Obeidi)*

U.S. Secretary of Defense Leon Panetta (right) shakes the hand of a Libyan freedom fighter in Tripoli, Libya, December 17, 2011. *(Courtesy of U.S. Department Of Defense / Erin A. Kirk-Cuomo)*

September 22, 2011: Two Diplomatic Security special agents raise the American flag as U.S. Ambassador to Libya, Gene Cretz (right), looks on, at a ceremony marking the reopening of the U.S. embassy in Tripoli, Libya. The ceremony took place one month after Libyan leader Colonel Muammar Qaddafi was forced to flee the capital, and seven months after the U.S. embassy staff was forced to depart. *(Courtesy of U.S. Department of State)*

U.S. Secretary of State Hillary Rodham Clinton is greeted by Libyan militiamen and military personnel upon her arrival at Tripoli International Airport in Libya on October 18, 2011. *(Courtesy of U.S. Department of State)*

U.S. Secretary of State Hillary Rodham Clinton departs the World Islamic Call Society headquarters after meeting with National Transitional Council (NTC) Prime Minister Mahmoud Jibril in Tripoli, Libya, on October 18, 2011. *(Courtesy of U.S. Department of State)*

After serving as the deputy chief of mission in Libya (2007 to 2009), and as the president's special representative to the Libyan National Transitional Council (March to November 2011), Christopher Stevens is congratulated by Secretary of State Clinton after being named U.S. Ambassador to Libya on June 7, 2012. *(Courtesy of U.S. Department of State)*

DS MSD personnel test satellite data and voice communications on a cargo ship en route from Malta to Benghazi. *(Courtesy of U.S. Department of State)*

The ambassador's villa at the Special Mission Compound in Benghazi. *(Courtesy of U.S. House Oversight Committee)*

The view north from the ambassador's residence, looking at the main gate and the February 17th Martyrs Brigade building, at the Special Mission Compound. *(Courtesy of U.S. House Oversight Committee)*

The DS villa on the east side of the Special Mission Compound. Note Mercedes G Wagon, believed to belong to Annex personnel. *(Courtesy of U.S. House Oversight Committee)*

The lavish interior of Ambassador Chris Stevens' villa. *(Courtesy of U.S. House Oversight Committee)*

The damage caused by an IED attack against the Special Mission Compound main perimeter wall on the night of June 6, 2012. *(Courtesy of U.S. House Oversight Committee)*

One of the blast-damaged vehicles from British Ambassador Dominic Asquith's protective detail, hit by RPG fire in Benghazi on June 10, 2012. *(Courtesy of U.S. House Oversight Committee)*

Blood stains the interior of one of the British ambassador's protective-detail vehicles struck by an RPG ambush. *(Courtesy of U.S. House Oversight Committee)*

DS Special Agent Mario Montoya teaches marksmanship and weapons handling to four of the National Transitional Council's local guards at Benghazi. *(Courtesy of U.S. Department of State)*

Sean Patrick Smith, a state department information management officer, assigned on temporary duty to Benghazi. *(Courtesy of U.S. Department of State / U.S. Embassy, The Hague)*

Glen Doherty, seen here photographed during an undated security assignment in the Middle East. *(Courtesy of the Glen Doherty Memorial Foundation)*

Al-Jazeera's Hoda Abdel-Hamid reports from the burned-out remains of the Special Mission Compound on the morning of September 12, 2012. *(Courtesy of Hoda Abdel-Hamid)*

Some of the damage that Hoda Abdel-Hamid's film crew found inside the burned-out destruction of Ambassador Stevens' villa at the Special Mission Compound. *(Courtesy of Hoda Abdel-Hamid)*

The burned-out shell of an unidentified vehicle found on the grounds of the Special Mission Compound. *(Courtesy of Federal Bureau of Investigation)*

The ransacked and burned-out DS residence at the Special Mission Compound. *(Courtesy of Federal Bureau of Investigation)*

The charred upper-level stairs inside the ambassador's residence that was ransacked and destroyed by both terrorists and looters on the night of September 11-12, 2012. *(Courtesy of Federal Bureau of Investigation)*

The ferocity of the fire inside the ambassador's villa is evident by the soot and ash on one of the building's chandeliers. *(Courtesy of Federal Bureau of Investigation)*

Fire damage to computers and other equipment, believed to be inside the TOC. *(Courtesy of Federal Bureau of Investigation)*

One of the buildings torched at the Special Mission Compound, marked with Arabic graffiti. *(Courtesy of Federal Bureau of Investigation)*

U.S. Secretary of State Hillary Rodham Clinton delivers remarks on the deaths of American personnel in Benghazi, Libya, at the U.S. Department of State in Washington, D.C., September 12, 2012. *(Courtesy of U.S. Department of State)*

A U.S. Marine Corps honor guard carries the coffin of one of the four men killed in the Benghazi terrorist attack. *(Courtesy of U.S. Department of Defense)*

President Barack Obama and U.S. Secretary of State Hillary Clinton honor the Benghazi victims at the Dignified Transfer of Remains held at Andrews Air Force Base / Joint Base Andrews, Maryland, September 14, 2012. *(Courtesy of U.S. Department of State)*

An FBI Wanted Poster, seeking anonymous tips in the Arab world and on social media, for assistance in the criminal investigation of the September 11-12, 2012, attack in Benghazi. *(Courtesy of Federal Bureau of Investigation)*

U.S. Secretary of State John Kerry tours the DS Operations Center at the U.S. Department of State in Washington, D.C., February 4, 2013. *(Courtesy of U.S. Department of State)*

Chairman of the Joint Chiefs of Staff General Martin E. Dempsey testifies during a hearing of the Senate Armed Services Committee on the Defense Department's response to the attack against the diplomatic and intelligence post in Benghazi. *(Courtesy of U.S. Department of Defense / Petty Officer 1st Class Chad J. McNeeley, U.S. Navy)*

The photo of three "persons of interest" released by the FBI in its investigation of the terrorist attack in Benghazi. *(Courtesy of Federal Bureau of Investigation)*

U.S. Secretary of State John Kerry, U.S. Vice President Joseph Biden, and American Foreign Service Association (AFSA) President Susan R. Johnson honor foreign affairs colleagues who have lost their lives while serving overseas in the line of duty or under heroic or other inspirational circumstances, at the AFSA Memorial Plaque Ceremony at the U.S. Department of State in Washington, D.C., on May 3, 2013. The names of the four men killed in the September 11, 2012, terrorist attack in Benghazi are seen in the upper right hand corner of the photo. *(Courtesy of U.S. Department of State)*

outposts of America's diplomatic and intelligence efforts was a series of parallel and perpendicular small side roads, a junction, and numerous spots that were ideal for hostile action.

The Special Mission Compound provided the semblance of a diplomatic cover to the Annex—a semblance. While the Special Mission was a small and isolated location, ramped up only when an ambassador or other dignitary made it to the city, the Annex was a 24/7 forward intelligence base. The exact nature of CIA operations at the base remains classified at the time of this book's writing. The conjecture surrounding its mission has been widespread, ranging from destroying MANPADs left behind by Qaddafi's military to sending those very MANPADs, as well as other battlefield weapons from Libya, to the Syrian rebels fighting Assad's forces. Some reports claimed that the Annex staff was trying to locate weapons of mass destruction. Some reports even claimed that the CIA was in Benghazi to round up stray RPGs that had become the jihadist weapon of choice all over Africa—from Mali to Somalia.[4]

Why the men were there was irrelevant; a whole intelligence and diplomatic front, the face of expeditionary conflict and presence, had been established in Benghazi. And, irrespective of its actual mission, the CIA's day-to-day operations were vibrant. Nearly twenty people worked there. The Annex had a base commander and a deputy—both answerable to the chief of station (COS) in Tripoli and CIA headquarters in Langley, Virginia. The Annex was staffed by analysts, communications specialists, linguists, researchers, case officers, and facilitators.

The Benghazi Annex fielded ten members of the agency's GRS—nearly half of the mini intelligence station's entire complement. The advent of the GRS is a by-product of the aftermath of the 9/11 attacks. CIA analysts and agents, deployed to some of the world's most dangerous locations, required tactical security to protect their travels and operations in the scorched-earth landscape of the Middle and Near East.

Years into the Global War on Terror, there was an ever-growing market for contractors to assist in the implantation of government operations throughout the war zones. Countless private military companies proliferated throughout the world to provide retired law enforcement and military personnel for service in Iraq and Afghanistan, but the CIA hired the best of the best to serve in the 125-man global force. Virtually all the operators hired by the CIA were retired members of the most covert elements of the U.S. special operations community; the top-tier operators were recruited and ultimately hired to be part of the GRS program. Many were from the SEALs or Special Forces; all had extensive combat experience and exemplary service records. The very best GRS members, those who sometimes are lent out to other clandestine services, are known in the slang as "Scorpions."[5]

For the CIA, the use of GRS operators was a natural extension of the paramilitary complexion of counterterrorist work. Before the 9/11 attacks, when the CIA was primarily an intelligence-gathering and data analysis organization, the agency's operational tradecraft of espionage required anonymity and invisibility. Afghanistan and Iraq redefined the metabolic chemistry of America's spies. In a region where warlords and militia leaders respected a show of force far more than a deft hand, GRS operators did not have to go to language school, they did not have to handle a bevy of agents, and they were never expected to write up reports, request funding to recruit a double agent, or deal with the bureaucracy of espionage and the backstabbing and office politics that were often the currency of day-to-day life in Langley. They had to come to meetings with a large entourage of heavily armed and commando-skilled shooters. GRS operators were shooters—pure and simple. They were highly skilled A-plus tactical talent designed to secure the spies no matter where they ventured. A CIA case agent with a suitcase full of cash was often accompanied by teams of heavily armed GRS specialists.

The CIA paid for the proper talent. A GRS tour of duty ran between 90 and 120 days; the salary for the contractors could be as high as $140,000 for the year; those on full-time contracts earned slightly less but received benefit packages—including death benefits. It was demanding work, and it required enormous physical stamina, absolute mental vigilance, and the ability to withstand fear and the longing for home. Teams operate in the most explosive locations inside the crosshairs of the Middle East and Africa; GRS operators have earned their share of scare and frequent-flier miles crisscrossing the globe to hot spots like Djibouti, Somalia, the Sudan, Mali, Iraq, Yemen, Pakistan, and Afghanistan.

The work was also quite deadly. Of the twelve CIA members killed between 2009 and September 11, 2012, three were GRS members; one GRS operator, Raymond Davis, was jailed in Pakistan for a lengthy period after killing two men in Lahore who he claimed were trying to rob him.[6] It is, however, widely believed that Davis's true mission was countersurveillance for a case officer meeting a clandestine informant without the knowledge of the ISI, Pakistan's notorious Inter-Services Intelligence.

Although the Annex and the Special Mission Compound answered to different masters and were subject to the rules and restrictions of very different bureaucracies, the security staffs of both the diplomatic and the intelligence facilities realized that their fates and survival were intertwined. The GRS personnel, together with heavily armed members of the February 17 militia, constituted what was classified as a quick reaction force. The QRF's mission was to respond to any active asset at the Annex out and about in Benghazi in need of support and rescue. One of GRS's primary missions was to assist the Special Mission in time of need. The handshake agreement between the intelligence community and the DS was how things rolled in expeditionary democracy posts; it was the currency of day-to-day life in volatile nations where the host government was incapable of providing support. The Scorpions were the backup plan. Their tactical skill sets and dynamic deterrence power would have to do. For the most part it worked. In June 2011, Special Envoy Chris Stevens had been prompted to seek shelter at the Annex due to credible threats against his personal safety that had reached the U.S. intelligence community via its networks in the city.

One of the GRS operators at the Annex was Tyrone "Ty" Woods. Born Tyrone Snowden Woods on January 15, 1971, in Portland, Oregon, Ty grew up in a religious home where doing the right thing was entrenched in the actions and visions of the family's children. Ty was reared in a setting straight out of central casting for the all-American hero—a five-thousand-acre cattle farm in Long Creek, Oregon. "He was the type of child that was fearless and could spend all day outdoors and tackle everything and anything that he put his mind to," his father, Charles Woods, remembered.[7] An avid hunter (he would spend days out in the woods with his .22 rifle, his father recalled), by the time he was thirteen years old, Ty Woods had earned an Oregon hunter's safety card and was also a certified PADI (Professional Association of Diving Instructors) diver. He was an all-state wrestler, and he was the kind of young man who would not quit until he achieved the goals he had set for himself—even if they were beyond the grasps of most men.

In 1990, Woods joined the U.S. Navy SEALs. He did not make it through the grueling, bone-breaking Basic Underwater Demolition selection process the first time out but was undeterred by the minor setback and tried again, going through the notorious Hell Week twice. He received his Trident, the iconic badge of the U.S. Navy SEALs, in October 1991. West Coast handsome, with a permanent look of righteous energy, Woods could have served as a recruitment poster for all that was unique about a close-knit brotherhood like the SEALs. Although much of his service record in the SEALs remains classified, he served as a medical corpsman and paramedic in SEAL Team ONE, SEAL Team THREE, and SEAL Team FIVE. He wore the Trident for nearly twenty years and served multiple tours of duty in Somalia, Iraq, and Afghanistan. "I never really knew where he was," his father remembered, "and I didn't think it was my place to ask. If they were sending Ty somewhere, I knew, though, that it was because he was needed."[8]

Although a trained marksman and an operator with an endless repertoire of tactical skills and combat experience, Woods was a dedicated lifesaver. His medical training was extensive, and it was reinforced by emergency room and paramedic real-world experience with the San Diego Fire Department. He was a licensed registered nurse and worked at his wife's dental practice in La Jolla, California. But with twenty years of active service on the teams, Woods still felt a duty to serve and to live the encapsulated reality of being the go-to guy on assignments in critically dangerous locations that required go-to men. In 2010, he took on the contract of serving the Central Intelligence Agency as a GRS operator. He traveled to various points of interest in South America, the Middle East, and Africa to support CIA operations.

As the primary 18-Delta at the Annex in Benghazi, Woods realized that the American presence in the city could go from threatened to full-scale catastrophic in the flash of a truck bomb detonating through the main gate. Days before September 11, he drove to the Special Mission Compound to provide a hands-on refresher class in emergency trauma care.[9] The DS agents at the Special Mission Compound had been through the rigors of the blood-and-guts classes during their high-threat training, but Woods was determined to keep them up to date and ready with techniques and suggestions in case they suddenly found themselves under fire and in need of treating a gaping chest wound. Everyone hoped that there would be no need to break out the medical kit or to have to apply the QuikClot agents for real.

Woods, as well as the other GRS team members at the Annex still awake, did not need to ask one another if the noise in the distance had been a gunshot. These men were expert enough not only to discern the difference between a car backfiring and a weapon being fired but also to identify the caliber of the round fired and in which direction the muzzle of the weapon was pointed.

There was absolutely no doubt when the percussive sound of the hand grenade exploding was heard. An attack was under way.

12.

Overrun

R. sounded the duck-and-cover alarm the moment he realized, by looking on the camera monitors, that the post had been compromised by hostile forces. The duck-and-cover alarm was a very loud warning device, reminiscent of the wailing European police sirens, that blared endlessly throughout the compound; the volume was eardrum pounding, and it continued without respite; each agent also carried a James Bond–like wireless switch to activate the alarm at a moment's notice. In the aftermath of the first explosive hit of the attack, it was not clear who sounded the duck-and-cover alarm first. Was it one of the agents outside the villa? The working theory was R. from the TOC. Regardless, the duck-and-cover alarm gave the agents a two-step lead on the terrorists. R., just to reinforce the severity of the situation at the Special Mission Compound, yelled "Attack, attack, attack!" "The order to retreat to the safe haven resonated throughout the sprawling facility.

From his command post, R. could observe a 360-degree panoramic view of the compound due to a bank of strategically placed interior surveillance cameras and the horizon painted what in the business is best described as an "oh shit" moment. He could see men swarming inside the main gate, and he noticed the Blue Mountain

Libya guards and several of the February 17 Brigade militiamen running away as fast as they could; they had, though, radioed the TOC to inform the RSO that the compound was under attack. The RSO's command of the video cameras gave the agents on the compound something of a tactical edge. Even though they were overrun and outnumbered, the TOC could identify where the terrorists were, and the RSO could provide the attackers' coordinates to the ARSOs. He immediately alerted the QRF at the Annex and at the embassy in Tripoli by cell phone. His message was short and to the point: "Benghazi under fire, terrorist attack." Nothing more needed to be said. The many REACT drills had become reality. This was any agent's worst nightmare.

A. was the agent on duty that night who, according to the Special Mission Compound's emergency protocols, or REACT plan, would be responsible for safeguarding Stevens and Smith in case of an attack. A. rushed into the residence to relieve, or "push," D., who rushed back to the barracks to retrieve his tactical kit through the access point in the alleyway connecting the two compounds. D. had to assemble his tactical kit and communications gear, as well as his M4 assault rifle. He was wearing a white T-shirt and his underwear when the alarm sounded. The terrorists had achieved absolute surprise. D. went into REACT mode without shoes or pants, but the duck-and-cover alarm gave him a few steps, which is all he needed.

The agents scrambled in an elaborate spiderweb to grab their M4 assault rifles, helmets, and battle kits, with a backdrop of explosions and automatic weapons fire rattling. The DS agents ran like sprinters toward their stowed weapons and equipment. Their hearts rushed up their chests to the back of their throats, causing their mouths to dry up in the surge of adrenaline. The agents attempted to stick to the plan, draw on their training, and keep their minds focused and fluid, as they hoped to avoid an encounter when outnumbered and outgunned. The sounds of guttural Arabic, noises that emanated from the back of the throat that were propelled forward, which to the

Americans sounded like angry mumbling, grew more unintelligible and numerous each stride they took toward the TOC and their villa; the odd angry shot was fired into the September sky. The night's clean and refreshing air was now polluted with a harsh and bitter smell of cordite, like a stagnant cloud left behind following a Fourth of July fireworks display. Numerous figures, their silhouettes barely discernible in the darkened shadows, chased the agents from behind, chanting unintelligibly and angrily.

The agents held their sidearms firmly as they raced across the compound to where their weapons and kits were stored. They were ready to engage any threat they encountered but hoped that they wouldn't have to yet. It was too early in the furious chaos to make a last stand. Each agent asked himself the basic questions: How many gunmen were inside the perimeter? What weapons did they have? "Combat was like a pickup game in the Arab world," a former DS agent with service in Yemen and the Gaza Strip commented. "When the gunfire begins, the terrorists and their supporters start sending text messages, and Facebook notifications follow. Soon it becomes a beach party, sans the beach and the party. And, of course, no one brings beer or hot dogs, but each will bring an AK to make the party interesting."[1] The DS agents knew that it didn't matter how many attackers were inside the post. Word of a dead militiaman would spread wildly, and soon there would be a thousand armed attackers inside the compound. One thing was absolutely certain, though, in the minds of each and every one of the agents in those early and crucially decisive moments, and that was that the U.S. ambassador, the personal representative of President Barack Obama, was the ultimate target of the attack. They knew they had to secure him and get him out of the kill zone.

Unlike an RSO whose tour at an embassy could last as many as three or four years, or an agent on the secretary of state's detail, the TDY agents in Benghazi hadn't had the time with Ambassador Stevens to get to know him properly. Agents assigned to an individual for an extended period of time get to know all the secrets of an ambassador or a secretary of state. The personal dynamics that develop between the agent and the man or woman he is tasked with protecting are a complex mixture of tactics, authority, personal bonds, and adherence to mission. The textbook requires that an agent never engage in protracted conversations that are unrelated to security and never develop emotional links to a protectee. The agents' emotions are irrelevant to the requirements and deadly realities of dignitary protection. But the agents are human. There have been secretaries of state and ambassadors whom the agents in the service—and the agents on their details— have absolutely adored. These principals made it their personal business to concern themselves that the agents who protected them were looked after and took the time to inquire about their families; some would celebrate the sacrifice agents made on a detail by inviting them to their homes for a summer's barbecue. Madeleine Albright was such a secretary of state. The men and women on her detail thought the world of her and affectionately gave her the nickname Fireball. Other secretaries of state did not treat the agents as kindly; one, the rumbles went, would never let the agents use the bathroom at his sprawling ranch and would charge them for food and water. Special agents on TDY details didn't have time to develop a personal rapport with their principals. At a UN General Assembly, or UNGA, as they are known, for example, a foreign minister or an Arabian prince could maintain a bizarre and reprehensible lifestyle as he ricocheted across the Manhattan nightlife, but it didn't matter; the DS agents were responsible for protecting these individuals in their temporary care from harm.

But the agents liked Stevens; there wasn't anything not to like. His fuel tank ran on high-octane dedication, and the smile never left his face. His dedication was absolute—even in a place as dangerous as Benghazi. The moment the duck-and-cover alarm sounded, the agents had to rely on their earpieces, their training, and their instincts.

In sticking to the REACT plan, A. rushed up the landing to round up Ambassador Stevens and Smith and ushered them to the safe haven inside the residence. "Follow me, sir," A. said in a calming, though immediate, tone. "We are under attack."

Both Foreign Service officers were startled by the deafening alarm; the worry was engraved in their faces. There was no time to get dressed or to grab personal items, such as a wallet or cell phone; there was no time to power down laptops or take them downstairs. A. insisted, however, that both Stevens and Smith don the khaki Kevlar body armor vests that had been pre-positioned in their rooms.

It was critical that the three men make it to the safe haven and lock the doors before the attackers knew where they were. A., in following the room-clearing tactics he had been taught in the training that prepared him for the TDY assignment, carefully turned each and every corner with his M4 poised to engage any threat he saw. He had a Remington 870 12-gauge shotgun slung over his shoulder just in case; the Remington was a no-nonsense tool of ballistic reliability that was an ideal weapon to engage overwhelming crowds of attackers. A.'s service-issue SIG was holstered on his hip. A. heard dozens of voices shouting outside the walls; these voices were interrupted only by the sporadic volleys of automatic gunfire launched outside. The lights in the residence were immediately extinguished. The unmistakable pop of gunfire caused both Stevens and Smith to realize the immediacy of the emergency, and the difficulty they encountered negotiating the darkened path toward the safe haven was exacerbated by the restrictive hug of the heavy vests over their distressed chests and midsections. Every few feet in the progression toward the safe haven, A. would make sure that Stevens and Smith were following close behind him. The fear of being separated was omnipresent in the coordinated dash to the safe haven. The roles were reversed. The special agent was in charge of the chief of mission. Stevens and Smith listened and followed instructions.

When the three reached the safe haven, the meshed steel door behind them was shut and locked, shielding the three from the assaulting force outside. The two diplomats, their eyes squinting in the darkness to see through the iron grating, expressed great fear. A. took aim with his M4 through the wrought-iron grating over the window, keeping his M4's sights on the heads of the men he could distinguish in the distance. The door, as well as the window, was supposed to be opened only when the cavalry arrived. When that would happen was anyone's guess.

A DS special agent's radio gear is called a surveillance kit. Each earpiece is custom molded and used for discreet communications. The clear plastic earpiece allows agents to move through crowds while listening to other agents or to keep an eye on a shady character in a crowd. In this case, the TOC was the lifeline to the safe haven. A. depressed the push-to-talk radio button to initiate the conversation.*

"TOC, A. here."

"Go, A.," said R., manning the TOC.

"Package and one guest secure, hunkered down."

"Roger that. TOC out."

A. updated the CIA Annex, the U.S. embassy in Tripoli, and the DS/CC via cell phone calls, with the message "Package and guest secure, hunkered down in the safe haven."

The safe haven enabled the three to remain unseen by the terrorists searching for them. Ambassador Stevens requested A.'s Black-Berry so he could start making calls to nearby consulates and to the embassy in Tripoli. Stevens spoke softly and in hushed tones, so as not to compromise their position to anyone outside. His first call was to his deputy chief of mission, Gregory Hicks, who was in Tripoli, at the U.S. embassy. Hicks[2] did not recognize A.'s cell phone number and ignored the call a couple of times. On Stevens's third attempt, Hicks picked up and learned of the attack.[3]

Stevens also called local militia and public security commanders in Benghazi pleading for help. Ambassador Stevens had developed a close and affectionate rapport with many of the most powerful men in the city—both the legitimate and the ruthless. He believed in the Libyan people, and he understood wholeheartedly how they had been brutalized and dehumanized by a megalomaniac dictator who terrorized on a whim. Stevens admired how the Libyan spirit had not been

---

*These radio transmissions would likely have gone along these lines, based on our understanding of the events as they unfolded. This is a summation of the communication and vernacular as per the events and as per security considerations. The same applies to communications appearing hereafter in the text.

broken by a tyrant, but rather emboldened by it. In his years in Libya, Stevens tried to sell the notion of America to just about anyone and everyone he met. He tried to convince them that the Libyan people—and those in power—had a friend indeed in the United States.

For an unknown reason, Stevens didn't call the Libya Shield Force, a group of relatively moderate fighting brigades that was, perhaps, the closest thing in the country to a conventional military organization. The Libya Shield Force did have Islamist-leaning ideology, but it wasn't jihadist. Under the command of Wisam Bin Ahmid, it answered to the Libyan Defense Ministry; Ahmid led a well-equipped and disciplined force in Benghazi called the Free Libya Martyrs. The Free Libya Martyrs fielded ample assets in the city; the militia even maintained a presence on social media, like Facebook, and was involved in numerous charitable endeavors. Reportedly, Wisam Bin Ahmid could have responded, but he was never asked.[4]

But perhaps Stevens feared that members of the militia were participating in the attack. Several reports linked this militia with al-Qaeda.

The Libya Shield militia, and concerns about its objectives and intentions, were part of the contents of a cable dispatched to the State Department early in the day by the ambassador. In the secret communications, there is mention of how two militia leaders, Muhammad al-Gharabi and the Libya Shield commander Wisam Bin Ahmid, would not continue to guarantee security in Benghazi, "a critical function they asserted they were currently providing," because the United States was supporting Mahmoud Jibril, a candidate for the office of prime minister. The report discussed the city of Derna and linked it to an outfit called the Abu Salim Brigade, which was beginning to enforce a harsh version of Islamic law that prohibited any commingling of men and women at a local university.[5]

Stevens, as close to an all-knowing expert on Libya as existed anywhere, understood that the country lacked the many moments of clarity it would need to muster from revolutionary chaos to a petrodollar-fueled vibrant democracy. Armed elements, with one foot in a pro-Western foothold and the other firmly fixed inside the jihadist camp, were turning the country into a failed state.

At just before 2200 hours on the eleventh anniversary of one of the darkest days in American history, Ambassador Stevens was hunkered down in a blacked-out basement, desperately seeking aid. The list of contacts whom Stevens phoned remains classified, but they included militia commanders who were quite proud to parade the president of the United States' personal representative in front of their ragtag armies but did not feel it wise or worthy to commit these forces for the rescue of a true friend.

C. had initially rushed to the TOC but then redirected back to the agents' quarters to grab his gear and back up D. It was procedure, and tactical prudence, for the remaining agents at the compound to work in teams of two. B. and R. were inside the TOC, which was locked down behind secured fire doors.

C. and D. rushed out of the barracks with weapons in hand, hoping to reach the residence on the western side of the compound, but the two young agents immediately found themselves seeking cover from an endless stream of armed men. Moving slowly, and peering around corners, the two men tried to crisscross the alleyway that separated the two halves of the Special Mission Compound, but they feared the connecting path would turn into an exposed kill zone. There were just too many gunmen racing about and screaming to one another in Arabic. Some were talking on smartphones; a few of the men barked orders on handheld field radios. The scene looked like something out of a science fiction film, in fact; small dots of light, the lit screens of mobile phones, vibrated in the darkness as the attackers moved into position. The DS agents realized that they were cut off. Hurriedly, they made their way back to the barracks. Some of the attackers carried RPGs slung over their shoulders, apparently to be used on the armored doors of the safe haven and the TOC or to repel any counterattack.

The DS agents knew they were facing superior firepower. C. radioed the TOC of their predicament and waited for the chance to attempt a breakout.

Along the way, C. and D. encountered a bewildered member of the February 17 militia who appeared panic-stricken and overwhelmed by the magnitude of the attack. They found him, weapon in hand, standing in front of the DS villa seeming to await the order of what to do. The man was frightened out of his wits. He had heard the screams of *"Allahu akbar,"* or "God is great," and he had heard the word *kafir,* or infidel, uttered by the gunmen as they raced about. Even though the February 17 Brigade espoused an Islamic agenda, and even though it was customary for members of the force to wear lapel pins with Libyan and Qatari flags, one of the hundreds of thousands of paraphernalia tossed about during the civil war to show Islamic solidarity with the tiny Persian Gulf oil-rich kingdom, the men inside the compound would cut the militiaman's throat if they had the chance for working with the Americans.

C. and D. ushered the guard into their living quarters and sealed the heavy doors behind them. It was going to be a long and difficult night.

The TOC was perhaps the most fortified spot on the compound. Just barely large enough for two or three individuals, it was bristling with communications, video surveillance, and other emergency gear. Hardened Pelican cases, the Louis Vuitton of the deployable and tactical, were stacked atop shelves, on tables, and laid out on the floor. Dell laptops were up and still running. The TOC was a logistics hub for the Special Mission Compound—complete with stationery and office supplies (including seals and labels for diplomatic pouches) and other tools to facilitate the day-to-day exchanges of diplomacy. A safe, complete with enough gear to hold off a determined adversary, was secured to the wall and floor; the TOC also housed the weapons that the British security specialists had dropped off less than an hour before.

As bad as it was, the TOC RSO had things in hand. Like an air traffic controller, he knew the stakes were high and that mistakes could lead to disaster. Ambassador Stevens was hunkered down, and so were the agents. The Scorpions and the QRF were gearing up and mustering the cavalry. Everyone just needed to hold tight. The TOC had visual surveillance of the "tangos," the slang for terrorists, and could update the agents. With notifications to Washington, D.C., he knew there must be other things happening behind the scenes.

The TOC was never designed nor intended to be a bunker, even though a heavy door separated it from dangers that could be lurking outside. Instead, as the eyes and ears of security operations at the compound, it was designed to serve as a command-and-control center. It was supposed to direct and coordinate the activities of the local guard force and the February 17 militiamen, but the Libyans paid by the Special Mission had fled the moment the attack commenced. Several Libyan guards were injured in the assault. Abdulaziz Majbiri, a Blue Mountain Libya guard, was ordered by the DS agents to assemble at the pool for REACT instructions, but he claimed that his comrades were incapable of defending themselves in light of the coordinated attack. "I was separated from the others and couldn't get anywhere near the swimming pool," he claimed, "before I was shot."[6] According to other reports, a terrorist grabbed one of the Blue Mountain Libya guards and beat him. "You are an infidel protecting infidels who insulted the prophet," the militant scolded the guard member as he beat him savagely.[7]

With pinpoint MOUT, or military operations on urban terrain, tradecraft, the terrorists assaulted the February 17 Brigade command post at the western tip of the northern perimeter by lobbing a grenade inside and then, before the smoke and debris would clear, firing dedicated bursts of AK-47 fire into the main doorway. Several militiamen, along with one or two Blue Mountain Libya guards, were seriously wounded in the exchange, though they still managed to use an escape ladder to climb up toward the rooftop, where they hid. The command post floor was spattered with blood.

As they watched the attack on the mission unfold in real time on the video monitors, R. and B. attempted to count the men racing through Bravo-1 and Charlie-1 gates. However, the men had rushed through the two entrances in such a quick and coordinated push, and flowed through the northern part of the grounds in such alarming numbers,

R. and B. could not ascertain their numbers or armament. It was only later, when reviewing the attack via the high-resolution DVR system, that the DS discovered there were thirty-five men methodically and systematically attacking the Special Mission Compound.

Those militants assaulting the compound were not members of a ragtag force. It was observed that the attackers were split into small groups, advanced throughout the compound methodically, and employed military-style silent hand signals to direct their progression toward their objectives.[8] At this stage of the attack it was impossible to assess if this was a spontaneous outburst of violence or a premeditated professional assault. To the agents inside the compound, these facts were irrelevant: the assailants were heavily armed and out for blood. They were under attack. Some were dressed in civil war chic—camouflage outfits, black balaclavas. Some wore white undershirts and khaki military trousers that were once worn by, or seized from, the Qaddafi military. A few wore Inter Milan soccer jerseys; Italian soccer was popular in Libya, even though Al-Saadi Qaddafi, the dictator's son—and former commander of the Libyan military's Special Forces—had purchased his way as a player onto several Italian professional teams.

Some of those who barked the orders wore mountaintop jihad outfits worn by Taliban warriors in Afghanistan. Virtually all of the attackers had grown their beards full and long. According to reports and shadowy figures on the ground in Benghazi, there were foreigners—organizers and commanders from nearby and far away—mixed in with the local contingent of usual suspects. Many were believed to have come originally from Derna, a city on the Mediterranean coast situated between Benghazi and Tobruk. Derna had been the traditional hub of jihadist Islamic endeavors inside Libya and beyond. It was also the birthplace of the Libyan Islamic Fighting Group (LIFG);* in the hopes of strangling it and once and for all choking

---

*According to a CNN report (Security Clearance, May 15, 2012), a U.S. diplomat who visited Derna in 2008 noted in a cable: "Unlike the rest of the country, sermons in eastern Libyan mosques are laced with phraseology urging worshippers to support jihad in Iraq and elsewhere through direct participation or financial contributions."

the jihadist elements dead, Qaddafi's forces surrounded the town for nearly twenty years. Most of the fighters, though, fled to the mountains and waged a lethal and highly organized guerrilla campaign against the regime. The LIFG command cadre had maintained lifelong relationships with their counterparts in Egypt, many of whom went on to become the core leadership of al-Qaeda. Hundreds of the most hard-core fighters from Derna traveled to Iraq, Pakistan, and Afghanistan to earn their spots on the front lines of the jihad. In 2007, allied forces in Iraq captured a list of foreign fighters working together with Sunni insurgents and jihadists. There were one hundred and twelve Libyan names on the list; fifty-two of the men were from Derna.[9] When they returned to Libya, many brought their international combat comrades back with them.

The men from Derna, as many of the jihadists were known, were specialists at asymmetrical warfare. They had waged an unforgiving campaign against the Soviets and then later the Americans in Afghanistan; they fought in Africa, in bloody conflagrations in the Sudan and Somalia. They were proficient in military hardware and in urban tactics. They were a lethal force to contend with, and they were social media and chat room savvy—using underground and ever-evolving sites to recruit, promote, and plan.*

It was clear that *whoever* the men assaulting the compound were, they had been given precise orders and impeccable intelligence. They knew when, where, and how to get from the access points toward the ambassador's residence and how to cut off the DS agents as well as the local guard force and the February 17 Brigade militia-

---

*An example of the power of such chat rooms, blogs, and social media communications, already one of the most effective tools of the Arab Spring, was found, following the terrorist attack in Benghazi, on a jihadist site. Among the comments and calls to action was the following: "All should strive together towards one goal; expelling US embassies from Muslim lands, persevering in demonstrations and protests, as has happened in a number of Muslim nations. Their embassies should be torched like zealous brothers did in Egypt and Yemen. And whenever a Muslim gets a hold of US ambassadors or delegates, he has the best example in the act of the grandsons of Omar Mukhtar in Libya—who slaughtered the US ambassador—may Allah reward them. Let the step of expelling embassies and consulates be a milestone to free the Muslim lands from American domination and arrogance."

men on duty that night. As is standard procedure, in the days leading up to the arrival of the ambassador (and thus the assault), the RSO and his team made a series of official requests to the Libyan government for additional security support to the mission. These communiqués included requests for an extra police and militia presence to coincide with the arrival of Ambassador Stevens, roving patrols at the front and rear of the compound, and bomb-sniffing dogs.[10] It appears that the attackers either intercepted these requests or were tipped off by corrupt Libyan officials. According to one European security official who had worked in Benghazi, "The moment notifications and requests went out to the NTC and the militias in advance of Stevens's arrival, it was basically like broadcasting the ambassador's itinerary at Friday prayers for all to hear."[11] The terrorists also had had sufficient time to map out the terrain. They owned the geography.

The attackers had known that there were new, uninstalled generators behind the February 17 command post, nestled between the building and the overhang of foliage from the western wall, as well as half a dozen jerry cans full of gasoline to power them. One of the commanders dispatched several of his men to retrieve the plastic fuel containers and bring them to the main courtyard. A gunman opened one of the cans and began to splash the gasoline on the blood-soaked floor of the February 17 Brigade command post. The man with the jerry can took great pains to pour the harsh-smelling fuel into every corner of the building before setting fire to one of the DS notices and launching an inferno.

A. watched from between the metal bars inside the safe haven as the eruption of the building caused a fiery clap followed by bright yellow flames. He updated the TOC with what he could see and, more ominously, what he could smell.

"A. here, I see flames and smoke."

"Roger that, me too, A.," said the agent in the TOC.

He keyed the microphone again and said, "Backup en route."

And then there was silence.

Silence on the radio means one or two things: either all is good, or things are very bad. There are no in-betweens. The TOC went silent on air after R. indicated that help was on the way. The silence initiated grave concern.

Thick plumes of acrid gray and black smoke billowed upward to cloud the clear night's sky. The terror-strewn landscape was painted eerily hellish as the grounds of the Special Mission Compound were lit up in an orange glow. For some added fury, some of the gunmen broke the windshields of several of the February 17 Brigade vehicles parked near the command post and doused the interior of the vehicles with gasoline. A lit cigarette, smoked almost to the filter, was tossed in to ignite another blaze. The crackling of flames introduced a wickedly violent cadence to the shouting in Arabic. Every few minutes or so, the sounds of shattering glass punctuated the terror.

The men carrying the fuel-filled jerry cans toward the residence moved slowly as they struggled to slice a path toward the ambassador's villa. The twenty liters of fuel contained in each plastic jerry can weighed forty-four pounds, and the gunmen found it difficult to manage the lofty weight with the gasoline sloshing around and spilling on their boots and sandals. Their grasps on the can handles were tenuous at best; the perspiration that turned their trigger fingers clammy made carrying a heavy load all but impossible. The men were forced to stop every ten or twenty feet to right themselves and to correct the slings for their AK-47s back across their shoulders. Several of the men in charge barked insults and orders to the jerry can–carrying crews, but intimidation was pointless. The jihad never turned away a martyr-to-be because he lacked upper-body strength.

The survival equation at the Special Mission Compound was growing dim. R. summoned C. and D. over the radio.

"Guys, TOC here, several tangos outside your door. Stay put. Do not move."

"Copy," replied one of the agents.

"Backup on the way."

In the background, the TOC agent could hear the sound of the angry mob in the hallways, over the agent's keyed microphone. R.

communicated his situation to the Annex, the RSO Tripoli, and the DS/CC via his cell phone. Well over a dozen terrorists were trying to break through the cantina at the residence. The agents had heard a crowd of men outside the building and then retreated inside once they heard the tumult and the AK rounds fired all around them. The layout of the Special Mission had betrayed the response capabilities of the armed agents. The sprawl had turned into a defensive handicap; being spread out enabled hostile forces to split and weaken any truly cohesive counterattack. C. and D. had shut the main door and had moved the refrigerator from its emplacement inside the kitchen and barricaded the door with it. They hunkered down low, with their M4s in hand, and prepared for the breach and the ballistic showdown. The agents' short-term objective was to remove the ambassador from his location, a mission they had trained and prepared for ad infinitum. However, in the backs of their minds the nagging question remained: Would they see the light of the next morning? This didn't matter. What did matter, however, was the knowledge that their colleague was alone in the safe haven and needed backup. They were, however, trapped.

In reality, so, too, was the TOC. But as long as some of the many cameras that were supposed to be functional still worked—and the terrorists didn't have the forethought to remove them from their rotating anchors—the TOC would be the Special Mission Compound's sole means by which to coordinate any and all rescue attempts of Ambassador Stevens and Sean Smith. The TOC's cameras gave them a chance.

A. leaned upward, glancing out the murky transparency of his egress window, peering across the bars toward the violence before him. He watched as the fuel bearers inched their way forward, and he limbered the fingers of his right shooter's hand as he laid a line of sight onto the multiple targets closing the distance to the villa. His breathing was controlled as he inhaled and exhaled in preparation for having to take that first and fatal shot. He found himself relying on his thoughts, his instincts, his experiences, and the responsibility for keeping Stevens and Smith safe. The very essence of those oh-shit moments in dignitary protection work was whisking a principal far from the kill zone—far from harm. The point of the training that an agent received was to instill the importance of using dynamic skill and pragmatic thought to buy time and space. It was, perhaps, a remarkable testimony to the means and measures that the Diplomatic Security Service took in recruiting its men and women that inexperienced agents who were thrown into the crosshairs of the new world disorder were able to assess threats analytically, with their minds and gut instincts, and not solely with their trigger fingers.

A. faced a life-changing or life-ending decision from the inside of the darkened bunker of the villa's safe haven that few of even the most experienced agents in the DS roster ever had to confront: Shoot it out and play Rambo, or remain unseen and buy time? Buying time takes brains, and according to a DS agent with a plethora of experience in counterterrorist investigations, "We hire people for their brains, not necessarily their trigger fingers."[12] Assessing threats and creating distance between a potential assassin and his target takes analytical judgment, and its takes being able to absorb a 180-degree view of the terrain and translate it into a chess master's plan of attack. "We're not there [in hostile locations] to engage," said Special Agent Dale "Chip" McElhattan, the acting DS chief of security and law enforcement training, at a training exercise at the Diplomatic Security Training Center in Summit Point, West Virginia, that was open to local media. "We're there to get the people we're protecting away from the threat."[13] McElhattan should know: he has had quite a lot of experience in protecting people from great threat. In 2002, McElhattan, the RSO at the U.S. consulate in Jerusalem, led a DS team that rescued citizens from foreign nations trapped in the Church of the Nativity in Bethlehem at the onset of full-scale warfare between Israeli and Palestinian forces. Under fire, the DS team rescued nine Americans, five Britons, several Italians, and one Japanese citizen from the church and a nearby hotel. For their courage under fire, McElhattan and his team were awarded the prestigious Federal Law Enforcement Officers Association National Award for Heroism.

Indeed, DS special agents are taught to cover and evacuate. This philosophy is the diametric opposite of the way that others who find themselves in critical-threat real estate are taught to operate; SEALs, after all, are trained to engage. A. found himself in an unforgiving position of being damned if he did and damned if he didn't. As the retired DS agent Scot Folensbee reflected concerning these life- and career-altering events while on a critical-threat assignment, "When you are faced with immediate life-and-death decisions, you know that ultimately, if you survive, you will be second-guessed and criticized. So, the only thing to do is realize that in these cases of 'should I shoot or not shoot,' you as the agent are the one making the decision and you, the agent, will have to live with that decision. There wasn't a right decision here, and there wasn't a wrong one, either. There was only the decision of the agent forced to make such a judgment call."[14] A. scanned the horizon, prioritizing the targets. He understood that depending on what outcome dawn's first light would bring, he would be either congratulated or criticized; dead or alive was a mere afterthought.

Had he had to write down the answer to this very pressing quandary, had such a question been on the basic agent test, he clearly would have answered it wrong. The Special Mission Compound in Benghazi on that night was not a textbook case. Benghazi—especially in the context of the Arab Spring and the fight against the new franchises of fundamentalist terror—was a dizzying and uncertain mosaic. It was a multidimensional mess with a border of whites and blacks that was filled with countless shades of confusing gray. No classroom, no training officer, and certainly no armchair general could understand the ballistic nuances of those terrifying, uncertain moments of the attack. The attackers had managed to cut off and isolate two two-man teams of armed support, and the local militia paid to stand and fight had cut and run. A. listened to the communications going back and forth between all the agents on the compound as best he could on the twisted coil earpiece connected to his Motorola handset radio.

A.'s decision was indeed his and his alone. And he chose to do whatever was humanly feasible to keep Ambassador Stevens and IMO Smith alive. If the time came to take out a few of the assholes who had invaded that night, then he wouldn't hesitate. But there was no honor in a suicidal last stand before it was absolutely the time to commit suicide. Every second that the three could hang on was another second of hope that rescue would come.

He hoped that the TOC had managed to reach someone who could help. He was waiting for the arrival of the operators from the "other government agency" down the road.

It was 2200 hours.

13.

Notifications

When the TOC first relayed the request for assistance to the U.S. embassy in Tripoli as well as to the Annex, Tyrone Woods knew what was needed. He and several comrades suited up. They checked their M4 carbines and semiautomatic pistols and loaded their tactical gear into several armored CIA Mercedes G-Wagons parked in front of their quarters. Some of the operators moved their heads slightly in the main staging area of the Annex, pointing their ears in the direction of the Special Mission Compound, in an attempt to listen to the events as they were transpiring. The crackle of the odd gunshot in the distance was an inconclusive yet optimism-building sign that the agents were indeed safe and hunkered down awaiting backup. The GRS team knew, from radio transmissions from the TOC, that the agents were still alive, although sudden bursts of AK fire from twenty or so weapons could hint that a massacre was taking place.

The operators wanted to move out immediately. They didn't understand what the delay was. As they assembled, some of the GRS members grasped their holsters, making sure one last time that their custom-made Kimbers and SIG ███████████████ semiautomatic pistols were ready; some removed their SIGs from their holsters to check out the SIGLITE night sights one final time. The men knew they would be using their weapons shortly.

The GRS team leader quickly briefed the February 17 Brigade commander on scene as to what they were going to do and prepared to depart. The CIA communications officer had been relaying the bursts of radio feed from the TOC to the chief of station in Tripoli. There was a fluid exchange of radio information and electronic messaging; communications between all points were working fine. The orange glow of flames flickered to the north as the radio communications between A. and the TOC became more desperate. Woods calmly reviewed the contents of his medic's bag and wondered what was next. Yet before the vehicles and armed specialists could traverse the mile or so separating the diplomatic and the intelligence compounds, the Annex commander emerged from his office and ordered the rescue force to stand down for a few minutes pending guidance from Washington.

The GRS rescue force stood in front of their vehicles with a perplexed mask of anger adorning their faces. The crackle of gunfire was heard to the north. Woods was reportedly unwilling to accept any delays coming from HQ or anyone else. As someone who had been in the center of combat where lives depended on rescue and medical treatment, he knew that seconds were precious. Woods knew that he was the lifeline and that the DS agents were pinned down.

The GRS operators made sure they had all their equipment and prepared to head out. They knew there wasn't a damn thing Washington could do at the moment for anybody.

It was 2205 hours in Benghazi, 1605 hours in Washington D.C., when the duty officer at the Ops Center at Main State received the following electronic cable:

Subject: U.S. Diplomatic Mission in Benghazi Under Attack (SBU)
SBU: The Regional Security Officer reports that the diplomatic mission is under attack. Embassy Tripoli reports approximately 20 armed people fired shots; explosions have been heard as well. Ambassador Stevens, who is in Benghazi, and four COM personnel are in the compound

safe haven. The 17th of February militia is providing security support.

The Operations Center will provide updates as available.

By established protocols on message dissemination, the inbound
cable had some thirty-five recipients, including those working for the
Department of Defense, AFRICOM (in Stuttgart, Germany), the
Federal Bureau of Investigation, and the Joint Special Operations
Command, or JSOC, secretly hidden inside Fort Bragg, North Caro-
lina, at Pope Army Airfield. The recipients of the message inside
Foggy Bottom would have included the office of Intelligence and
Research (INR), the Office of the Coordinator for Counterterrorism
(S/CT), and the Near Eastern and African Affairs Bureaus.

The Department of State handles the notifications process of international incidents, especially attacks against American installa-
tions, very well. The DS agent at the Ops Center ensured that copies
of the cable went to the SWO, senior watch officer, and the State Staff
Secretariat, the staffers assigned to Secretary of State Hillary Clinton.
The DS/CC was also simultaneously notifying the special agent in
charge, or SAC, of the secretary's Personal Protection Detail, known
as SD. The SD SAC could always whisper in the secretary's ear or pass
her a note or, as has been the case, interrupt what she was doing to
bring her a message. It had been that way forever. Besides the secretary, "positive notifications" were made to the regional bureaus, INR,
and S/CT. The agent assigned to the Department of Homeland Security command center was also called. Within minutes, hundreds inside
Foggy Bottom alone knew exactly what was unfolding in Benghazi.
Word spread like wildfire inside Foggy Bottom as employees tuned in
to WTOP and BBC radio for updates; remote controls were pointed at
wall-mounted television sets to see what Al Jazeera was reporting. The
mission was under a terror attack.

At the J. Edgar Hoover Building at 935 Pennsylvania Avenue, NW,
the duty officer immediately ensured that the Director's Office, al-

ways referred to as Mr. Mueller, was notified, along with the assorted list of assistant directors, who worked in the firing line at HQ until a more lucrative post, such as the Salt Lake City Field Office, popped up. The FBI's elite Hostage Rescue Team, or HRT, was also alerted— "just in case"—even though the chances of them getting involved in any operations in Libya would be slim to none. Since the 1986 Omnibus Diplomatic Security and Antiterrorism Act created extraterritorial investigative authority for the FBI, the facility attack was now a U.S. federal crime.

DS agents had gotten used to working with the FBI, although the relationship was historically challenged. In February 1995, the FBI took credit for the apprehension of Abdul Basit Mahmoud Karim, also known by his pseudonym/nom de guerre of Ramzi Yousef, in Islamabad. A walk-in to the U.S. embassy in Islamabad told the DS special agents Bill Miller and Jeff Riner, the two ARSOs, that he had information on Yousef's whereabouts; the walk-in had presented the two special agents with a matchbook, distributed by the Diplomatic Security Service's Rewards for Justice Program, offering $2 million for any information leading to Yousef's arrest. The RSO, Art Maurel, was a tough-minded investigative veteran who was willing to absorb any bureaucratic punches and allowed his agents to work the case; they avoided informing anyone outside DS, including the DCM, so as not to compromise the mission. Yousef was apprehended at an al-Qaeda guesthouse linked to Osama bin Laden before he could embark on a notorious plot, code-named Operation Bojinka, which targeted the destruction of ten American airliners as they flew over the Pacific Ocean. After being interrogated by Pakistani security services, Yousef was turned over to the FBI HRT, who secured his return to the United States. The bureau took credit for his capture and forbade elements of DS to "claim the collar," as a DS agent from the New York Field Office put it.

The Yousef capture was a low point in DS-FBI relations. Subsequent investigations, including the bombings of the U.S. embassies in Nairobi, Kenya, and Dar es Salaam, Tanzania, as well as the bombing of the USS *Cole* in Aden, Yemen, in 2000, did little to repair the difficult working relationship between the two agencies. After 9/11, a plethora of FBI agents were placed inside embassies overseas, exacerbating what was already a difficult coexistence. When operating overseas, in the eyes of many RSOs, the bureau was known to wield a heavy hand and display poor bedside manner. "Investigating a crime in Hoboken was one thing, but in the third world, where there is no process, the bureau struggled," said a veteran DS agent who had worked with the bureau. "DS agents were always saddled with either holding the bureau's hands overseas or smoothing over ruffled feathers. They came and left in most cases," he reflected. "The RSO still had to live there."[1]

As much infighting as existed, both agencies had no choice but to work together—especially as the definitive lines separating law enforcement, military, and intelligence operations blurred during the evolution of expeditionary counterterrorism. It had become the norm for MSD agents to protect FBI criminal case agents working investigations overseas.

Buried inside the Hoover Building is the FBI Strategic Information and Operations Center, known as the SIOC. At the SIOC, the supervisory special agent, or SSA, in charge was putting together a team of agents that could be mustered to respond to investigate the crime. In the past, the bulk of the agents came from FBI Washington Field Office or New York Field Office. The Assistant U.S. Attorneys in New York City had plenty of experience in prosecuting terror cases, so the venue was usually the Southern District of New York. In this case, a special agent in charge from the Denver Division was chosen to lead the FBI team. Reportedly, the agent was James Yacone. Yacone had been in Mogadishu, Somalia, as one of the elite 160th Special Operations Aviation Regiment–Airborne 9 MH-60 Black Hawk pilots involved in the operation to capture the warlord Mohammed Aidid that resulted in the Black Hawk Down incident; in the battle he was able to land his crippled Pave Low chopper in a protected area after sustaining militant gunfire.*

---

*On March 9, 2013, it was announced that Yacone would head up the FBI's elite Critical Incident Response Group out of Quantico, Virginia (the same unit that coordinated the rescue of a five-year-old who, in February 2013, was held hostage for several days in an Alabama bunker).

The SIOC was typical FBI: SSAs wearing heavily starched white shirts and blue ties walked around with their jackets off and sleeves rolled up. Multiline phones rang incessantly in the SIOC; the agents on duty shifted their eyes from computer monitors in front of them to the BlackBerrys they kept on their desks. The SSAs rushed from workstations to various offices where the OGAs, or other government agencies, were represented: the Diplomatic Security Service, the CIA, DOD, Department of Homeland Security, and a dozen or so other intelligence and law enforcement entities, each with a specific interest in the developing crisis abroad. The events unfolding in Benghazi were, in the multidimensional world of global crisis management, a critical challenge. The day had been busy with reports flowing in from Cairo and the demonstrations outside the U.S. embassy. Benghazi was clearly more than a demonstration and a chance for the Arab street to get its fifteen minutes of camera time yelling this and burning that. A rather hush-hush American diplomatic post was under attack; the likelihood of an even more covert intelligence outpost being overrun and publicly revealed was now a virtual certainty.

The developing cyclone of events, all coinciding with the eleventh anniversary of the September 11 attacks, metastasized into a perfect storm of worst-case scenarios. Real-time perfect storms are virtually impossible to neutralize in real time; distance and dynamics sometimes thwart the most dedicated of efforts and most noble of causes.

The most immediate objective involved getting Ambassador Stevens, IMO Smith, and the five DS agents to safety and making sure that the Annex received the protection it needed to hunker down until help could arrive or at least buy time for the CIA staffers to destroy their classified apparatus.

Both the CIA and the Department of Defense fielded special operations assets that could have been rushed to Benghazi to rescue personnel from both the Special Mission Compound and the Annex. The CIA fielded two top-tier special operations assets that had the resources and the tactical skill sets to secure enough of the terrain in

Western Fwayhat to properly neutralize the threat to American personnel. One unit, known as the Special Activities Division, or SAD, worked directly as the covert command arm for the agency's National Clandestine Service. SAD personnel were the super-spooks—Rambos and James Bonds put together in one top secret operative. The Special Operations Group, or SOG, a section within the SAD, was responsible for the collection of intelligence, as well as operations with the military, in countries that were hostile threats to the United States or in locations where a U.S. presence had to be covert. But there was no CIA response. The agency did indeed have personnel on the ground in Benghazi, but they weren't under attack. And, as vulnerable as the Annex was, an assessment must have been made that the GRS personnel were more than capable of neutralizing any outside threat "in house."*

The Joint Special Operations Command's two counterterrorist forces—the U.S. Army's First Special Forces Operational Detachment–Delta, or Delta Force, and the U.S. Navy's DevGru—always had an on-call element ready to respond anywhere in the world on an immediate basis to a critical-threat incident, a hijacking, or an incident at sea. These units traveled heavy. And when these secretive teams were given the green light to deploy, they crossed time zones with an enormous support and logistics contingent. These units were most effective when operational circumstances were optimum, such as host-nation approval and support; the last thing that a Delta or DevGru commander wanted was to land or parachute his forces into a hostile environment, only to have to fight their way toward the mission. These units were designed to react, respond, and remedy critical situations—

---

*As a result of the terrorist attacks in Benghazi, and other events (such as the arrest of a GRS staffer in Pakistan), there has been a great deal of media spotlight into the secretive world of the CIA's special operations assets and the GRS program. Some of the open sources, include the December 2012 article in the *Washington Post* referenced in this book. Other sources include: Matthew Cole, "Raymond Davis Is CIA Contractor, U.S. Officials Say," *ABC News* February 21, 2011; David Ignatius, "Death in Benghazi: CIA timeline of how a tragedy unfolded: Multiple errors were made, but there's no evidence the White House deliberately impeded rescue efforts," *Washington Post*, November 5, 2012; Geoffrey Ingersoll, "Missteps By CIA's Shadowy Military Wing Highlight The Agency's Troubling Shift To Militancy," *Business Insider*, January 2, 2013; and, of course, Mark Mazzetti's outstanding book, *The Way of the Knife: The CIA, A Secret Army, and a War at the Ends of the Earth* (Penguin Press, 2013).

situations that were clearly defined. These units were not designed to participate in a rapidly flowing incident that could, like Mogadishu twenty years earlier, result in disaster.

The elite of the elite, the two-pronged dagger of JSOC, did not respond to protests and fires. Governments did not dispatch their most elite units, men who are truly not replaceable, unless the situation warranted a razor-sharp slice and not a wide-handed slap. Anyway, deploying one of the JSOC units from the continental United States would take hours.

There was always the Marine Corps—a branch of the armed forces with an illustrious combat legacy and entrenched history with Libya. In 1987, in the aftermath of nearly twenty years of global terrorist attacks that seemed endless and without solution, the U.S. Marine Corps adhered to a presidential directive mandating all branches of the military to enhance their counterterrorist capabilities. The USMC response was the FAST, Fleet Antiterrorism Security Team, companies, which could respond quickly to incidents around the world where Americans required emergency military aid.* FAST units saw action in 1989 in Panama and in 1991 during Operation Desert Storm. FAST companies worked security in Somalia following the withdrawal of U.S. peacekeepers from Mogadishu and then secured the evacuation of the U.S. diplomatic presence in Monrovia, Liberia, during the civil war. FAST platoons provided tactical security to investigative teams following Saudi Hezbollah's bombing of a U.S. Air Force barracks in Saudi Arabia in 1996. FAST platoons were on site immediately after the bombings of the U.S. embassies in Kenya and Tanzania in 1998; FAST marines secured the damaged USS *Cole* in Aden, Yemen, following the deadly attack on the warship in October 2000. They were a globally on-call force.

---

*On September 27, 2012, Secretary of Defense Leon Panetta and the Chairman of the Joint Chiefs of Staff General Martin E. Dempsey convened a press conference where the deployment of U.S. Marines, a FAST team, to augment security at the embassy in Tripoli, was confirmed. Even prior to this news conference, on September 18, 2012, USMC Commandant General James F. Amos addressed the deployment of the FAST Marines at the Atlantic Council. Additionally, the limitations of the U.S. military's reach were expressed quite specifically by General Martin E. Dempsey when he testified before congress concerning Benghazi on February 7, 2013.

The FAST unit closest to Benghazi was FAST Company Europe, which reported to the Marine Corps Security Force Regiment, II Marine Expeditionary Force. Based at the Naval Station Rota, Spain, FAST Company Europe was no stranger to crisis and response work in the Mediterranean. Secretary of Defense Leon Panetta ordered that appropriate forces respond. A task order flowed from the Pentagon to NAVSTA Rota, Spain: "Lean forward and get there as fast as you can." The marines mustered into their transport aircraft on the tarmac in their combat fatigues and full battle kit. However, logistic challenges such as airspace and overflight clearances are not easily sorted out, especially involving a nation like Libya. Sending armed U.S. Marines into a sovereign nation became a complex foreign policy decision with multiple moving pieces between the Libyan Foreign Ministry, the Pentagon, and the State Department. The marines waited on the tarmac for their orders. The FAST platoon wouldn't make it to Libya, to augment security at the embassy in Tripoli, until the next evening.[2]

AFRICOM, headquartered at Kelley Barracks in Stuttgart, Germany, was responsible for Libya and the closest operational command to have the assets, especially special operations forces, that could respond. AFRICOM was founded in 2000, with the looking-glass forethought that Africa would become a continent of vital interest to the United States, especially as it related to the war on Islamic terrorism, and AFRICOM was announced prior to the 9/11 attacks. The hell of Mogadishu was a wake-up call to American military planners, as was the realization that Africa was so volatile, so precariously steeped in failed-state chaos, that it was an ideal petri dish inside which the plague of Islamic fundamentalism could morph into an all-encompassing pandemic. AFRICOM is tasked and equipped to handle U.S. military operations and straight-on relationships with fifty-three African nations; it covers the entire continent with the exception of Egypt, which for reasons of geopolitical importance is still the focus of U.S. Central Command, or CENTCOM. The fledgling post-revolution dysfunction that was Libya was the true personification of why AFRICOM was created—as a focal point of American military interests and operations to stem the seemingly unstoppable growth of Islamic-inspired violence, led by an implacable al-Qaeda in the Islamic Maghreb. AFRICOM was General Carter F. Ham's shop.* The general realized—before the September 11, 2012, attack—that Libya would have an intrinsic influence on the future of terrorism on the continent and especially in the northern half of the continent.

Even though AFRICOM was closer, geographically, to Benghazi than any other major American military command center, there was still an inescapable issue of logistics. Even for AFRICOM, assembling the personnel and the aircraft, addressing the operational intelligence, and securing permission from the Libyan government in order to respond forcefully to the developing situation in Benghazi were going to take hours. As much as technological innovations and the U.S. presence throughout the world—especially following the 9/11 attacks—had turned the planet into a condensed theater of operations for the United States and its global interests, issues of logistics and kilometers still required adequate start-up and deployment times for even the most immediate of global emergencies. There was no U.S. Air Force AC-130 gunship anywhere near the African continent that could have been diverted to fly close air support and aid rescue efforts.[3] The fastest response boiled down to an unarmed drone that AFRICOM diverted from a mission "somewhere" over the continent.

There was never a question concerning U.S. resolve or the overall capabilities of the U.S. military to respond to Benghazi. There was, however, nothing immediate about an immediate response. There

---

*As was conveyed by Lt. Col. Andrew Wood, the SST commander, in the October 2012 hearing before the House Committee on Oversight and Government Reform, a request was made to extend the unit's tour in Libya because of the security predicament in the country and, indeed, inside the city of Benghazi. General Ham agreed. The SSTs, though, did not belong to AFRICOM; they belonged to U.S. Special Operations Command (USSOCOM) and, reportedly (based on interviews), USSOCOM did *not* want the team to extend in its embassy support role but wanted it to get back to doing spec ops elsewhere in the region where it was needed. The impression given, though, was that DS and the Department of State did not want to extend the SST mission any further, and this appears to be incorrect.

were logistics and host-nation approvals to consider. An immediate response was hampered by the equation of geography and logistics.

Inside the State Department's Operations Center, there was a bank of secure color video screens where senior government officials had the ability to talk to each other at the top secret level; it was an advanced and highly secure adaptation of the Skype concept for those engaged in classified videoconferencing. When news of the attack in Benghazi began to reach the various law enforcement, military, and intelligence agencies, the response could not be instantaneous or in real time; it took quite a bit of effort and time to get cabinet-level officials into these rooms for a single secure videoconference. The initial attack on the villa had taken place *before* the assembled appointed officials could gather and figure out what to do. Government agencies and bureaucracies are not made for speed. As many DS agents will say, "By the time the bosses get involved, it's too late."*

At Foggy Bottom, Secretary of State Hillary Clinton and Undersecretary Patrick Kennedy, known simply as M. (for Management), discussed response options with John Brennan, President Obama's national counterterrorism adviser, at the White House. The decision was made not to launch a Foreign Emergency Support Team, or FEST, from Andrews Air Force Base. FEST teams are always on call to respond to international terrorist incidents—their personnel are able to depart Andrews Air Force Base within four hours of notification. Since its inception in 1986, the FEST has deployed to more than twenty countries.

FEST teams deploy under short-notice requests by U.S. ambassadors. They can be deployed to assist U.S. diplomatic posts with internal crises (such as Benghazi) and can also be deployed through bilateral requests to support host nations facing crises not related to or directly affecting U.S. diplomatic posts. Made up of intelligence operatives and experts from the State Department, FBI, Department of Defense, and

---

*Secretary of State Hillary Clinton, in her January 23, 2013, hearing on Capitol Hill, stated, "We did not have a clear picture" of events on the ground as they transpired.

Department of Energy, FEST's job upon arrival at the scene is to manage operations based on its assessment of the emergency and to advise the ambassador on a subsequent course of action.

FEST packages are multiagency security and intelligence teams sent by the U.S. government within three hours of an attack anywhere in the world to prop up, support, or provide technical assistance. The composition of the team varies, depending upon the assignment, but generally includes DS agents, intelligence analysts, JSOC operators, FBI hostage negotiators, bomb techs, and communications and military logistics experts. Once in country, the FEST mission is operational. By long-standing orders, put together by various NSC directives from the early 1980s, attacks and hostage takings at U.S. diplomatic facilities dictate a FEST response, even if the team gets turned around in the air. A little-known issue that always becomes a kludge on international terrorist attacks is the complexity of overflight and host-government clearances in order for a FEST team to move in. Country clearances are required and are worked through Foggy Bottom with the respective government permission.

With Libya's nascent and fairly dysfunctional government, a move would have to be unilateral and covert, without host-government knowledge. This is always the course of last resort, and such operations are conducted solely under extraordinary circumstances; the May 2011 killing of Osama bin Laden, in Abbottabad, Pakistan, where the host government's approval was never sought, was one such undertaking. Despite what you see in the movies, the U.S. government doesn't like to go down this path, absent extraordinary conditions. The foreign policy blowback from such unilateral moves is simply too great.

FEST packages are usually deployed in "permissive environments" only, where local security arrangements can be coordinated and generally assured; such was the case, for example, in previous deployments to Kenya, Tanzania, and Yemen, when the host nations provided official authorizations for the American specialists to operate in their countries.

In Benghazi, the decision to deploy FEST was held up by State, reportedly by M., because of the risk of putting American assets on the ground in a place where the local militias could not prevent another attack and where the host government could not ensure a safe and secure environment. A FEST response to Benghazi was possible only when thinking of life inside the bubble of a perfect world. The FEST assets could not have gotten to Benghazi in time to do anything for Ambassador Stevens or the DS agents under fire. It was doubtful, even in a perfect world, if the package could have arrived in Benghazi by mid-morning (local time) the following day.

The situation report from Benghazi was still murky. Everybody wanted more eyes, visibility, and ground truth. The drone, on an unknown classified mission somewhere over North Africa, was immediately reassigned by AFRICOM to Benghazi.

"Real time" was a befuddling sort of term that was a cliché with many meanings. For someone sitting inside an air-conditioned command center in Washington, cradling a cup of coffee and watching men face life-threatening challenges and threats, real time provided a thirty-thousand-foot view from above. Perhaps John le Carré said it best: "A desk is a dangerous place from which to watch the world."[4]

For someone inside a besieged diplomatic compound, under fire and on fire, real time all too often translated as a day late and a dollar short. The shock and awe of the world's most powerful military was an impotent entity when the air strike was needed five minutes ago, rather than five hours from now. The DS contingent in Benghazi fully comprehended the might of the U.S. government; they were part of that large and often slow-moving bureaucracy, but they understood the resources and scale that the U.S. government could bring to bear on any foe or to anyone in need of rescue. But for the five DS agents in Western Fwayhat, and for Ambassador Chris Stevens and IMO Sean Smith, real time was stale. Backup couldn't come from an aircraft carrier rushing to the Gulf of Sirte from a port of call or an exercise near Gibraltar. It was about now and an hour from now.

Support would have to come from nearby, the agents knew. It would have to come from the Annex, and it would have to come from inside Libya.

14.

The Fires of the Martyrs

The armed men moved quickly into the villa, creating an unmistakable rumble of fast-paced disturbance. The front door had been locked, and it took some effort to get it open, but even the most ornate of heavy security doors will eventually give way once dozens of men use fists, hammers, and rifle butts to make entry. Finally, an RPG was employed to blow a hole through the main front door.

The penetration of the villa was furiously violent and resembled an animal-like rage that was hard for civilized minds to fathom. It was clear that the throngs who flowed into the villa were looking for Ambassador Stevens, but they happily satisfied their appetite for destruction on anything before them.

The attackers began to rip the upholstered furniture to shreds, and then they assaulted the main sofas; anything upholstered was ripped to shreds with daggers and with fingernails. The cushions were torn apart and thrown about with all the charm of an urban America blackout and the bloodlust of tribal genocide. Bookshelves, lighting fixtures, vases, and throw rugs were bashed and crushed with hyped-up wrath. TVs were thrown to the ground and stomped on with crushing force, and the kitchen was ransacked with a looter's lust. The computers left behind, perhaps containing gigs of sensitive and possibly even classified information, were simply trashed; the gunmen didn't even have the common sense or tactical forethought to steal the communications gear and forward the intelligence bonanza to al-Qaeda commanders in the Maghreb, in Egypt, or even in Yemen and Pakistan. Devastation was the sole order of business. Nothing else mattered.

The Arabic voices upstairs were hard to decipher through the thick walls and raging flames of the command center at Charlie-1 gate, but it was obvious the men had no intention of leaving until they found what they were looking for.

A. raised his M4 at the ceiling, trying to follow the footsteps of the invaders as they stomped on the shards of broken glass above. The TOC was providing him with a foreboding play-by-play of the frenetic orgy of destruction playing out in front of the villa, and B. told his colleague that they were in essence surrounded and cut off. As the gunmen searched through the house, determined to retrieve a captive, either a defiant ambassador or the corpse of one, they headed down toward the safe haven.

All that separated A., Stevens, and Smith from the grasps of heavily armed men was a steel-reinforced security gate usually installed inside the apartments of diplomats serving in "normal" locations in order to prevent criminal intrusion.[1] The metal gate wasn't a State Department–spec FE/BR door, like the ones that were used at various entrance points and access areas in embassies and consulates that were Inman buildings. It was a commercial, off-the-shelf steel door designed to keep intruders away; it could be bolt locked from the inside, which made it an ideal stopgap security measure for locations that need an additional layer of steel to keep intruders out.

B. wished that he could offer some glimmer of hope to the three men trapped inside the villa, but no words were needed. A. knew that unless help arrived soon, they were, to use a DS euphemism, "screwed."

It was an understatement. A. thought that the terrorists would use explosives or an RPG to blast their way into the safe haven; they had, reportedly, used an RPG to blast through the doors at the main entrance.[2] RPGs and satchels of Semtex were virtually supermarket staples in Benghazi, and one pull of the grenade launcher's trigger or one timed detonation, and the armored door to the safe haven would be an easily entered smoldering twist of ruin. But fire was a much cheaper and far simpler solution to a frustrating obstacle.

Burning down an embassy or a diplomatic post was so much easier than blowing it up. Historically, when a diplomatic post's defenses had been breached, the end result always ended in an inferno. It had happened before in Benghazi when, in June 1967, a mob set fire to the U.S. diplomatic post in the city:

> *I was at the foot of the wide marble staircase when the breakthrough occurred. Fanatical knife-carrying intruders, bleeding from cuts received as they were pushed through broken windows, ran down the hall. Putting on gas masks and dropping tear gas grenades, we engaged them on the stairs with rifle butts. In seconds tear gas saturated the area. We then moved into the vault, securing the steel combination door, locking in ten persons. My greatest fear, which I kept to myself, was that gasoline for the generator would be found, sloshed under the vault door and ignited. When after minutes this did not happen, our hearts sank, nonetheless, as outside smoke wafted in and we knew the building had been set afire.*[3]

As the frenzy of destruction began to simmer down, the roar of a fire being set bellowed loudly and ominously. The fuel that flowed from the jerry cans proved to be an ideal accelerant to spread a blaze inside the debris of the ransacked mansion. All that it took to turn bedlam into homicide was a cigarette. R. radioed A. with the ominous news. "Smoke is seen from the villa's windows, over." The message was superfluous. The three men could hear the flames engulf the building, and they could feel the oven-like heat growing hotter and more unbearable as each moment passed. The lights from behind the door began to flicker. The electricity began to falter, and then it died.

Once the fires began and the gunmen discovered the path to the safe haven, A. moved onto his knees, behind a wall, to take aim with his M4 and engage the attackers if they made it through this final barrier. The men were basically indistinguishable from one another. They flailed their hands wildly in the attempt to pry the gate open, looking for any opportunity to manipulate the door that was securely locked from inside. None fired into the room; the mesh steel made it difficult for them to poke the barrels of their AK-47s to a point where they would be able to safely launch a few rounds into the darkened room. Stevens, Smith, and A. were all safely out of view; had the attackers known that their target was behind the gate, they would have spared no effort to puncture through the metal barrier. A. cradled his long gun with his left hand, wiping the sweat from his right hand in brief moments to be ready for the breakthrough and the three-shot bursts. He knew he had to be frugal with his ammunition. His magazine held ▮▮▮ rounds of ▮▮ mm ammunition. Each round traveled at 3,020 feet per second. He knew that he would bring down whomever he hit. A.'s service SIG held ▮▮▮▮ ▮mm rounds. He didn't know, should the men burst through, if he had enough rounds to stop ten or fifty. The crowd of mustached men shouting loudly in Arabic appeared all the more menacing concealed by the darkening clouds of smoke; as A. moved his sights from target to target, the fiery orange glow behind them made the dozen or so men look like a hundred.

Just before the fire was set, the gunmen emerged from the villa joyously animated by the engulfed destruction. They fecklessly fired their AK-47s into the air and watched the villa erupt in a wild and uncontrollable inferno. They stood by with a sense of satisfaction. Whoever was inside the doomed building would most certainly die. Their work for the night was partially done.

The smoke spread fast, a wild and free-moving metastasized vapor of burning wallpaper, fabrics, and plastics. A. ordered Stevens and Smith to drop to their knees and led them in a crawl from the bedroom, where he had been taking aim with his long gun, toward the bathroom, which had a small exterior window; interestingly, and perhaps shockingly, diplomats, even those destined for critical-threat posts, were not mandated to undergo survival-type instruction before leaving the United States. Towels were taken off their fancy racks and doused quickly with water. A. then rolled them loosely and forced them in between the doorjamb to keep the poisonous air from entering the smaller space the three men retreated to. The black acrid vapor was eye searing and blinded the men in the safe haven. The three crawling on the ground, hoping for a last gasp of clean air to fill their lungs, couldn't see a thing in the hazy darkness. The men began to vomit inside the toilet. At first they expelled the lunch and dinner that they had yet to digest. They then began to puke sputum laced with lines of burned tar and other carcinogens that were the natural by-products of the plastics and cushioning that so easily erupted into an out-of-control blaze.

Getting some air was more important than facing the wrath of the attackers; without oxygen they could only hold out a few more minutes. The situation from the safe haven was direly critical. A. attempted to pry open one of the windows, but in seeking ventilation he exacerbated the situation; the opening created an air gust that expanded the intensity of the flames and the smoke. The safe haven became a gas chamber. Both Ambassador Stevens and Sean Smith struggled to inhale; their lungs were singed, and they couldn't remove a word from their blackened mouths. A. signaled the two to follow him to an egress emergency window, but he couldn't see his protectees through the smoke. He banged on the floor as he crawled, hoping that both Stevens and Smith would hear him. A. found himself in a predicament of absolute terror. He was, however, unwilling to surrender to the dire environment. He pushed through toward the window, barely able to breathe or retain focus. With his voice box damaged by smoke, he mustered whatever energy he had remaining to yell and propel Stevens and Smith forward.

The egress window was grilled, and within the grille was a section that can be opened for emergency escape. It had a lock with the key usually located near the window but out of reach from someone outside the window. It did not open easily. Pushing his body strength into his arms and shoulders, A. managed to pry the window slightly ajar. He yelled and motioned to both Stevens and Smith to follow him as he slunk his smoke-blackened body through the opening. The taste of fresh air pushed him ahead, even though his inner survival resources were already signaling his brain to acquiesce. He was determined to get his ambassador and his IMO to safety no matter what.

A. coughed up generous portions of soot at the windowsill as he reached inside to help Stevens and Smith out. There was no response, though; Stevens and Smith had not followed him out. There was, however, gunfire. A. heard the crackling explosions of AK-47 gunfire in the distance, and he heard the whooshing shots flying overhead. Some of the gunmen, who had by now slowly begun to retreat from the bonfire, started firing at the figure emerging from the building's lower section. A. didn't care about the gunfire at this point. Showing enormous courage and dedication to preserving the lives he was charged to protect, he went back into the safe haven several times to search for both men. The heat and the intensity of the tornado-like smoke beat him back severely each time he made entry; he could only remain behind inside the room for brief suffocating periods.

The agents inside the TOC, as well as those at the DS quarters barricaded behind a refrigerator and a heavy wooden door, were helpless to render assistance. Fifteen armed men were trying to break through, pounding furiously on the door. The DS agents were besieged and taking fire. The TOC offered them eyes-on-target intelligence of what the gunmen were doing and where they were positioned, but being trapped behind the door made any breakout or counterattack impossible.

The utter confusion and chaos of the horrifically unfolding events was all encompassing. The U.S. embassy in Tripoli informed the TOC, through radio and mobile phone communications, that help was on the way, but there was no word as to when the help would arrive. In any other critical-threat setting, the RSO would have been able to summon emergency medical and firefighting assistance; even at posts in Baghdad, Peshawar, Islamabad, and Sana'a, there was in place government infrastructure standing on call to respond to emergency needs. In a perfect world, the villa would have had sprinklers, foam, and smoke hoods. The Benghazi Fire Service station was approximately three miles from the Special Mission Compound, in the northwestern parcel of the city near the bay; it was situated adjacent to a hospital, a twenty-four-hour convenience shopping mall, and the March 2 School for Girls. The station accommodated dozens of Italian-produced firefighting vehicles; five were on call at any given time. With lights and sirens blaring, it would have taken less than five minutes for the trucks to be through the gates of the Special Mission Compound and hosing the blaze down.

It is not known if any of the Western Fwayhat residents summoned the fire service begging that they hurry up and help put out the fires blazing at the Special Mission Compound. It was hard to ignore the gunfire—even harder to ignore the stench of burning plastics and melting metals. The smoke had by now sifted through the entire neighborhood. The city's who's who, sitting on their verandas drinking the *haram* nectar of the Westernized well-to-do, simply refused to get involved.

The wafting smell of smoke and the unmistakable sounds of gunfire littered the not-so-distant landscape at the Annex as well.

A. would not remember the number of attempts he made in order to search for Stevens and Smith, but there had been many. His hands were already severely burned, and the smoke inhalation had already battered his body to the point where minor movement caused excruciating pain. He was not going to leave until he found them; he was determined to get them out of the inferno dead or alive. Even the most determined of men, fueled by dedication to mission and the surges of adrenaline, are halted by unbeatable elements of heat, fire, and pain. At about his fifth reentry into the safe haven, the area had become too hot to enter. The oven-like hell of the rooms buttressed by window grating and armored door was simply inaccessible to a properly equipped firefighter, let alone a man who had been trying to survive a large-scale terrorist assault for nearly thirty minutes. At approximately his sixth attempt inside, A. couldn't go back anymore. His body, weakened by a lack of oxygen and unimaginable pain, had been humbled by a hellacious reality. His body reeling from the suffering and his lungs attempting to recover and relish the breaths of air that he was inhaling, A. gathered himself stoically as he fought on. He ran toward an emergency ladder near the egress window and raced up to the roof as he tried to clear an air path, coughing up the toxins as he climbed. Flames rushed upward from the windows that had exploded open in the fiery violence. There was a metal grate over a skylight on the top of the roof he tried to pull off, while rounds were flying by him. The building resembled a funeral pyre.

Atop the building, A. struggled his way toward the wedge-shaped sandbag firing emplacement that the MSD operators had affixed the last time they had been to Benghazi. The sandbags protected A. from the odd shots still ringing out in the night; greenish laser beams of tracer fire littered the roofline as the gunmen were still hoping to have a chance to engage some of the Americans in a battle to the end. A. used his radio and weapon to smash open a skylight in the hope of ventilating the building. In better times, on a night like this, the skylight was a beautiful accoutrement to the villa and opened up the sparkling stars of a Benghazi night onto the main sitting area of the palatial home. Tonight, A. prayed, it would allow the fire to burn itself out and enable him to rush down into the labyrinth of destruction and hopefully save the lives of the ambassador and Sean Smith.

As pillars of fire and smoke rushed upward through the shattered remnants of the skylight, the collapse of the weakened roof was near imminent. A. refused, however, to get down. Struggling with every breath he took, he gathered his strength and pressed down on the talk button of his Motorola handset. "I don't have the ambassador," he yelled, knowing that anything he said in his regular voice would be unintelligible. "Repeat, over?" B. responded, having a hard time hearing what he said; the flames around him were still roaring, and A. found it hard to utter a complete sentence. A. struggled to gather his voice and his thoughts. He found it hard to hold the radio in hands burned severely in the fire; he found it excruciatingly painful to grip the call button to talk to the TOC. But they had to know. He righted himself slightly and took one last lung-filling gasp of air. "I don't have the ambassador!"

It was 2220 hours.

Part Three

RESCUE

15.

End of Siege

2205 hours (approximately): Benghazi, Libya.

The attack on the Special Mission Compound provided great theater to the who's who of Western Fwayhat. Some neighborhood residents emerged from their homes to watch the flames burn in the distance; these concerned neighbors, some wearing robes and flip-flops, shot video of the chaos and called family and friends to let them know of the live-fire Benghazi vaudeville transpiring right before their eyes. The chief Italian diplomat in Benghazi, identified as Guido De Sanctis,* reportedly watched the attack unfold from his vantage point, a reserved table at the Venezia Café.** There was no wine with dinner.

---

*On January 12, 2013, Ambassador De Sanctis was targeted by terrorists as he drove through Benghazi. Terrorists had ambushed his motorcade and hit his vehicle with automatic weapons fire; he had been issued an armored Mercedes G-Wagon following the attack on the Special Mission Compound and the Annex. De Sanctis was not injured in the attack. Italy ruled Libya until the Allies liberated the country from the Axis, and it remains Libya's closest ally in Europe. Still, the attack, which followed nearly a year of lethal strikes against Western interests in the city, prompted the Italian government to close down its consulate in Benghazi and to call home its diplomatic personnel. Interestingly enough, nearly seven years earlier, on February 17, 2006, eleven people were killed and the Italian consulate burned to the ground during mob violence protesting the publication of cartoons depicting the Prophet Muhammad.
**According to a source and resident of the Western Fwayhat neighborhood in Benghazi.

The Italian diplomat did not have the assets—or the authorization—
to intervene. And after all, the violence ended almost as suddenly as it
began; the fires of rage still burned wildly out of control, but a semi-
silence returned to Western Fwayhat. The attackers fell back into the
perimeter of the compound, but they never truly disappeared. Instead, they lay in wait, firing random bursts from their AK-47s into
the compound. The attack had hit the Special Mission Compound
like a twirling tornado twisting out of control across the American
plains. The devastation came with little warning, was indiscriminate,
and departed with a whimper. Like someone who had been impris-
oned inside a cellar awaiting the storm's departure, R. scanned the
areas of the compound on the DVR camera monitors that were fixed
to their mounts and still transmitting imagery to see if the coast was
clear. It was not a particular surprise that the camera system was still
functioning. This was not an off-the-shelf system purchased at
RadioShack. It was designed and produced for DS to function through
the most difficult of circumstances, including extreme heat and fire.
This not only reflected the prescient thoughts of the DS SEOs but
provided insight as to what U.S. diplomats expected to occur in dangerous outposts.

The TOC had lost its cohesive link to A. and the villa. There was
silence. The two DS agents inside the cantina were still barricaded,
along with the February 17 militiaman, behind the battered door and
the refrigerator awaiting a showdown with the terrorists. The custom-
molded surveillance earpiece with discreet communications with the
TOC was their lifeline.

The RSO's office in Tripoli, as well as the powers that be representing a dozen or so law enforcement, intelligence, and military
commands, were assessing the situation in Benghazi and attempting
to respond in as timely a fashion as possible. The Annex instructed
R. that help was en route. In this day and age of digital communications and instant messaging, the fog of terror had rendered definitive
immediacy into an absolute unknown; interestingly enough, *unsecure*
(those not deemed safe for the transmission of sensitive or classified
information) cell phones were the primary means of communications

between Benghazi and Tripoli. Nevertheless, R. relayed over the radio to the agents in the line of fire that backup was coming: "Help on the way." Though R. would have preferred to have heard more specifics about the "help," the mere thought that they were attempting to send reinforcements assured him that the powers were well aware of the gravity of the situation, and this also allowed him to refocus his thoughts solely on staying alive. In this world of fighting terrorists in places such as Benghazi, "help" could be crashing through the main gate with guns ablaze, or it could be a day away in the form of an AC-130 gunship and a company of marines.

"TOC, B. here, we are moving." B. grabbed his M4 and braced for a fusillade of terrorist gunfire. He removed a smoke grenade from his vest carrier and pulled the pin. Holding the spoon down forcefully, B. aligned his back against the north wall while R. slowly unlocked the front door and yanked it open. He flipped the grenade underhand to a halfway point between the TOC and the DS villa, and then R. slammed the door shut to shield the two from potential terrorist fire. The grenade erupted in a slapping thud and then dispensed a thick and impenetrable white smoke. B. raced through the cloud, the EO-Tech 512 holographic combat sight fitted to his M4 raised firmly at eye level. He ran as fast as he could into the murky darkness, searching for targets that could be lurking in the distance. Distance was good. He knew that the AK-47s that the attackers were carrying might be the most reliable and robust assault rifle in the world, but they were certainly not the most accurate. B. had ninety feet to traverse to make it to the DS villa—the distance from home plate to first base—but under fire that distance could feel like an eternal divide. The sprint through the night took seconds, but it felt as if it lasted hours.

B. used the armored layer of Kevlar wrapped around his shoulders and torso to burst through the door; the terrorists had battered it off one of its hinges. He reached the cantina and radioed that help had arrived. C. and D. used their combined strength to throw the refrigerator aside and open the door. The February 17 guard was grateful to have been rescued, and he embraced the lone member of the cavalry that rushed in. The DS villa was in shambles. The terrorists had thrashed through the living quarters and around the building. There wasn't an emotion on earth, the agents felt, that could propel another human being into such an act of explosive rage. The destructive lust of the men was daunting. The agents could only imagine what the bastards might have done to the ambassador at the residence. Operating as a small tactical team, the agents knew there was strength in numbers. The high-threat tactical course at Bill Scott Raceway in West Virginia that was part of the DS training curriculum had set the stage. Fortunately for the agents, the DS Training Center in Dunn Loring, Virginia, had written training modules for ground-zero worst-case-scenario possibilities. Even the best training in the world, however, cannot replicate the sheer fear and feeling of loneliness.

The alleyway separating the ambassador's half of the compound and the DS half had the potential of being a kill zone—a trap where well-positioned men, either seizing the high ground or in superior tactical locations, could pick off anyone attempting to pass in a cross fire of death. The three DS agents rushed to their armored Toyota Land Cruiser, threw an extra ballistic vest and helmet, as well as extra ammunition, into the vehicle—just in case—and rushed to the villa; a fully armored vehicle, or FAV, was also a weapon and could be used, in the vernacular, to "run the bastards over." The agents still didn't know what was out there awaiting them. R. attempted to use his DVR surveillance camera system as a guide, but there were so many blind spots and potential firing positions for a terrorist with an RPG; the wall separating the two compounds would provide ideal cover for an armed assailant with an RKG-3 antitank grenade.

A. was on the roof. He was burned and in dire condition; his face, hands, and forearms were red and black. The agent, known to barrel his way through any obstacle, was vomiting and coming in and out of consciousness. "I can't find the ambassador, we need to find Stevens," A. kept uttering to himself. The medical training that the agents underwent prior to shipping out proved to be a lifesaver. The sandbags on the roof provided safety, allowing the agents who climbed up the ladder that was positioned next to the villa to check on A. The agents knew that Stevens was missing and A. was under fire. As the trio deployed from the safety of the armored Land Cruiser, they climbed the fixed ladder to the roof. "We'll find Stevens and Smith," the two agents offered in unison. It was imperative to show confidence to a victim in shock, and A. was in a state of shock. The agents had been trained in the TacMed course to conduct a quick patient assessment: airway, breathing, and circulation (known as the ABCs) become the first responder's mantra; they were taught to check for severe arterial bleeding and neck injuries and to stabilize major trauma with Quik-Clot from the trauma kit. Burns were evident, but there was zero time to assess. Blood was on his sleeves. He could squeeze his hands in a quick handshake. His legs were movable. No major back or head trauma was visible or evident.

Emergency first aid was administered to the agent in distress and great care given to stabilize him and bring him safely from the burning building. A. motioned down, waving his arms and pointing toward the egress window, struggling to get the word out to his colleagues that Stevens and Smith were still unaccounted for and probably *still* inside the smoldering remains of the safe haven. "We gotta get Stevens and Smith," A. expressed. "I'm okay."

The three agents needed to improvise in order to survive. They immediately grabbed a rope from their Land Cruiser, tied it around their waists, and cracked open the egress window to enter the safe haven and search for Smith and Stevens. In such situations, all of the men thought, "At least we won't leave an agent behind," but no one dared say it aloud. They all thought, "Hell, you could feel it. If we go down, we'll go down together."[1] There was no time to ponder the outcome. A gunshot from the perimeter whizzed by; most likely someone had taken a sniper shot at the agents, but looking back, it was as if someone had fired the gun to signal the start of a race. In this case, it was a race for their lives.

The brunt of the blaze was still roaring inside the main reception area of the villa, and the building was hot—skin-roasting hot. The gaping hole in the main door, as well as the smashed skylight, ventilated the fire and let it breathe and grow. Waves of cream-like smoke wafted toward every opening and crevice throughout the building. Entering the safe haven was like diving into murky and treacherous waters with zero visibility. One wrong turn inside the blinding mess would result in death, and hopefully that death would be a rapid one.

One agent remained with A. at all times to tend to his critical smoke inhalation; a second agent ventured through the window opening to search while always tied to a third agent. It was impossible to yell for either Smith or Stevens; even attempting to breathe was likely to result in a spiraling-out-of-control domino effect of respiratory distress. It was unlikely that either man was still conscious in the suffocating smoke. The search was conducted on hands and knees. It was a grisly undertaking. When the agent emerged from the safe haven, he hovered on all fours and pointed his head down, hacking heavily and spewing out the poisonous elements that had raced into his lungs. His nostrils were blackened like West Virginia coal miners'. When he raised his eyes, his fellow agents poured water over his eyes from a Kevlar helmet, scooped up from the swimming pool. Cushions from a couch, as well as other assorted debris, floated in the pool. The sky overhead had turned reddish gray.

The process repeated itself without respite. The three agents, their M4s at the ready and their fingers outside the trigger guard, protected A. and tended to his medical condition, and ventured into the smoky confines. A slight breeze blew across the compound. All of the agents were beginning to suffer the consequences of smoke inhalation. R. checked in from time to time; he was coordinating communications at the TOC but knew that the lack of chatter over the airwaves was a foreboding sign. He looked at his watch and checked with the GRS crew at the Annex. It was 2225 hours.

Six GRS operators and a "regional specialist" divided themselves into two teams and entered their armored Mercedes G-Wagons and at least one armored four-door BMW 5 Series. The regional specialist was a translator, someone who spoke impeccable Arabic, probably with North African dialect, and could provide an immediate agency-filtered ear to any word that locals, friendly or otherwise, would have to say. The translator would be essential if the GRS team encountered a wounded terrorist or a prisoner that the DS contingent might have secured. The regional specialists were an interesting collection of intellectuals, native sons, and first-generation American-born Arabs who found their interests and backgrounds offered them unique career opportunities following the new demands forged by the September 11, 2001, attacks. The regional specialists weren't necessarily operators; most times they weren't. But in the field, when some Islamic cultural keys were warranted or a dialogue needed to be established, they could be more valuable than an entire entry team of former DevGru triggermen.

The Annex security officer lowered the wedge gate—a barrier that could stop a fifteen-thousand-pound truck traveling at fifty miles per hour dead in its tracks—and the two Mercedes G-Wagons raced out into the darkness. There was silence in the cars, as in all tactical missions, except for the shooter in the right front of the second car, who keyed his push-to-talk microphone: "We are less than ten 'mikes' out."

"Roger," said R. Ten minutes. He phoned Tripoli and updated the RSO.

The GRS drivers drove with their headlights off. The vehicles made a left turn, heading west for approximately 925 feet, and then, at a sleepy corner, made a sharp left heading north, racing toward the main junction some 2,080 feet away; there were no traffic laws in Benghazi, which was a good thing because the CIA GRS operators were reputed never to drive at the speed limit.

At the junction, the two vehicles made a left and raced a mile down the road toward the militia compound. The Mercedes G-Wagons crossed a median and pushed forward in both the west and the east lanes, careful to avoid being bottlenecked in a possible ambush or RPG attack. The two agency vehicles passed Charlie-3 gate at the Special Mission Compound and could see an orange glow in the northerly sky and smell the acrid stench of smoke. The rescue mission suddenly became more urgent. Nothing needed to be said;

you could see it and smell it. From the right front of the first G-Wagon, the former SEAL Tyrone Woods had rolled up on countless similar battles in the past. Rescue operations had been his life.

"COBRA five to seven minutes out."

"Copy," was the reply from the TOC. There was a saying among many of the DS "Dirty Harry" agents who had served in the civil wars of Africa and South America, as well as in the fratricides of the Balkans and Beirut: "When rolling into hell, keep moving forward. Reverse is not an option."

The February 17 Brigade maintained a base at the junction southwest of the Special Mission Compound, and the GRS team leader wanted to have his men lead a much larger and more substantive force to break through any terrorist opposition still lurking inside or near the besieged post. The GRS force was geared for war: full battle kit, night-vision equipment, helmets, and face-concealing balaclavas. Some of the men wore their lucky team baseball caps from their SEAL and Marine Corps units. To the commanders at the militia's headquarters, it was time for tea—it always was. Anytime a guest ventured into the office of the senior officer, the revered *fa'ed*, or commander, the guest would be offered a small and sinister cup of rocket fuel, Bedouin coffee laced with cardamom, followed by cup after cup of sweet tea; the hosts were generous, and the teacup was stuffed with mint leaves. There was one civilian, employed by a Middle Eastern military unit, whose sole job was to make tea, clean the thin glasses in which tea was served, and then offer the tea to the commander and his guests. With refreshments being served, the militiamen seemed to be in no hurry to suit up and enter into battle. The team leader and the interpreter entered the commander's office and, in very diplomatic terms, said something to the effect of "What the fuck? Why aren't you guys ready?"

"TOC, COBRA. We've hit a roadblock. Stand by."

"Copy," said R. "Shit." There were formalities, acts of honor, that had to be attended to before business could be discussed. Outside, in the courtyard of the base—actually, a small compound that the militia had taken over—men in camouflage fatigues wandered about inside their compound without their personal kit, or weapons. The pickup trucks with multibarrel machine guns stood idly by; some had no fuel inside them, and none of them were fired up and ready to go.

But the February 17 Brigade still had enough mobility and fire-power to beat off any possible threat; the Soviet-era 12.7 mm and 14.5 mm heavy machine guns were game changers in any free-moving battle, and the GRS operators could certainly have inflicted enormous damage with such weapons at their disposal. "Borrowing" the weapons would require some finesse. So the GRS leader, through his interpreter, tried to bargain a compromise—another Middle Eastern specialty—where the CIA operatives would return the weapons and pay handsomely for any ammunition used. With great respect, though with a typical sense of American urgency, some sort of deal was offered for the heavy weapons. The militia commander would have none of it. The notion of the multinational QRF was a farce. Host-nation security in a host nation without any semblance of host-nation central government was a bizarre and untenable reality. The CIA shooters were uninvited and unwelcomed foreign fighters on Libyan soil. Libya was a nation with a violent past of being colonized, and the centerpiece of the national identity was its resistance to the Italian occupiers.

The February 17 Brigade had been embroiled in a pay dispute with its State Department paymasters; brigade members were, in effect, down-and-out with a Libyan case of blue flu and were under no compulsion to head into harm's way for a client that was nickel-and-diming them. Ambassador Stevens was supposed to have met with the local commander on September 11. The meeting was supposed to have transpired at the Special Mission Compound just after a long and leisurely breakfast, but the meeting was mysteriously rescheduled for a later date by Stevens; a handwritten note confirming the need to move the meeting to later in the week was scribbled on Ambassador Stevens's official itinerary.

The February 17 Brigade demanded the protocols of Middle Eastern foreplay before engaging in discussions concerning tactical backup, but the GRS force had no time or patience for it. The team leader radioed the TOC at the Special Mission Compound that his men would be there in a matter of minutes.

Three members of the militia, though, volunteered to accompany the GRS operators to the Special Mission Compound. The DS contingent, and the MSD teams before them, had developed a unique rapport with some of the Libyan fighters. They equipped them, they trained them, they ate together, and ultimately they became friends. The DS art form of gaining support through human interaction and respect was paying off a dividend under the most desperate of circumstances. The response force now numbered ten men.

"COBRA rolling, two-three mikes out."

"Copy, COBRA. Our guys at VICTOR building," which was improvised code for the villa. R. felt it was possible the radio frequency had been compromised and the terrorists were listening in to the radio channel.

"Roger, VICTOR," said the shift leader. R. checked in with Tripoli on his cell and learned that a drone was up and in the area. With luck, we may get out of here, he anxiously hoped.

The GRS vehicles sped out of the February 17 compound and headed west for a few feet before making a sharp turn north along a busy thoroughfare; the motorcade was observed by armed men emerging from a mosque on the southwest corner of the nearby junction. The men watching, and the motorists whizzing past, knew that the men in the Mercedes weren't Libyan. Libyans, recent history had shown, honked their horns and waved flags when they went to war. These men didn't.

The rescue team pushed north for five hundred feet and then moved in toward the Special Mission Compound, making a right, traveling east, until they hit Charlie-1 and Bravo-1 gates. The operators readied their HK416s and their heavy machine guns in anticipation of pulling up in front of the gate. The GRS team did not know what to expect once they arrived. Eerily, one of the shooters flashed back to FDNY and NYPD running toward the World Trade Center buildings, eleven years ago this day. Would the response force be met by thirty or so armed men with AK-47s and RPGs? Would an IED be waiting for them in front of the diplomatic mission? These threats were very real concerns to the team from the Annex, especially as sporadic gunfire from the direction of the Special Mission Compound was now thrown toward them.

The terrorists, taking cover, threw down a gauntlet of AK-47 fire at the GRS operators, creating an impenetrable wall of fire. The northeast corner of the Special Mission Compound became a kill zone, and the shooters would have to engage in a full-blown firefight just to gain access to the villa and the DS agents inside. They were it. They were the only tactical rescue force that would and could be coming. The GRS team would have to find another way in.

Instinctively, the GRS vehicles rushed forward toward the fire and then J-turned, retreating west. They reversed their route toward the compound and backtracked on ground they had already traversed. The two vehicles banked a sharp left turn once they reached the junction with the Fourth Ring Road and then proceeded west in the eastbound lane. The vehicles pulled up in front of Charlie-3 gate. The gate, locked from the inside, was also reinforced by two vehicles parked next to the entrance; the vehicles were parked in such a way so as to mitigate the risk of the compound being rammed by a VBIED.

The GRS operators rolled out of their vehicles, in tactically defensive positions, while two men threw their HK416s over their shoulders and scaled the gate. The terrorists had not identified their movements yet, as the smoke billowing from the ambassador's villa covered their entrance. Once the gate was open, the two G-Wagons pushed their way past the blocking parked vehicles and rolled up to the villa, coming in from the rear and then positioning the vehicles in front of the main entrance.

The GRS operators immediately radioed the TOC that they had arrived. R. was grateful that help had finally reached the scene. His mind thought solely of Chris Stevens and Sean Smith. The thirty-thousand-foot view of their predicament, the big picture of what was transpiring for U.S. foreign policy in Libya, mattered little. Henry Kissinger's view that there was a "higher purpose" to all this was irrelevant. Men were down, and they needed to be saved. The higher purpose was to save as many men as possible now.

16.

Diplomatic Pouch

An embassy is not the usual setting for the frenzy of emergency late-night contingency planning. An embassy is where meetings are conducted in the polite foreign language known as "diplo-speak"; direct language, "real-speak," is never used. Embassies are lavish bastions that display a nation's wealth and influence; these buildings are fancy, blessed with Michelin-star-capable chefs, and have banquet halls that are stocked handsomely with enough Moser crystal champagne flutes to enable a brigade of men to make toast after toast and can hold annual gala balls. Embassies are places of business and bureaucracy. These sovereign grounds in foreign lands are designed to promote diplomatic relations and commerce between nation X and host nation Y and to serve expatriates in need of consular and emergency assistance.

American embassies are bastions of the "yes, ma'am" and the "no, ma'am." From the local uniformed guard manning the identity check and the X-ray machine at forward gates to the Marine Corps sergeant at Post One (located at the front entrance to all embassies), an American embassy is a city of pure polite. With the exception of a few lavish grounds, located in the historical linchpins of U.S. foreign policy, embassies are cookie-cutter antiseptic fortresses. The State Department is very much into the trappings of government purchasing and bureaucracy. Brussels, Athens, Tel Aviv, or Prague, the inside of an embassy looks and feels the same: the incandescent light, the artwork, the computers, and the people—it is all interchangeable. It's designed to be. The company that had the contract for photograph frames must have made a fortune: there were framed eight-by-ten photographs of President Obama and Secretary of State Clinton on just about every office wall in the city. Staffers—from the ambassador to the deputy assistant of a deputy—swap postings every three or four years. Embassies, thanks to American cleaning products purchased en masse on Government Accountability Office solicitations, even smell like federal office buildings in the United States.

American embassies are also intelligence stations. Some embassies field CIA stations, as well as various representatives from the other intelligence agencies and departments that make up the espionage and intelligence-gathering community; it was probably safe to say that there were more spooks at the U.S. embassy in London than in Wellington, New Zealand, or Santiago, Chile, for example. Reportedly, there were numerous American assets represented at the embassy in Libya.

Embassies also field military attachés: the men representing the army, navy, air force, and even sometimes the Marine Corps. There are top secret areas of embassies where few can venture. These Sensitive Compartmented Information Facilities, or SCIFs (pronounced "Skiffs"), are "for your eyes only" areas where the spies and the soldiers converge to convene court.* Sometimes, entire buildings or compounds at an embassy are SCIFs. Embassies are mini-extensions of Washington, D.C.—mini-extensions of the global power that the United States can wield.

As a result of this projection source of American power, American embassies around the world *are* inherently prepared to deal with disasters. The U.S. embassy in Tripoli was ideally prepared to deal with the news of the September 11 attack on its mission in Benghazi.

---

*For a larger discussion of SCIFs, see Rajini Vaidyanathan, "Barack Obama's Top Secret Tent," *BBC News* (U.S. and Canada), March 22, 2011, as well as other public domain sources.

The embassy began formulating its emergency response the moment the TOC relayed news of the attack to the RSO's office. The RSO grabbed the CIA station chief and the senior defense official and met in the DCM's office to get everyone on one sheet of music. The reporting from B. and R. was steady and calmly crafted; they never overreacted, and given the circumstances the remarkably professional manner in which they provided detailed and precise information helped to paint a thorough, though foreboding, portrait of what was transpiring in Benghazi at the Special Mission Compound. This was a worst-case scenario for RSO Tripoli—his worst dreams realized. The young agents in Benghazi were his responsibility; the well-being of the ambassador and the communicator was his responsibility. But RSO Tripoli was 640 miles away. His men under fire were a thirteen-hour drive (no gas or bathroom breaks, no flat tires, no jihadist checkpoints, no Qaddafi-loyalist highway carjackers, and no warlord robbery attempts) away. Benghazi could have been on the moon for all it mattered. He could not provide them with an immediate tactical response and rescue. When things went bad for SY and DS in some far outpost of the world, things usually went very bad, with missions littered with body bags. Some lived for this environment, but others were better off behind desks. RSO Tripoli silently hoped and prayed D.C. would get off their asses quickly.

By the time the DCM took the call from the unidentified number on the Libyan mobile phone network and heard Ambassador Stevens's voice, the notifications were already being disseminated to the men and women who would be facilitating the response. The DCM had prayed, when he heard Stevens's voice, that word of the attack was some sort of unannounced drill or tabletop exercise, but no surprise drill ever contained a voice fraught with so much terror and fear. And then the line went silent.

Notifications followed immediately as the embassy's emergency response triage went into full gear. Even in an age when everyone carried an embassy-provided BlackBerry and was reachable 24/7, it still took an effort to get everyone out of bed, out of the gym, and away from the dinner table to return to the embassy. An emergency action committee, or EAC, was convened immediately; the DCM, now in charge, chaired the fastidiously paced contingency planning.* There was little time to spare.

The DCM, the RSO, the defense attaché, the political officer, the public affairs officer, and the IMO would have all been present, along with note takers and various members of the administration staff. Secure laptop computers, capable of facilitating classified information, were open on the large faux-wood conference table; the cups of coffee filled the room with the aroma of an early morning board meeting. The red light outside the door meant serious business was being discussed inside.

The EAC was convened to provide the besieged DS contingent with support and rescue. The DCM briefed the gathered and explained, word by word, the message he received from Stevens; RSO Tripoli briefed the gathered on the reports from the TOC, and the chief of station briefed everyone as to reports that he had received from the Annex, as well as from assets—who would remain nameless forever—on the ground in Benghazi and even in Tripoli who might have a handle on what might, from the CIA perspective, *really* be happening at the Special Mission Compound. The DCM might have, on paper at least, been in charge, but in a post like Tripoli the chief of station, in times like this, was the man who ran the show and called the shots. Libya was different, and some would whisper after the fact the true reason they were there in the first place was to support the CIA.

As the men whose decisions mattered planned the next move, the assistants worked the phones. The bosses looked at maps and at options, while terse, urgent, and sometimes pissed-as-hell calls were made to members of the fledgling Libyan government and members of the underground Libyan militia movement (friend and not so friend), as well as to friends—murky friends from dubious backgrounds or from other nations' intelligence services who served secretly or not so secretly in Libya—and mere contacts. They called anyone and everyone who just might be able to lend a hand.

---

*For more personal detail of the night of September 11, 2012, as per events at the U.S. embassy in Tripoli, see the May 8, 2013, testimony of former DCM Gregory Hicks before the House Oversight Committee (Benghazi: Exposing Failure and Recognizing Courage).

Outside the confines of the protected "U.S. ears only" area of the embassy, a "helper" was working the phones at a furious pace. Every embassy and consulate had local helpers. He or she was someone with exceptional networking skills and a vast Rolodex, who had the magical gift of knowing just about everyone and anyone who mattered in the host nation; if the helper didn't know the right person, the right person didn't exist. Helpers were experts in clearing items through customs, locating guesthouses and residences, and, most important, dealing with the maddening bureaucracy that could often be found in foreign lands. The helper greased the wheels and enabled people to move about without having to deal with the dirty little tidbits of graft that third-world nations called the currency of day-to-day life. The helpers knew whom to visit and whom not to visit; they knew which police chief could get anything done if somehow, miraculously, a bottle of Johnnie Walker Blue ended up in the backseat of his car and which customs agent was taking his family to Disney World and wanted tickets to the Magic Kingdom. More often than not, no one at the embassy wanted to know just how the helper got things done as long as he got them done; this was especially the case at isolated and critical-threat posts.

And in a crisis, if the embassy needed to charter transport, the helper was the one person who could locate a reliable provider and make sure the pilot had all his certifications and that fees and protocols would not delay or disrupt any critical mission. Private transport wasn't hired unless something critical was going on. It had been done before, after all. In May 2012, the State Department had denied a request by the U.S. embassy in Tripoli to have the SST continue using an official DC-3 aircraft to shuttle personnel to and from Benghazi. According to declassified cables, the State Department suggested that the embassy charter an aircraft instead; the e-mail stated that Undersecretary of State for Management Patrick Kennedy "has determined that support for Embassy Tripoli using the DC-3 will be terminated immediately."[1]

Inside the bureaucracy that was Foggy Bottom, DS worked for, and reported to, M. Some of the DS agents hated that the Diplomatic Security Service was not a stand-alone agency like the FBI, but the old-timers knew this would never happen. M. controlled the Bureau of Diplomatic Security purse strings, and money drove missions; whoever controlled the purse strings controlled the outcome. Some inside DS, especially the top-tier management, viewed him as an ally; others viewed him as the problem; the truth, of course, rests somewhere in between. At minimum, Kennedy had been a survivor. The key players in Washington—the cabinet-level roster—were all kept abreast of the developments courtesy of their personal representatives stationed in Tripoli. The response from Washington was monolithically unified: get our people out. A private jet, or some sort of aerial transport, would definitely be needed. And, in the chaos of a crisis, when the local political and military representatives of the embassy could get the local government to supply a C-130H aircraft and a supporting crew for the quick flight to Benghazi, the helper was ready to serve to make sure that all military protocol at the airport, as well as any other Byzantine protocol, was properly attended to.

The U.S. embassy in Tripoli was well staffed to execute a dynamically tactical response to the attack. The Joint Special Operations Command happened to have a covert top-tier counterterrorist presence in country. Its mission was classified, but reports have hinted that it was in Libya trying to prevent terrorist elements from acquiring remnants of Colonel Qaddafi's WMD (primarily nuclear) program. The agency was also hunting down loose MANPADs that had possibly fallen into the hands of al-Qaeda or its affiliates in North Africa.[2]

There was also deep speculation—unconfirmed, of course—that the CIA (or other elements of the U.S. intelligence community in country) was training Libyan mercenaries to topple the Syrian regime. But there is no doubt that Benghazi's intelligence mission was driving the show. According to one former DS veteran with a wealth of service in the Middle East, "Libya was the agency's circus."[3]

The CIA, reportedly, also had a sizable GRS support element in Tripoli. These men, like those at the Annex in Benghazi, were veteran operators who had years of combat experience in the top tier of the JSOC and USSOCOM order of battle. These men were experienced professionals whose dedication to mission was unrivaled.

A muster was called in the RSO's office to find a volunteer rescue force to send to Benghazi. Virtually all available—the precise number is classified—volunteered. Two JSOC shooters volunteered to fly to Benghazi, as did five GRS operators. One of them was Glen Doherty.

Glen Anthony Doherty was born on July 10, 1970, in Winchester, Massachusetts; he was the second of three children born to Ben and Barbara Doherty. He grew up in a Norman Rockwell landscape of outdoors, trees, and winter wonderland adventures. His parents raised their children to appreciate nature and to develop themselves athletically. Rugged, handsome, and blessed with an inherent sense of success, Glen could accomplish just about everything—from the academic to the hard charging—that he put his mind to. He was one of those people who didn't have the word "failure" in his molecular structure.

Glen Doherty attended the Embry-Riddle Aeronautical University in Prescott, Arizona. He did more in his formative years between being a teenager and being a man than most people do in their entire lives. Doherty flew airplanes, he motorcycled, he skied, and he excelled at white-water rafting. And, just for an added test to his stamina, he became a triathlete. In 1995, Doherty joined the U.S. Navy and volunteered for the SEALs. He wanted to push himself even further than most humans could imagine, and he wanted to change the world.[4] "Glen was pretty much a hippie," said Clint Bruce, a former NFL player with both the Baltimore Ravens and the New Orleans Saints who left a very lucrative professional football career to join the Navy SEALs and who worked with Doherty. "He was carefree without a worry in the world. Some men stressed at work inside the teams; they had to work very hard at their cardio strength or their shooting skills. Not Glen. He looked at something, heard someone talking about it, and without as much as breaking a sweat, he would master it. One day he could be at the range, making us all look bad with his M4 or an AK, and then the next day you would find Glen by himself strumming a guitar."[5] Bruce—who served as a SEAL officer in the Pacific and Middle East in multiple leadership positions prior to, and during, the Global War on Terror and is the founder and president of Trident Response Group, a risk and threat management firm headquartered in Dallas, Texas—said that he was one of the many commanders who was taken aback by Doherty's unique and unrivaled style. "He was the kind of SEAL everyone wanted to be around," Bruce added. "He always provided a sense of confidence that even we in this confident setting always wanted to be near." Doherty was, like many SEALs and members of the special operations community, a recruitment poster for all that was grand about the American spirit. But he was also an enigma. When he wasn't working for the CIA, he worked security for the Grateful Dead.

Glen Doherty served as a paramedic and a sniper in SEAL Team THREE; the unit's responsibility was the Middle East. He was in a force that was no stranger to terrorism, having responded to Aden, Yemen, in 2000, following the suicide bombing of the USS *Cole*. Knee issues almost forced Doherty out of the military, but after he re-upped following the September 11, 2001, attacks, he served two grueling tours in Iraq and believed that the sacrifice of serving in the war-torn nation was worth it if the action of the SEALs and the coalition could help rescue a nation from the grips of a tyrant.

Doherty left the SEALs in 2005 and entered the world of military contracting, working for the U.S. intelligence community in hot spots around the world, including Afghanistan, Pakistan, and Yemen. The work was lucrative—especially considering that he was deployed for only three months out of the year. His work in Tripoli for the CIA was one such assignment.

17.

Linkup

Once inside the compound, a two-man team of GRS operators ran up to the villa from their access point at Charlie-3. They had point. The rest of the rescue squad followed immediately behind in their G-Wagons and set up a defensive perimeter once they reached the ambassador's residence. Looking north, the operators saw the fires at the February 17 Brigade command post burning wildly. The villa was also aflame. Bloodstains were noticed on the pavement leading to the building's entrance, and one of the pickup truck weapon carriers was completely engulfed by flames; the vehicles that the attackers had torched burned ferociously, almost to a white fire. It was Detroit or Newark on a hot summer night in the 1960s during the height of ballistic anarchy. The six operators and the translator moved cautiously but swiftly into the grounds. They hoped that they could conclude their business at the Special Mission Compound in a matter of minutes and pull everyone out.

Several operators took up rear security in case any of the attackers were lying in wait with an RPG or RPK in hand looking to pick off the rescuers. It was classic terrorist modus operandi that was reenacted time and time again in Mogadishu, southern Lebanon, the Gaza Strip, Iraq, and Afghanistan: enemy elements launched an attack that exacted heavy casualties and then waited for the rescue forces to arrive so that they, too, could be drawn into a larger and more involved kill zone. The GRS operators wanted to be in and out. They didn't want to be there fighting until dawn requesting backup. They were the last line of defense in Benghazi. There were no other good guys to call.

The team of operators moved forward in the choreographed silhouette of engaging threats; their eyes never moved off their weapon sights. Their weapons forward and their backs curved downward, the former SEALs and marines reduced their target profiles and silhouettes and flowed as they positioned themselves. Their motion was a precisely choreographed advance. Quick movements jotted up and down, right and left, seeking targets to engage. Peering through their Trijicon ACOG sights, they moved cautiously toward the villa to the agents at the egress window outside the safe haven. The heat emanating from the burning buildings and vehicles was severe. The red sky looked absolutely hellish.

Radio communications enabled the CIA security staffers and the DS agents to link up without any possibility of a blue-on-blue engagement. R., in the TOC, identified the location where the agents were hunkered down, and he updated the DS staff that relief was close by.

The GRS force did not know what to expect when they linked up the DS agents. They thought the DS personnel would be deployed in tactically defensive positions but instead found the four men covered in blackened burns, coming in and out of the safe haven, searching for the ambassador and Sean Smith. The men were in a dreadful state. Their eyes were swollen and awash in cleansing tears. Their clothing was singed and blackened. Their mouths and noses were painted with a black sheen from inhaling through the heat and smoke; the DS agents had crawled to the swimming pool and soaked their T-shirts and wrapped them around their faces in order to be able to endure the flowing thick of the cream-like poison smoke. The agents remained undaunted, however. They were not leaving until they found the ambassador and the IMO. The GRS team leader shouted a predetermined code name before moving in closer.

The DS agents didn't say much, though the sense of relief was etched on their blackened faces. There was no time for niceties of "glad to see you." Once the required situation reports were exchanged—and updated through the TOC—the agents resumed their search for Stevens and Smith.

The GRS operators immediately split their forces in three. One team remained behind with the DS contingent to search for the two missing diplomats, and Ty Woods used a trauma kit and administered emergency first aid to A., who was in respiratory distress and badly burned. Two GRS operators—a sniper and his spotter—climbed the roof of the villa and from behind the concealing veil of flames and smoke set up a perch overlooking a 360-degree field of fire to detect and terminate any encroaching threats. The GRS snipers were good—very good—and they were determined to keep any hostile elements from getting near the search-and-rescue operation going on for the two missing Americans. The third two-man element rushed over to the TOC to rescue R. and bring him back to the villa. R. had time to secure weapons and equipment, including the firearms of the British specialists, and make sure that the laptops were destroyed and any sensitive material on them would be impossible to retrieve; it was all very old-school and a "back in the day" sort of thing, but smashing hard drives with a hammer was quite effective.

R. grabbed his M4 as he prepared to leave the TOC. He paused for a moment, almost as if made unable to move by anger or shock, before being assisted out by one of the GRS operators. There wouldn't be time for any of the DS agents to retrieve their personal belongings. Their personal kits—their iPods, books, and photographs of their families—would have to remain behind.

At the villa, the two GRS snipers scanned the horizon from their rooftop perch. Each wore an IR/overt strobe, night vision, binoculars, parachute cord, and "blood chit." The chit has an American flag on the front of a laminated card, with four perforated corners that have a unique number assigned to each operator. Below the flag on the card is a request for help in the local language: the person rendering assistance is told that he will be rewarded for his benevolence. If the torn corners show up in friendly hands, the spies will know who needs help and is missing. The snipers listened carefully on their secure frequency for any sign of life from either Stevens or Smith. They gauged the sense of anguish on the faces of the DS agents. The faces told of men who would not stop looking for the ambassador and the IMO. The snipers asked for but did not demand a status update. They knew that the situation down below was tenuous and emotionally charged. The men had enough experience in the "Sandbox" to know that explosive eruptions of Islamic-fueled rage did not blaze a path of destruction only to fizzle out so meekly. The GRS snipers knew that more was coming. They hoped to be far away when the real shooting began. It was 2245 hours.

In downtown Benghazi, and throughout the city, it sounded as if the Libyan national soccer team had just won the World Cup. White-and-tan trucks belonging to the various militias moved slowly through the narrow streets of the downtown markets and the medina, honking their horns in celebration. The vehicles barely squeezed through the narrow alleys in residential areas—their residential areas—where the believers flew the black flags of the jihad where their laundry hung to dry. The vehicles played songs of the jihad, and young men, screaming into microphones and megaphones, called the residents of the city to war. "Today we have attacked the infidels," one such call went. "We have avenged the honor of Islam and struck the heart of those who have insulted the Prophet. Let's go and finish the job!"*

On the eleventh anniversary of the September 11 attacks, the jihadist militiamen in Benghazi had hoped to replicate history and

---

*According to interviews conducted with Benghazi residents on the day immediately following the attack by the Al Jazeera correspondent Hoda Abdel-Hamid, the militiamen drove through Benghazi looking to generate a mob that could, reportedly, be similar to the crowds and the TV-spewing rage that was witnessed earlier in the day outside the U.S. embassy in Cairo.

launch a repeat of the lethal battle that transpired in Mogadishu, Somalia, on October 3–4, 1993, when a U.S. military special operations abduction raid led to a two-day battle that resulted in the deaths of nineteen Army First SFOD-Delta operators, 160th Special Operations Aviation Regiment–Airborne (Night Stalker) aviators, and elite infantrymen from the Seventy-Fifth Rangers Regiment–Airborne and the 10th Mountain Division (Light Infantry). The operation was viewed as an epic failure of the reach of American power, and a hefty sum was paid for the release of one of the aviators, Mike Durant, captured in the raid. The raid in Mogadishu all but put an end to U.S. military intervention in the famine-struck and Islamic-combustible Horn of Africa nation.

In Benghazi, the militiamen flying the black flag of the jihad had hoped that they, too, could mobilize an entire city into a cascading and costly debacle of American intervention, but Benghazi was not Mogadishu, and the militants had chosen the wrong night to get the men of Benghazi away from their television sets. Many of the city's men were at home watching the after-match coverage of two soccer World Cup qualifiers with great impact to the Arab world: Jordan's 2–1 victory over a superior Australian side, and Lebanon's defeat of Iran 1–0, which caused much glee among the country's Christians and Sunnis; the Lebanese star Roda Antar had scored the game winner in the seventy-first minute. Men, even those wearing the fatigues of those hoping to bring Islamic law to Libya and all of North Africa, put their guns down to watch the sports highlights. Benghazi's wives and mothers, even those in the poorer neighborhoods where fundamentalist fervor was strongest, found the militia noise to be a true nuisance; the odd magazine-emptying bursts of AK-47 fire that the militants launched into the night's sky were excruciatingly aggravating. Some threw garbage at the jihadists from their kitchen windows; it was night, after all, and calls for a holy war interfered with risqué soap operas that the MBC, the Moroccan Broadcasting Company, showed after dark. Syrian TV was once famous for the forbidden pleasures of late-night risqué, but programming had been impacted by the fratricide of civil war.

Still, a few men grabbed their AK-47s and began their journey toward the Special Mission Compound. They hopped a ride with some of the armed pickup trucks, or they tried to see how many armed men could ride on a dirt bike at once. The pillaging of an American target was good entertainment for a Tuesday night.

Late evening winds intensified the fires at the Special Mission Compound. The blaze roared wildly, and the villa began to make noises indicating that it was becoming structurally unsound. The GRS operators became concerned that the building could soon collapse, but the agents were not leaving until they found Stevens and Smith and, realizing that they would be in a terrible state, could resuscitate them. The DS agents went in again and again; each time they emerged, Woods and the other GRS operators would splash bottled water in their eyes and on their faces to relieve the burn of the heat and the acrid smoke. The GRS operators on security watch scanned the grounds of the compound, wary of a possible next wave of attackers.

The DS agents working inside the blinding oven of the safe haven came across a body lying on the ground in one of their many searches. They couldn't see who it was, but they immediately hoisted him up in an over-the-shoulder "fireman's carry" style and brought him to the egress window, where the other agents and the GRS operators were waiting; the individual was carefully removed from the safe haven and brought into the fresh air. It was Sean Smith. The medics checked Smith for a pulse and vital signs, but he was dead. The agents saw him and were overwhelmed by sorrow and adrenaline. The typhoon of emotions that raced through them even as they gasped for breath after having their lungs fill up with smoke was enough to knock any man down. The GRS operators, looking on, could see that the DS agents were devastated over the loss of the IMO. The agents ventured back into the cauldron to search for Ambassador Stevens, but it was becoming too dangerous. One of the agents suffered a deep laceration resulting in severe bleeding during a search of the safe haven. R., trying to gain entry to the villa through the front door that had been blown open by an RPG warhead, had to retreat when elements of the buckling ceiling caved in and collapsed, showering the agents with a plume of debris.

An IED landed near the feet of the agents and the GRS team, hissed, and then exploded in a surreal scene. Debris and fragmentation landed on the group. The men looked around at each other, but nobody was hurt by shrapnel or killed. It may have been a hand grenade or a "gelateena" bomb. How nobody was killed at this moment simply defies logic and remains a mystery even to date. One agent opined that it was divine intervention. Even nonbelievers become believers after moments like this.

The three February 17 Brigade militiamen rushed from near Charlie-1 gate and warned the DS agents and the GRS operators that they had to get out immediately. The February 17 militiamen appeared nervous and fearful of the threat that was building outside the perimeter walls. The GRS interpreter attempted to calm them down, but the militiamen were panicking; their speech pattern became rapid, and their hand gestures became more animated. The militiamen claimed that a large force of armed men was moving in on the compound. The snipers on the roof scanned the grounds one more time. The reticles of their sniper scopes revealed a target-rich environment; these men excelled on target-rich evenings.

It was hard for the GRS operators to count the number of tangos, or terrorists, who were positioned inside and outside the compound. Who was a terrorist and who was a looter? Did it matter? The Annex shooters were laser focused on finding the agents, then locating Stevens and Smith. The GRS operators had learned, from the TOC, that there were at least thirty-five armed intruders who had to be dealt with. Yet from the impassable mob of armed men who had seized control of the main Charlie-1 gate, the team leader assessed that there were many more terrorists who now controlled the northerly escape routes as well. None of the GRS crew knew how many more belligerents were on their way.

There was an impetus to conserve ammunition. Many years earlier, inside the teeming slums of Mogadishu, JSOC learned that the finest fighters a nation could assemble could sometimes be critically wounded inside a city determined to engage a foreign enemy to its death. The GRS team was determined not to fight the terrorists' battle. The terrorists' combat skills were pure Taliban—relying on familiar ground and overwhelming numbers rather than precision and weapons proficiency. The GRS team wanted to be in and out of the compound in minutes. Hopefully without any of their own killed or wounded in action.

18.

Departures

It would have cost approximately $30,000 to hire a private jet to make the unscheduled 404.49-mile flight between Tripoli and Benghazi; it was $30,000 that the CIA wouldn't have thought twice about spending. Certain elements of the U.S. government handle fluid emergencies with enormous speed and decisiveness. Some don't. The CIA excelled in this little bit of tradecraft; the RSO, of course, lent whatever support he could provide. The agency pulled out all the stops when it came to removing its own from harm's way, and it did a respectable job making sure that others were extracted before a crisis could become a catastrophe. The CIA had learned, especially in the years following 9/11, that speed and secrecy—not to mention hefty piles of discretionary cash—enabled it to achieve the many immediate and sometimes unsavory missions it needed to accomplish while deployed so many miles from home. But, as would later be revealed, the Libyan government responded to the pleas of assistance. A Libyan Air Force C-130H Hercules was made available to the rescue team from the embassy to fly from Tripoli to Benghazi.

The RSO's office and the chief of station often worked hand in hand in posts around the world and here, specifically, in Tripoli. Supporting the CIA chief of station was not in the DS job description, but RSOs often lent whatever help they could to the needs of the agency. Conversely, the CIA complement in country—or in any country—was not officially responsible for safeguarding an embassy or the diplomatic staff, but they would—and did—if asked. The rush to Benghazi was not one agency helping out another. It was what the spies and the diplomatic security staffers did all the time. They made sure the other was safe and could function in countries where the word "function" was not part of the vernacular.

The two JSOC operators and the five GRS staffers retreated to their quarters to fetch their tactical gear; the weapons were held under lock and key at the chancery. Each man had at least one or two kit bags lying in a locker or under his bed filled with his favorite personal items: a pair of desert boots, an Emerson knife, or an Under Armour shirt. Camel-Bak hydration packs were filled with fresh water, and the operators made sure that shiny Velcro-adhesive patches with their blood types were affixed to their Dragon Skin custom-fitted body armor. They made sure that their SureFire flashlights were close by. The volunteers had no time to e-mail home or make any personal notifications concerning their side trip to Benghazi; most of their loved ones and friends didn't even know that they were in Libya. Anyway, good-byes were bad luck, and these men were a superstitious lot; it was against regulations for their wives and children to know where they were and, more specifically, what they were doing. The operators used the precious preparatory time to check their HK416s and M4s; they determined which high-tech items of gear were needed and made sure they absorbed all of the actionable intelligence available on the situation in Benghazi.*

Each operator carried varied bags. As part of the SF world, you carried what you liked. More important, your load was made up of what worked. Some of the operators had GORUCK GR1s and the smaller Radio Rucks and Red Oxx bags, manufactured in Montana. Both brands were high-end, reliable bags, created by former operators, that housed everything from spare magazines to PowerBars.

---

*The weapons and gear used by operators in the field are often a personal choice and are reflective of equipment that the individual might have found useful, functional, and comfortable in his previous military career. A reference into some of the weapons and equipment used by such personnel can be found in Jack Murphy and Brandon Webb's book *Benghazi: The Definitive Report*.

Most operators carried an Emerson folding knife, the preferred knife of the Special Forces community.

The seven men mustered outside the main entrance of the chancery shortly after 2300 hours. It was a clear night in Tripoli, and the stars were starkly visible toward the south and east, away from the built-up city areas. Two armored SUVs transported the group to Tripoli International Airport. The RSO and the chief of station stood outside to make sure the send-off was quiet and efficient. The military attachés also came outside into the cool autumn night to see the men off. The helper worked his juggler's kit of multiple mobile phones, making sure that the Hercules would be ready and fueled and that there would be no snags at the airport. An airport official, feeling slighted by the lack of a bribe, could, in a country as bureaucratically dependent and nepotistic as Libya, halt the plans of armies, let alone a seven-man force of special operators.

Had the U.S. embassy in Tripoli been a normal post—one in a functioning nation and one whose day-to-day agenda was not run by the CIA—Marine Security Guards, or MSGs, would have been on duty safeguarding the integrity of the classified material behind the fortified walls of the chancery. There would have been a marine, usually a lance corporal, standing behind Post One, checking the credentials of any visitor attempting to gain entry to the embassy proper. If the U.S. embassy in Tripoli had had its own MSG contingent, then the force headed to Benghazi would have been much larger and more formidable. The fact that both Tripoli and Benghazi were operating under unique criteria *without* marines underscored how precarious security was for both locations—especially given the departure of the SST earlier that summer.

Outside the embassy's main entrance, a small crowd had gathered to assist in loading the "Tripoli Task Force" gear into the Suburban and Land Cruiser SUVs that would ferry the seven men to the airport. The embassy was rarely fired up for an all-nighter, but no one was heading to bed until Ambassador Stevens, Sean Smith, and the five DS agents were "wheels down" in Tripoli. Some of the administrative personnel joked about having enough cold beer on hand to celebrate their homecoming; others wondered if the embassy would throw a small banquet to honor the group for making it back from the hell of Benghazi. The common hope—prayer—was that the seven volunteers would not need to fire a single shot to secure everyone's well-being. All hoped that the September 11 attack would soon be forgotten. The chief of station certainly hoped that the incident would remain quiet. It would be a pity for the operations in Benghazi to become breaking news on al-Arabiya TV. After all, hush-hush was always preferred to the inquisitive headache of publicity.

Security concerning the rescue sortie to Benghazi demanded absolute secrecy. The ride from the U.S. embassy off al-Jarabah Street close to the city center to Tripoli International Airport some eighteen miles due south, in the town of Ben Gasher, was a straight run into the sparsely populated fringes of the desert. Other than passing near Tripoli University and some lower-income neighborhoods, the path was a simple push into emptiness. There was a fear that if the attack in Benghazi was somehow linked to a larger plot, the embassy itself could be targeted, or at least an embassy convoy could be put inside the crosshairs.

The gear that was loaded into the two armored SUVs was checked and rechecked—one last time. The good-byes were solemn. Men with misgivings tended not to volunteer for the most dangerous of assignments, but these were not ordinary human beings by any stretch of the imagination. Confidence to them was a layer of their genetic body armor; swagger and style were their calling cards. Many had their bodies marked with the "I've been there, and I've done that" arrogance that only men who have actually been there and done that can wear painted forever on their forearms, necks, and chests. Many of those departing the U.S. embassy that night had already served seven or eight tours of duty in the worst places in hell. Some, men in their late thirties or early forties, were working on marriages three and four; the number of years they had spent away from their wives and children were astounding.

As the convoy, which had now swelled to a small armada with support personnel and helpers, departed the embassy, the glimmer of the metal letters that proudly proclaimed EMBASSY OF THE UNITED STATES OF AMERICA slowly disappeared behind them. A floodlight focused its beam on the large American flag that was hoisted atop the chancery. The flag snapped angrily in the strong September breeze.

19.

Contact

The two-man sniper team atop the fast-melting roof at the villa could hear the voices in the distance, the loud cadence of the flames crackling, and then the clanking of weapons slung over shoulders banging against bodies. The sniper team had used the sandbags on the roof for cover, emerging to scan the horizon, but much of their focus was facing north and northeast, from where the first attackers had launched their initial strike against the compound. These voices were coming from the southeast, Charlie-3 gate. Then there was the flash of an RPG being launched and soon afterward the explosive whoosh of the antitank warhead falling far short of its mark.

"Hostiles on the south gate," the spotter reported in a calm, though immediate, voice, and the sniper quickly pivoted his body and the sights of his long gun to engage. SEALs, U.S. Army Special Forces, and especially U.S. Marine Corps scout snipers are considered among the finest in the world, and those whom the agency selects to cover its most secret operations are the overachievers of this elite group. Snipers are an eccentric group, each with his set of quirks and superstitions, but each also is most effective with a rifle that is the proper caliber and the proper weight and has the right feel. Snipers working for the black world of the OGAs, or other government agencies, are permitted great indulgences when selecting the weapons that they would use in lands that are most certainly in harm's way; these weapons include the Mk 12 SPR 5.56 special operations rifle, the SR-25 7.62 mm rifle, the gas-operating rotating-bolt AR-10, and the bolt-action Marine Corps M40A2 7.62 mm rifle. Many of these designated marksmen, having had the chance to ply their trade in Iraq and Afghanistan, prefer the SCAR, FN's 5.56 mm Special Operations Combat Assault Rifle with Nightforce optics; a 7.62 mm variant, known as the "SCAR Heavy," is also available. Those seeking enough firepower to stop a tank in its tracks may also prefer the seven-shot-capacity CheyTac M200 Intervention .408 with bipod.[1] A sniper's rifle is like an athlete's favorite sneakers—a matter of personal choice. Every sniper rifle, though, is personalized by the shooter. The sniper would position adjustable cheek welds and rail systems for mounting lasers and optics, high-end Advanced Armament Corp suppressors, and Nightforce optics.

To maximize their visual reach, the snipers and their spotters would have also carried Leica spotting scopes and laser pocket range finders. Other gear included thermal optics, night-vision optics, and the Insight M6X Tactical Laser Illuminator.*

When the spotter glanced south, toward Charlie-3 gate, the shadows revealed a target-rich environment; it certainly appeared as if there were a large mob assembled behind the wall. But the high fence shielded many of the terrorists now mounting a second phase of the attack from the GRS sights.

The perch showed a large mob was gathering near the south gate.

"COBRA 3 to TL [team leader]."

"Go, 3."

"Tangos mustering, fifty to seventy-five. Recommend we exfil [exfiltrate]."

"Copy."

"We gotta get out of here. The next wave is coming."

The gunfire went from sporadic to intense in an instant. The fact that more fighters were now assembling at the compound was ominous.

---

*For a discussion of laser capabilities deployed in Benghazi, see Jennifer Griffin, "What Laser Capability Did Benghazi Team Have," *Fox News*, November 4, 2012.

The terrorists, confident in their growing numbers, became brazen. Small groups, using the flaming vehicles in front of the February 17 structure for cover, unleashed magazine-emptying bursts of AK fire as their comrades inched closer to the GRS positions. The GRS response was measured and double-tap accurate: two shots to the chest, one to the head for good measure, sight alignment done quickly with the red-dot lasers. Suppressors muffled the sound, to also help the ears of the shooters.

The operators encountered men coming toward them with a hodgepodge of weapons. The operators split up and worked in teams of two, moving about in a dizzying fashion of bouncing red dots, the laser sights tap-dancing on terrorist center mass. The movement resembled a combination of combat ballet and a strange game of Twister. When a threat was discovered coming from behind the burning trucks in front of the militia building, the team would coordinate their response as one. "Hostile left" would be heard in the earpiece, "RPG northwest corner." Time slows down for the shooters, with a fixated tunnel vision on the target. In each case the operator would raise his shoulder weapon and fire two rounds into the chest, followed with a third round into the head. The threat was considered over once the terrorist's AK-47 dropped to the floor.

Head shots were an imperative. The GRS shooters had no way of knowing if any of the terrorists were wearing body armor. The Gulf Arabs had delivered enormous supplies of top-flight combat gear to the Libyan rebels during the civil war, and these tools of the trade—everything from combat radios, flashlights, cases of QuikClot, and body armor—were available in the markets of Benghazi and at smuggler bazaars in the desert.

GRS operators communicated among themselves on Motorola radios. Amid the roar of the fire and inside the earsplitting noise of the firefight, the operators' high-decibel-mitigating Peltor earmuff headsets ensured that the triggermen could talk to one another during the firefight. Some carried communications gear produced by Silynx, a world leader in tactical hearing-protection/enhancement headset systems.

Communication was critical; it was essential each GRS operator vocalized which target he would be engaging. With a limited supply of ammunition there was no need for overkill.

The terrorists seemed defiantly arrogant in challenging the GRS responders. Even when a three-round burst of 5.56 mm fire took out one of their comrades, they simply continued to advance. Spent shell cases littered the area where the GRS operators stood; spiraling plumes of smoke emerged from the ejected brass. The terrorists made little effort to retrieve those cut down by the GRS fire. Their religiously fueled courage in the face of such daunting firepower was impressive. The terrorists didn't care about their brothers in arms being hit. There would be time later to grab the wounded or, God willing, transport a martyr toward a hero's burial in town or at his ancestral village. Even when they were wounded, the terrorists didn't cry or beg for aid. Many didn't stop their push against the American line until they were shot dead.

The terrorists knew that there were another six hours until daylight. Time was on their side.

Gunmen began to take aim at the villa and the area in which the GRS and DS contingents had gathered to continue their search for the ambassador. Entering the burning building was challenging enough without 7.62 mm rounds whizzing by overhead. But the DS agents were unencumbered by the gunfire, which was now directed from the south and the east. Even though they were, man for man, suffering from the effects of smoke inhalation, they were fueled by sheer determination and raw adrenaline. Their faces were wrought with anguish, and their hearts sank lower each and every second that passed in which they could not locate Stevens. Although rounds were impacting quite close to their location at the villa and the GRS team was engaged in a pitched battle with a seemingly endless flow of men with RPGs, assault rifles, and even Soviet-produced light machine guns, the agents were not going anywhere until Stevens was found.

The assault on the compound was coordinated and serious. It was not a spontaneous explosion of firepower that had suddenly and surreptitiously commenced. This wasn't the Benghazi take on a pickup basketball game where anyone with a ball and a pair of Converse All Stars was allowed to play. It was evident to the GRS operators, as well as to the three February 17 men engaging the marauding terrorists, that this was another coordinated attack launched by men with military training and firearms skills who were seizing ground with military precision. This was a battle and one that grew in scope and intensity with each and every round fired. None of the GRS shooters wanted this battle to become a Libyan version of Custer's Last Stand. Yet Woods and the GRS team lived for moments like this. As clichéd as it might sound, this is what they did for a living.

The battle was one of sheer volume versus pinpoint talent; in the lineups that constituted the order of battle, the sides were very uneven. The militiamen, zealous in their approach and overwhelming in their numbers, initiated the engagement in true al-Qaeda fashion—a swarm of firepower attempting to overtake an already-battered position. In Kabul and other locations where jihadist terrorist elements had engaged their opponents in open battle, this tactic had proven effective. The terrorists weren't necessarily concerned about success; they simply wanted to kill as many of the enemy as possible. This tactic, known as the swarm attack, was designed to scupper an enemy's defenses. Such attacks usually began with a suicide bomber detonating himself near where the defending forces were concentrated. The blast was followed by a secondary suicide strike and then wild gunfire. The attackers in such instances, reminiscent of infantry charges from a century earlier, would wave war flags and scream wildly at the top of their lungs to inject fear into the hearts of the forces they were intent on overrunning. In Benghazi, the calls of *"Allahu akbar,"* or "God is great," were heard coming from the darkness.

The exact number of attackers remains unknown, though there were, according to sources close to the investigation, "many." Nobody bothered counting or had time to tend to the enemy combatant wounded. It is believed that the GRS and February 17 force was outnumbered at least ten to one, and certainly the CIA gunmen did not have RPGs or anything near the firepower of the flip-flop-wearing force closing in for the kill.

The GRS operators would have enjoyed complete technological superiority; their capabilities were augmented by night-vision devices for ballistic helmets (also called NODS) and thermal optic devices.

The GRS staffers fielded Dragon Skin flexible body armor. The terrorists did not possess advanced combat optical gun sights. They did not have advanced night-vision capabilities, nor did they have bullet and blast-resistant SUVs that cost hundreds of thousands of dollars. Yet the jihadist force—from one militia or, perhaps, fringes of several—managed to push close inside the Special Mission Compound to overrun it a second time.

The men who attacked the compound found tactical comfort in the size of their assault. They pushed inside the grounds—slowly, ferociously, and confidently. They lurked in the concealing shadows and emerged when the winds pushed the flames to the east or west and provided them with a few seconds of darkness. Their movement into the compound was likened to an infestation.

In battles where fervor is pitted against proficiency, proficiency usually wins. But this battle was different from the conventional firefights that the men might have experienced during their military service in the alleyways of Fallujah or a desolate village in Helmand Province. The GRS combat philosophy was decisively dynamic firepower to protect a source, an asset, or even an ongoing operation from being terminated or compromised. The GRS teams were not on the agency payroll to fight long, drawn-out battles that ultimately could warrant the intervention of additional resources. They, like the DS agents, were mandated with creating a safe distance between themselves and hostile threats any which way they could.

But the battle for the Special Mission Compound already involved an entity that was critically compromised. This was a rescue-and-recovery operation. One man was known to be dead, and another missing and presumed dead; A. was in serious respiratory distress, and all the other DS personnel were injured. The GRS team had rapidly secured a 360-degree perimeter around the smoking building, while the rescue efforts continued, taking the high ground, or perch, on a rooftop. Two or three terrorists would wander into the kill zone toward the rescue team and be very quickly shot by the suppressed weapons. Some were seen running away; others were talking into cell phones. There was a general feeling of angst among the shooters, though; the noose was tightening, and ammunition was running low. But time was dragging on, and even though the GRS ring of fire had already left a dozen or so terrorists dead, the American force was very susceptible to being overrun.

The terrorists sprayed their gunfire in inconsistent yet steady bursts. The GRS operators were frugal with their ammunition. They had to be. For all they knew, there were a thousand armed men descending on Western Fwayhat that night, and even though the operators knew that help was arriving from Tripoli, there was no estimated time of arrival established; it could be in one hour or in one day.

Many of those hit by GRS fire were struck by the sniper team from their high-ground emplacement. The attackers near Charlie-1 and Bravo-1 gates were roughly two hundred feet away; those attacking the compound from the south were four hundred feet away. Engaging targets from such distances enabled the sniper to terminate the heavy-weapon threats attempting to enter the grounds. It was a priority for the GRS team to neutralize any attempt by the terrorists to introduce the weapon-carrying pickup trucks into the fray. Some of the trucks carried crew-served multi-barreled 23 mm cannon shells and could chew apart the GRS/DS position without the slightest difficulty. Another weapon that the terrorists had at their disposal was the 14.5 mm heavy machine gun, whose armor-piercing projectile could penetrate an inch and a half of armored steel at a range of a hundred meters. The terrorists also managed to fire an ample arsenal of RPGs at the American defenders.

Firefights usually last for a minute or two before they end abruptly (of course, anyone who has ever been in battle will always say that those seconds have felt like hours), but the battle for the compound lasted more than fifteen minutes. The fight was so fierce that, it has been reported, Tyrone Woods was down to a spare magazine for his pistol. The manicured lawn was quickly filling with the dead; the bodies of the killed terrorists were illuminated by an eerie orange light coming from the roaring flames shooting into the dark crimson skies. The smell of the fires did not mix well with the sweet and pungent smell of blood and the bouquet of ripening guava fruit.

For every terrorist killed, two would take his place. Those shot and injured by GRS gunfire were quickly evacuated behind Charlie-1 gate and brought to safety. Sedans and pickup trucks raced about outside the main perimeter. This jihadist ambulance service proved to be quite effective.

The DS agents continued their search for Ambassador Stevens unfazed by gunfire, but each time they ventured deeper into the safe haven, the smoke and heat forced them to retreat. The GRS operators were awed by these young men and their unbreakable determination to pull the ambassador out of the inferno, but after close to an hour on the compound, the time had come to withdraw and return to the Annex. The GRS operators were not known for being long-winded or for adding hyperbole to any statement of tactical fact, but in the middle of the search for Stevens, under intense terrorist fire, the team leader pulled R. aside and said, "We have to get the fuck out of here." The February 17 militiamen concurred, but in a somewhat more animated manner. There was no choice anymore. The DS agents were ordered out.

The combined efforts had found Smith, but where the hell was Stevens? The agents were adamant about not leaving Stevens behind, but after approximately twelve trips in, they believed Stevens could have been kidnapped. They were working off the theory that perhaps one objective was to kidnap, not kill, the ambassador. They argued and they struggled with the decision, but the GRS team leader realized that Stevens was most likely dead already, and if they remained behind any longer, there would be a dozen dead Americans in Benghazi before dawn's first light. He pulled rank and tried to articulate his case in a loud and unshakable voice. It was a struggle to hear him over the sounds of gunfire and bullets whizzing over the heads of the American contingent.

It was 2330 hours.

20.

Breakout

The breakout plan called for both the DS and the GRS teams to depart simultaneously from the Special Mission Compound and burst their way through the kill zone in a motorcade configuration, through Charlie-1 gate, and to then head west, before heading south on a primary thoroughfare, and then east again to the Annex. The Annex would be a true safe haven. It was fortified, and the remaining security staff at the location was already mobilized and at the ready in defensive firing positions. The DS agents would take one of the armored Land Cruisers that was on the compound, and the GRS team would return in their vehicles. It was decided that the GRS personnel would take Sean Smith's body back with them since they had more room in their two G-Wagons. It became a logistical issue, even though the agents wanted Smith with them. The GRS and DS contingents made sure, even under heavy terrorist fire, that Smith was treated with the utmost dignity and respect.

The five DS agents were in no condition to drive; the GRS team leaders should have realized this. Their throats were smoked dry, their eyes boiled to a teary mess. They were heartbroken and angry; they were exhausted beyond the usual definition of the word. The worst-case scenario that they could have envisioned, the nightmare scene that went through every rookie agent's mind the moment he graduated from the Basic Special Agent Course, the loss of not one principal but two, had happened on their watch. But this was no longer training. This was the real world of outposts of diplomacy where the norms of civil decency were dictated by religious and other fanatical rage and at the barrel of an AK-47. What had happened in a remote section of a city that had been abandoned by the rule of law and governance on this night was of course not their fault. They did exactly what they had been trained to do—buy time, buy distance, and keep a level head. The job put them in a position that they should never have been in, and they did the best they could. Their lives, if they made it through the night, would never be the same. As they gasped for air and attempted to sharpen their fight-or-flight senses into focus, they realized that, like Al Golacinski thirty-three years earlier in Tehran, they would forever second-guess themselves, thinking that they could defend eight acres against the rage of an entire city.

Still protesting against leaving Stevens behind, the DS agents entered the Land Cruiser and moved out. They were equipped with their battle rattle and their M4s. A. was the wheelman. The GRS operators and the three February 17 militiamen laid down a hellish field of fire to cover the DS agents as they pushed toward Charlie-1 gate and safety. Many of the terrorists had hidden behind the thick trees that separated Charlie-1 and Bravo-1 but were cut down by the barrage of 5.56 mm firepower thrown their way. It is not known how many bodies were left in the trees.

Other gunmen waited outside Charlie-1 and Bravo-1 with their weapons at the ready. When the gate swung open for the DS agents to emerge, they laid down a full-auto turkey shoot. There were twenty-two bullet holes counted in Charlie-1.[1] Errant rounds flew into the night sky or landed in the rows of guava trees.

The route called for the American vehicles to make a left turn, heading west, back to terrain owned by the February 17 Brigade; the concern, of course, was that the hostile elements would pursue the DS and GRS operators. But A. erred, perhaps overcome by the effects of the smoke inhalation, perhaps confused by a sea of Arab humanity that was awaiting them outside Charlie-1. A. made a right turn, instead of a left, and headed east—just where a large contingent of men in galabiya robes and Afghan jihad uniforms were waiting. A. suddenly found his access out blocked off by men waving black flags and angrily raising their AK-47s in a gesture of defiant victory. The mood in the Land Cruiser was one of absolute exasperation. "What next?" the agents thought. "We have to get out of here now!" A. J-turned out of the danger zone. A J-turn is when a driver breaks suddenly (attack recognition), then backs up at approximately twenty miles per hour, and then turns the wheel sharply to the left, whipping the vehicle around 180 degrees and heading in the opposite direction of the route entered. It is a skill learned after many hours of training at the Bill Scott Raceway in West Virginia. The other agents were belted in, of course, but were jerked violently. But unlike the J-turns that he was trained to execute at the raceway, where DS agents hone their skills in handling ten-thousand-pound FAVs at speeds that sometimes exceed a hundred miles per hour, A. was wary of running over the crowds that had gathered and possibly being entangled in an inextricable cobweb of legs, arms, and chaos. A. reversed course, slowly, and returned close to Bravo-1, before reversing course again and moving onto an easterly path. He heard gunfire; angry hands pounded on the windows and on the hood of the car. The agents clutched their M4s and SIGs; if the crowd managed to swing open one of the doors or the rear hatch, they were ready to fight it out, even though they would have been easily overwhelmed. Several of the agents suffered serious burns on their hands from crawling on the ground at the safe haven. It would have been hard for them to engage a numerically superior enemy even under the best of circumstances. Fighting for their lives with hands barely able to clutch a weapon would have been virtually impossible. The bullet-resistant windows prevented the agents from shooting, unlike in the movies. There was no "well position" in the vehicle where an agent would sit in a rear seat facing traffic ready to shoot at attacking vehicles.

A. swung sharply to the right, rising up on the curb to avoid hitting the men, and then moved cautiously through the roadway filled with a sea of heavily armed men. The terrorists, and those who were summoned from the roundup in town, were huddled too close together to start firing without the real risk of hitting one another. Otherwise they would have simply emptied as much ammunition into the Land Cruiser as possible.

Once A. saw a bit of daylight on the road, he distanced the Land Cruiser away from the mob. But as the DS vehicle moved farther down the road heading east and purchased some real estate between itself and the crowd, the Land Cruiser began to take fire—heavy fire. The bullet-resistant windows began to absorb incoming rounds. The glass fractured in telltale spiderweb patterns; in some cases, rounds nearly penetrated, causing the glass spall to spray into the vehicle's interior. It was deadly to breathe the toxic fragments of glass and polycarbonate. When the small particles and chunks were sprayed into eyes already damaged by fire and smoke, it significantly cut down the agents' ability to see. Bullet-resistant, after all, did not mean bullet-proof.

It was difficult for A. to control the vehicle. He swerved at an accelerated speed in the attempt to race clear of the men still firing wildly behind him. The terrorists were not truly skilled at the inner workings of the RPG—especially when firing at a vehicle twisting and turning at top speeds. They bounced several grenades, like a father and son skipping stones on a pond, at the fleeing Land Cruiser; the bright green light of 7.62 mm tracer rounds made the DS agents and their attempt to flee the area resemble the center of a fireworks display.

The fast-moving vehicle, and the rounds impacting nearby, created a difficult-to-negotiate cloud of smoke and kicked up dirt and sand. A. was wary of crashing the vehicle or being overturned in a mangled wreck. It was doubtful that the terrorists carried the Jaws of Life in their armored pickups. The fear was that if the vehicle was disabled or wrapped around a light pole, the terrorists would simply set the agents alight in a death trap. They would either burn to death, with the footage aired a few hours later on one of the jihadist Web sites and chat rooms, or be overcome and overwhelmed and beaten to death. The images of past instances where Americans had been killed or mutilated on camera for the shock-footage appeal were never far from their thoughts. The ghoulish images of the Black Hawk pilots in

Mogadishu, Daniel Pearl in Karachi, and Nick Berg and the Blackwater contractors in Iraq came to mind. DS was at all of these locations after all; DS special agents participated in the investigations.

As A. proceeded east, he made a point of recalling the landmarks of the neighborhood so that he could solidify his bearings—the Rishwan villa on the left, the resort-looking estate to the right. In daylight the real estate looked so familiar and so extravagant. The plants and trees were so exotic and wondrous and the grounds so magnificent, even though some were vacated by their owners because Benghazi had simply become too dangerous for themselves and their families.

Approximately three hundred meters east of the Special Mission Compound, A. squinted and saw a man standing on the south side of the road. He carried an AK-47, but so did just about everyone in Benghazi. A. slowed down, wondering if the man was a member of the SSC or the February 17 militia. He appeared calm and looked as if he wanted to help. After all, had he been intent on killing the occupants of the car, he could have simply opened fire. The man motioned for the Land Cruiser to veer off the main road and make a right into a small private dirt road surrounded by walls and concealing trees that separated the properties of two very lavish estates. The road, large enough to accommodate two lanes of traffic, led to a small and grubby patch of land that the neighboring villas used as a dumping ground. The man motioned as if to direct the Land Cruiser away from the gunfire; instead, he was leading the DS agents into a death trap. Hidden inside the darkness of the alleyway and concealed behind the trees were a dozen or so men armed with RPGs and PKM squad-support machine guns capable of firing up to 650 rounds per minute.

Remarkably, given his smoke inhalation and burns, A. maintained his wits. All of the battered men inside the Land Cruiser did as well. They realized that the gesture could have catastrophic repercussions; A. glanced at the man and sped off east into the darkness. The terrorists waiting inside the darkness emerged from their firing positions and unleashed whatever they had at the fleeing DS agents. Two or three RPGs were fired; one or two impacted at the rear axle and set the vehicle ablaze. The tires, run flats, were shredded by the explosion and the penetrating shrapnel of the cone-shaped grenade. Hundreds of PKM rounds were thrown down range, many punching the armored exterior of the Land Cruiser. A Land Cruiser that was *not* armored would have already been destroyed, chewed up like a plastic toy by the RPG hits and the machine gun fire. But the run flats proved true to their name, and the armor specifications that dictated the level of protection to the Toyota SUV enabled the vehicle to push on.

Smoke filled the Land Cruiser's interior. The underside of the vehicle was ablaze, and the agents were unsure if they would make it back to the Annex. They couldn't roll down their windows; all they had by way of firefighting equipment was a small fire extinguisher. Stopping for anything before they reached the gates of the Annex was not an option.

The agent in the right front was in direct touch with the Command Post at the Annex. He called out the initial departure, then radioed in the ambush and taking incoming rounds, then gave the Annex a five-minute out with injuries. "Please have medical help waiting." Like those of air traffic controllers during the most tumultuous days, the communications were surprisingly measured.

The Land Cruiser continued east for another quarter mile before making a sharp left turn on a main road heading south. A. steered the difficult-to-maneuver, heavy, and hulking Land Cruiser another 675 feet down a main road. He still had control of the vehicle, however, even though it was a struggle. He drove down the central median in order to bypass vehicles that had been stopped by the gunfire or that had been used to transport the terrorists to the compound. A. made it a point to drive in the center of the road and was prepared to crash into anyone or anything that got in his way. The DS agents were close to the Annex—too close to stop.

The Land Cruiser left a burning trail as it struggled to make it the last mile or so. Two vehicles initiated a pursuit of the DS agents. A. floored the gas pedal. The agents inside the car checked their weapons once again. They braced for a firefight. One of the pursuing vehicles, a pickup truck with a mounted heavy machine gun, it is believed, followed the Land Cruiser east, along a main road another 650 feet, and then followed close behind heading south, until it suddenly turned right into a maze of warehouses and industrial buildings. Relieved, the DS agents moved south another 1,100 feet until they banked a sharp right and drove the last 900 feet toward the Annex. The security guard anxiously standing watch in his full battle kit lowered the wedge gate to help the agents in. The agents pushed into the compound and veered right, in front of the two main buildings of the secret CIA base. A.'s driving skills showcased during this escape from hell were extraordinary; DS personnel back in Washington would later speak of his cool under fire as an example for game-board training to teach young agents how to get out of the "X," the kill zone, to save yourself and your team members.

A medic rushed to the Land Cruiser and began treating the agents. It was 2330 hours.

The GRS team could not leave with the DS agents. Their sniper team was still atop the villa's roof, and several of the agency security specialists were still inside the safe haven looking for Ambassador Stevens. They remained behind for another five minutes. The drone footage would have shown a herky-jerky start/stop of the two G-Wagons, as the second wagon waited for the operators from the perch to get off the rooftop. But they were losing the high ground. The drone took over being the eyes then, with calls from Stuttgart, relayed to Tripoli, then passed along to the Annex Command Post, then passed by radio to the GRS team.

The roaming gun battle continued. The encroaching force of armed men became cockier with each inch of real estate they gained; inexplicably, their numbers grew minute by minute. The three February 17 militiamen urged the CIA men to leave. It was impossible to hold on for much longer. The southern gate, just in front of the Venezia Café, had been compromised. Grenades were being hurled over the wall. Gunmen moved quickly amid the guava trees and the dark grounds and got as close to the villa as they could before being engaged by the GRS operators. The TOC and the DS residence had been overrun. The villa was slowly becoming surrounded. The GRS team leader knew it was time to leave—especially with the DS agents en route already to the Annex. He ordered the sniper tandem off the roof, and he ordered the search for Stevens to end. Sean Smith was respectfully loaded into one of the G-Wagons.

The GRS operators would have to shoot their way out of the compound. Nothing was ever easy in Benghazi. The men advanced in a synchronized brilliance of tactical choreography, moving in on the encroaching threats rather than retreating from them. By closing the distance between themselves and the attackers, the operators forced the terrorists to retreat and flee. When the terrorists retreated, seeking cover, the CIA shooters would be able to push their way out of the battle zone.

Just as the team prepared to exit, the AFRICOM drone made it to the skies over the Special Mission Compound. At a command center deep inside a labyrinth of buildings at Kelley Barracks, the drone's video feed was transmitted at first telephonically to the U.S. embassy in Tripoli, AFRICOM, and the top levels of government in various locations in Washington, D.C., including the Pentagon and CIA headquarters. An eye in the sky, it was hoped, would help the decision makers understand exactly what was transpiring on the ground. It was good that someone somewhere knew what was happening; the men on the ground inside the kill zone were most certainly reacting to the chaos one minute at a time.

The GRS two-vehicle convoy pushed out, absorbing hellish gunfire. The G-Wagons had a platform atop the roof where gear could be stored, and a spare tire was tied to the top. Fearing that the Americans had brought a weapons carrier with them, the terrorists aimed much of their fury at the spare tire and not at the transparent armored windshield or the doors. It is not known exactly *how many* rounds hit the vehicle, but the sounds of the 7.62 mm rounds impacting the doors, tires, and windows resonated as if angry men with ball-peen hammers were pounding at it with all their might. The thirty seconds seemed endless. As the lead vehicle burst through Charlie-1 gate, anyone caught in its way soon found himself under its tires.

The vehicles headed west in a high-speed rush. They covered a quarter-mile stretch in a matter of seconds and then headed south. They would maneuver back the way they had come until they reached the Annex. The operators knew that the night was far from done. There were too many armed men with lethal intent riled up so close to the Annex. Ambassador Stevens was still missing.

It wasn't known how many terrorists had been killed in the battle for the Special Mission Compound or how many had been wounded. Some estimates at enemy killed in action are a dozen; others list the number of enemy dead at over fifty. Bodies had been strewn all along the lawn, but there was not time to verify the numbers. In this fog of war, all that mattered was that the Americans who were alive departed the kill zone. The battle was just a bloody chapter in what was becoming a bloody long night.

21.

The Cavalry

In Tripoli, the ride to the airport was conducted in typical agency and JSOC manner—high speed and low drag. The armored SUVs flowed along the smoothly paved highways that Qaddafi insisted connected key areas of the country. The headlights picked up dust and large desert flies along the way. Near the airport, as is so customary along main roads in Arab countries, families settled under the stars to grill fresh meats and pigeons for a hefty night's feast.

The darkness of the Airport Highway enhanced the somber mood of the men who would soon depart for Benghazi. There was no chit-chat inside the SUVs, no levity or even the gallows humor so often expressed by men about to enter battle who struggle to maintain a macho veneer to shield their fear and apprehension.

The light in the distance was the airport, Libya's primary gateway to the rest of the world. International airlines had by now, since the overthrow of Qaddafi, resumed commercial service, though air traffic into oil-rich Libya paled in comparison to the international list of carriers that landed twice daily in Dubai, Abu Dhabi, Doha, and Riyadh. Officially, Tripoli International Airport operated 24/7, but most commercial flights had ceased by 2300 hours.

The vehicles rushed into the airport's government section protected by soldiers and militiamen. The DCM's calls to the interim

Libyan prime minister, Abdurrahim el-Keib, and foreign minister, Ashour Bin Khayal, ensured that the motorcade would be free from the bureaucratic bullshit that would usually have been meandered through; the helper's calls made sure that everything inside the military terminal ran smoothly and with great ease. There were instructions that the men departing for Benghazi were to be left alone and allowed to proceed unencumbered by procedure or delay. The soldiers, militiamen, fueling personnel, and other airport workers who milled about at all hours of the night inside hangars were told to mind their own business. Libya's "in tatters" intelligence services, the internal spy operations that always had people planted at the airport, were ordered to look away. The heaping amount of grease applied to ease the departure of the rescuers illustrated how a few phone calls to the centralized government could make anything happen. The need for the expeditious treatment on the tarmac also illustrated that there was no centralized government in Libya; had there been one, one call could have brought a thousand heavily armed soldiers to the front door of Ambassador Stevens's villa seconds after the first attack commenced.

The two JSOC operators and the CIA personnel did not let the locals touch their gear. Every weapon, every piece of high-tech equipment, every bag of cash was loaded onto the aircraft by the Americans and under the watchful eye of the senior man who would lead the rescue bid.

C-130H was in good shape. The crew was prepped and ready.

It was just about midnight, as September 11 bled into September 12, when the seven operators boarded the aircraft. The estimated arrival time was shortly after 0100 hours.

Part Four

FIRE BEFORE DAWN

22.

The Anonymous Target

If there was one man in Libya who believed that the CIA didn't have a secret intelligence-gathering base in the country, he most certainly wasn't in Benghazi. According to a local Libyan source, even before the first armed men waving black flags pushed their way into Charlie-1 gate, just about everyone in the city knew of the existence of the American *Mukhabarat*, or intelligence service, site in Western Fwayhat.

The CIA didn't even go to the trouble to camouflage its existence there with some sort of cover story. There was no fake import/export company created to work inside a cookie-cutter warehouse complex somewhere near Benina International Airport far from prying eyes; there was no elaborately choreographed ruse created with fake offices, fake business cards, and even fake secretaries. There was no need. The cover story of the CIA station in Benghazi was simply that it was an extension of the unofficial U.S. diplomatic presence in the city.

The CIA never seemed to think through the geopolitical ramifications of its Benghazi outpost being discovered. And, apparently, the agency believed that the local GRS contingent could defend the position against most threats. Yet even the formidable veteran special operators of the GRS team could not withstand a siege by an overwhelming force of militants for very long. The State Department, for its part, had failed to effectively support the CIA mission in the city. Had the State Department simply declared the Special Mission Compound as something more than an unregistered ad hoc outpost, it would have been protected by the terms of the Vienna Convention; the Libyan NTC would have been responsible for the safety of the diplomats and the diplomatic grounds. By being the worst-kept secret in the city of Benghazi, the Annex was a huge red pin on jihadist maps all across Libya.

When the battered and burned Land Cruiser entered the Annex compound, the five DS agents thought that they were safe at home. Looking at the charred and smoldering vehicle, staffers were amazed that anyone could have walked away from it, let alone drive it for more than a mile. The agents, having negotiated a path through hell, finally took a moment to breathe deeply and ponder the horrors that had just transpired.

Those in the Annex tended to the agents' wounds; some of the lacerations were serious. The DS agents were given bottles of mineral water to drink. Some of the Annex staffers who came outside didn't know what to say to them, but words would have been superfluous. The agents were in a state of shock. They were heartbroken, and they were full of rage. The burden of survivors' guilt was evident on their faces and in their body language.

A few of the agents sat on the steps of the main building with their legs spread wide and hands clasped over the napes of their necks. As they sat on a stoop inside the CIA's fortified compound, their faces were sullen, their shoulders dropped in grief. The agents closed their eyes to alleviate the pain from the burns and piercing gut kick of self-imposed guilt. These young men, whose thoughts were racing wildly, were having a terrible time digesting the fact that those they were charged to protect were now dead and missing.

Libya was an assignment of great risk and great promise; ultimately, service in such a post was considered a badge of honor—especially for younger agents—and requirement for advancement. Many young agents thought that having a Libya or a Yemen on one's résumé was a privilege; after all, so many of these agents joined the DS as a result of the 9/11 attacks. Yet even the best of intentions, for those young agents who volunteered and for those for whom Libya was the luck of the draw, could have a cruel outcome.

It would soon be dusk in New York and Washington, D.C. How many of their classmates at field offices throughout the United States were working criminal cases, putting individuals behind bars for passport and visa fraud, punching out and heading to the local tavern for a few beers? How many in Brussels were serving in the comfortable parlors of NATO headquarters, augmenting security? How many were stuck in traffic on I-95 listening to WTOP radio? How many were in Pakistan or Iraq as nameless faces added temporarily to an understaffed post? Which unlucky classmate was doing a ninety-day tour in Conakry, in Guinea?

In the field of expeditionary diplomacy, the lines separating security duty and combat were blurred. DS special agents, after all, are law enforcement officers, not combatants. And, had the five DS agents been involved in a shooting while working a passport-fraud case out of the NYFO, the New York Field Office, or had they taken fire while on a dignitary protection detail in California, they would have been pulled off the street immediately and evaluated for shock and trauma. What happened in Benghazi was war, but the DS agents were not soldiers. "We are college kids doing grunt work," a retired DS agent commented. "We go to college, we are put in charge of huge operations, we are given this great authority, yet there we are, roping ourselves together and moving into a den of death. Soldiers and elite warriors like the SEALs and Delta are bred and trained to be warriors. We are bred and trained to be mostly managers and suits, and yet we are still drawn to the most dangerous of missions in the most dangerous parts of the world."[1]

And the night's combat was far from over. The Annex was under attack. The initial barrage of AK-47 and PKM fire was furious; the sounds of 7.62 mm fire punctured the darkness. Dozens of rounds were ricocheting off the northern, eastern, and western walls. The unmistakable swoosh of an RPG being fired was heard in the distance. The rocket-propelled grenades exploded in fiery bursts of light and the splintering glow of fragments spraying wildly into the night.

A fusillade of heavy small arms and machine gun fire followed the

GRS rescuers as they burst through the unhinged Charlie-1 gate in the mad rush out of the Special Mission Compound. Several of the attackers, grasping at their PKM light machine guns by their carrying handles, fell to their knees and then squeezed the triggers forcefully, going through a hundred-round belt of 7.62 mm ammunition in a matter of seconds. The tactic looked good on those video moments shot on mobile telephones to be uploaded later to the jihadist Web sites, but the tactical accuracy of such bursts was more Hollywood than heroics. The machine gun fire was sprayed wildly in the darkened distance; the incandescent rounds bounced all around, spiraling like a kaleidoscope of crisscrossing beams, but they were ineffective against the speeding G-Wagons. The GRS team exited the kill zone quickly and without suffering serious damage.

The GRS team retraced its path back to the Annex. It drove by the February 17 barracks and then east on the Fourth Ring Road past the Venezia Café and the Italian diplomatic attaché south to the Annex. As the vehicles passed the café, though, the operators noticed what appeared to be the fuzzy silhouettes of suspicious-looking characters walking on the north and south banks of the roadway heading east. As the G-Wagons sped ahead, the silhouettes became the outlines of armed men, who glanced curiously at the vehicles zooming by. The men tried to engage the G-Wagons, but by the time they could take aim and fire, the G-Wagons were a mere fast-moving blip in the distance. The GRS drivers, whose skills could make a Formula 1 race car champion blush with envy, were flying across the major thoroughfare, near 110 miles per hour.

As the two G-Wagons banked a sharp right turn off the Fourth Ring Road and headed south, the vehicles sustained heavy terrorist fire from the direction of a patch of land with fruit groves and trees. The gauntlet of weapons fire was heavy and dedicated; the mesmerizing muzzle bursts flashed like fireworks and provided the impression of thousands of gunmen lurking in the darkness. The GRS operators, along with their bosses in Tripoli, were convinced that the attack against the Special Mission Compound had been an attempt to assassinate or kidnap Ambassador Stevens; how symbolic it would be for members of one group or another to dispatch the video clip of President Obama's personal representative to Libya begging for his life—or worse. But as events that night unfolded, and the magnitude of the assault grew with scores of armed attackers rushing to the scene, the GRS operators wondered if the CIA post was the ultimate target and if the attack against the diplomatic compound was a clever tactic designed to split the CIA's defenders in half. When the flashing warning came over the CIA frequency that incoming rounds were impacting the Annex's outer defenses, the team leader's concerns were reaffirmed. The night was far from over.

The DS agents were relieved to see the GRS rescue team return to the Annex. The agents heard the sounds of gunfire in the distance, and as the sounds grew louder—and closer—they realized that the CIA operators had had to fight their way back from the Special Mission Compound. The scene at the Annex resembled what nighttime must have been like at an isolated American outpost somewhere in Vietnam that was under siege. Heavy bursts of machine gun fire were sprayed above the walls, racing like lethal fireflies on a summer night into the darkened sky. Explosions rocked the outer walls, and shrapnel and debris showered the grounds. DS and CIA personnel raced to find defensive positions from where they could engage the invisible enemy that was slowly but surely advancing inside night's shadows.

The GRS operators who returned from the Special Mission Compound were highly experienced tactical professionals and would have always wanted to be ready for the *next* fight. The first thing they would have wanted to do upon returning to the Annex was to head to the armory and grab a fresh supply of thirty-round magazines for their HK416s; most of the shooters had also depleted the six or seven fifteen-round magazines for their SIG P226 MK25s and their custom-crafted Kimber 9 mm semiautomatics in the battle for the compound, and they needed to reload. Rounds were also readied for the garrison's Mk 46 5.56mm light machine guns. Reinforcements were en route, but this was Libya after all: a one-hour flight and a ten-minute ride from the airport could be a journey that lasted a day or more. Seventy minutes, as was witnessed at the Special Mission Compound, was, simply stated, "a very long time." There was also concern that the rescue force could be ambushed at the airport. The night was full of doubt and threat. The events were quickly spiraling out of control and out of reason. The Annex was on its own. It was truly an Alamo, or Pork Chop Hill, moment.

Noncombatants at the Annex—the analysts, case agents, supervisors, and translators—prepared the classified materials for destruction. Computers, files, phones, and classified communications gear, such as satellite phones and other devices that enabled secret communications with Langley and the NSA, were all moved into piles—in case they had to be destroyed. Even if the Tripoli rescue force arrived, what would the next morning bring? There was little doubt in anyone's mind—let alone Washington, D.C., and Langley—that the Annex had been forever compromised. The not-so-secret secret base in Benghazi would have to be abandoned.

Top-secret equipment and files were all backed up and replaceable; the human assets weren't. The chief of base checked in with his boss in Tripoli. Where was the rescue team? The CIA communications officer maintained constant radio communications with the station in Tripoli. Just like Sean Smith, he facilitated all contact of a routine, sensitive, secret, and top secret manner between the Annex and points beyond. A quick glance at the clock indicated that it was after midnight and therefore September 12. In reality, the battle was not yet over, and with any event that starts on one day and ends the next, history will attribute the events that occurred and will occur to the date it started: September 11.

The midnight shift working at Tripoli International Airport didn't pay much attention to the C-130H taxiing slowly out of one of the military hangars. The aircraft had the markings of the Libyan Air Force. In the new Libya, after all, armed men usually ventured by private jet. It was common for the occupants of these aircraft to remain anonymous. The Libyan revolution shattered forty-two years of nepotistic wealth distribution into a free-for-all of oil-rich opportunity.

Private jets were more common than commercial airliners in the skies over Libya. Sheikhs from the Gulf emirates and kingdoms, princes from the Kingdom of Saudi Arabia, oligarchs from Africa's mineral-rich dictatorships, and CEOs from European-based multinational corporations crisscrossed Libyan airspace determined to stake a claim in the untapped wealth of an oil-rich nation in, as some have called it, "opportunistic transition." These men all traveled with armed entourages. The Tripoli Task Force that the U.S. embassy had mustered was nothing out of the ordinary on the Tripoli tarmac.

The C-130H moved out of its hangar on its slow roll to takeoff position. Air traffic controllers at Tripoli International worked slowly. The Hercules pushed past several Toyota pickups and the armed men who garrisoned the tarmac. None of them wore ear protection, even though the engines of the military transport produced an eardrum-pounding roar. The militiamen seemed bored watching the plane move by; they clutched their weapons, smoked cigarettes, and sat inside their truck awaiting the next chance to grab some tea or a bite to eat. Some of the militiamen wore the long beards usually associated with the jihadists.

Months earlier, Tripoli International Airport was the center of the war to topple Qaddafi; the smoldering tail fin of an Afriqiyah Airways Airbus A300, an aircraft caught in the cross fire as rebel fighters descended on the airport, became a symbolic image of the revolution. Now the C-130H passed rows of Afriqiyah Airways Airbus A320s and CRJs as it moved toward takeoff. The men in the aircraft fastened themselves in and waited. The jump-off from the runway was smooth and brief. Benghazi's Benina International Airport was an hour away—a blip in time for those who travel by aircraft; an eternity for those in Benghazi anxiously awaiting reinforcements.

The attack on the Annex was an odd sort of battle. Heavy and sustained automatic weapons and RPG fire subsided as easily as it erupted. The terrorists, the militiamen, or whoever they were had experienced the lethal skill of the GRS operators at the Special Mission Compound, and they seemed wary of mounting a full-scale swarm assault against defenders who were very skilled at hitting what they were aiming at. The Libyan fighters could not have seen or heard the small propeller-driven drone flying thousands of feet above Western Fwayhat, but the operators at the Annex had the luxury of maintaining a computerized link with the unmanned aircraft through ROVER.[2] ROVER, or Remotely Operated Video-Enhanced Receiver, was a high-powered laptop inside a hardened shell of a case that enabled soldiers on the ground to see, in real time, the video feed off what an aircraft or drone was seeing. ROVER was an invaluable tool in the Global War on Terror, and it allowed forces, especially special operations units, to acquire real-time ground intelligence on targets they were operating against. ROVER allowed spec ops commanders to call in air strikes, and it enabled small teams of operators (with the twenty-thousand-feet-aboveground vantage point) to avoid ambushes and other threats. In Benghazi, ROVER enabled the GRS and DS agents to pinpoint their shots and to lay down effective fire against attempts by the terrorists to rush the Annex's outer defenses. On the night of September 12, the drone became the Annex's perimeter eyes from the sky.

Several GRS operators stood at the ready at the main entrance of the Annex with their Mk 46 light machine guns. Because they feared that the terrorists might attempt to drive a vehicle laden with explosives through the main gate of the facility in order to breach its formidable defenses, the GRS's personnel were positioned at the main entrance, facing south, along the main road, and the east, at a side gate, and the dirt road that led to the industrial area adjacent to the CIA compound. The rest of the shooters—DS and GRS—were on one of the three rooftops facing a 270-degree field of fire. The terrorists and the Annex defenders played a deadly cat-and-mouse game of attempting to pick each other off in the darkness. A half-moon illuminated part of the night, though much of its glow was already negated by the fires from the Special Mission Compound a mile away. The smell of burning furniture and other unnatural materials crept through on the gentle night breeze.

The attackers had the luxury of cover. The area around the Annex was for the most part shrubs, fields, and abandoned buildings. The north side of the compound faced an industrial complex with some 850,000 square feet of warehouse area; the prefabricated warehouses, with their narrow and concealing alleyways, created a labyrinth of cover for snipers and machine gunners. A small house and an empty field lay directly to the west of the Annex, and behind the dirt path was a row of hedges and trees and a dirt embankment. The area surrounding the Annex was not the open terrain suitable for fluid and open warfare. It was, though, ideal for a nerve-racking urban quagmire. Without some sort of decisive move from either side, the battle of sniping, rapid-fire bursts, and RPG fire could go on for hours or even days.

Well concealed and enjoying—for the most part—the advantage of the high ground, the Americans waited until one of the terrorists exposed his position or fired a burst of AK-47 fire. The muzzle flash compromised the terrorist's position, and the GRS and DS shooters tried to pinpoint the light with bursts of their own. It was a game of patience and correcting one's hunch. Often, American weapons fire would result in some dirt or debris being kicked as the 5.56 mm volleys hit the dirt embankment or the side wall of a concrete home. Other times, though, the fire would result in silence or the moan of a man cut down by gunfire. Cries of the wounded cut through the surrounding darkness. Whenever an RPG was fired, or there was a burst of 23 mm or 14.5 mm fire from one of the militia trucks, the operators and special agents defending the Annex put their hands over their heads and sought cover. In some cases, the exchange of gunfire was furious.

And then, just as quickly as it began, the terrorist gunfire ceased. Shouts were heard in the distance, all unintelligible, even to the Annex translator. Some engines rumbled nearby. But the attacking elements, the mysterious and faceless muzzle flashes in the night, had simply had enough and appeared to have headed home.

The defenders didn't know what to make of the sudden cessation of hostilities. Nothing about the night made sense. Those working for the CIA and the State Department looked at one another with a sense of confusion and relief. The shooters propped themselves up from lying flat on their chests and stomachs and righted themselves to a resting position on one knee; the GRS operators wore knee pads to protect their limbs, while the DS agents were simply sore from the searches inside the safe haven for Sean Smith and Ambassador Stevens. The men looked on the ground and saw hundreds of spent shell casings. The respite was welcome, of course. The quiet gave the shooters a chance to reload and the intelligence folk time to prepare for being overrun. It also bought time for the reinforcements to arrive from Tripoli.

So much about the night just didn't make sense, but one question everyone was asking was, where were the good guys? Two and a half hours of war had been waged in the city of Benghazi, and everyone in the know—and many who weren't—were aware that the U.S. presence in the city was under full-scale attack. There was no cavalry charge of men in white hats eager to save the day and rescue the besieged American positions. None of the militias—not even the one on the State Department payroll—had mobilized their forces to mount a large-scale and deterring show of force to Western Fwayhat. Militia commanders who had worked with Chris Stevens and called him their friend disappeared that night, as did their soldiers. There was no police response at all. This absence of the most basic pillars of law enforcement was illustrated in an interview with Salah Doghman, Benghazi's latest police chief, when he told Reuters, "This is a mess . . . When you go to the police headquarters, you will find there [are] no police. The people in charge are not at their desks."[3]

News of the attack against the Special Mission Compound and the Annex had spread like wildfire throughout Benghazi, though the security staffers who worked at the friendly consulates didn't bother calling or sending aid. The diplomatic staffs in besieged cities were kindred spirits, and they all looked out for one another, but these representatives abandoned the United States that night in Benghazi. The Turks, who had been at the Special Mission Compound an hour before the attack, did not send any assistance, not even an agent with a walkie-talkie and a mobile phone to call *someone* for assistance. The

Moroccans didn't offer any help, neither did the small German liaison office; the Egyptians, recipients of hundreds of millions of dollars of U.S. aid, sent nothing. The other countries represented in Benghazi offered nothing—not even a slight display of concern, not even an armored car.

It was 0100 hours on September 12, 2012.

23.

The Looters

The C-130 flying from Tripoli to Benghazi traversed its westerly path without even the slightest turbulence. It was a smooth and easy flight, even though the mood on board was one of concern. The aircraft was reported as "wheels down," having landed, at just before 0100 hours.

Also at 0100 hours the first curious "visitors" hesitantly walked through Charlie-1 gate at the Special Mission Compound. The entire Benghazi metropolitan area had been alerted to what had happened in Western Fwayhat and knew that an American "consulate" and "spy den" had been overrun and destroyed. The news was spread along the pulsating mobile telephone networks: calls were made throughout the night's bloodshed, and SMS messages were typed quickly on Samsung and Nokia smartphones; the MMS messages, with their multi-megapixel video and picture high-res detail, showed a complex on fire and the men who seized it waving their AK-47s in victorious rapture. This was what instant messaging was like in Benghazi, and this was how violent acts of murder became nighttime social events in a city bereft of law and order.

The first curious onlookers who arrived at the Special Mission Compound waited for the shooting to end before wandering inside and seeing what they could steal and plunder; no point, after all, in entering a kill zone unnecessarily. The onlookers were, for the most part, young and bored; most, according to witnesses, and as seen on home movies they filmed with mobile phone cameras, were unarmed. It would, after all, be difficult for someone to steal a television set from the ambassador's bedroom while struggling with a fifteen-pound RPG launcher slung over the shoulder. Looters had to travel light in order to go home heavy.

The first looter wandered into a surreal setting of destruction and emptiness. The February 17 command post and the villa were still on fire, and tornado-like plumes of black smoke still bellowed out of control. The sounds of gunfire had been heard for nearly two hours, and the thuds of explosions were still noticeable coming from a mile down the road to the south. Text messages sent out throughout the evening spoke of a vicious and deadly battle that honored the memory of those martyred in the fight, but when the first men entered the grounds looking for some treasure, there were no bodies to be found; there were no wounded men praying to be seen by a doctor. Casualty evacuation was incredibly effective and immediate in the asymmetrical battlefields. Bodies were thrown onto the back of a pickup truck—both the dead and the wounded. Those who moved were taken to an emergency room. Those who didn't move weren't. The combined casualty count of wounded and dead was, it is believed, well over one hundred.

Still, there were the telltale signs of a fight. Bloodstains and shiny chunks of human tissue littered the grass and the paved path leading from Charlie-1. A few bloody AK-47s could be found on the ground, as well as a few spent shell casings. The terrorists sanitized the crime scene as best they could before departing the compound. No one really wanted a thumbprint or some spilled DNA to help the CIA identify any of the attackers.

For someone looking to steal whatever he could carry, the Special Mission Compound was like a Neiman Marcus outlet. Vehicles, AK-47s, ammunition, MREs, bottled water, furniture, and other military tools of war were available at the February 17 building. The militia was never known for its protocols in the safe storage of weapons, and when the attackers came over the gate, the militiamen simply fled. The DS villa, across the compound, had personal effects of the agents who withdrew—iPods, personal computers, cell phones, photographs, clothing, televisions, cigars, and other items that were worth stealing. There were televisions at the DS residence, and there were running shoes. The looters, many wearing T-shirts and Adidas shorts, looked as if they had been at home, possibly even asleep, when their mobile phones vibrated and invited them to an orgy of theft. Many, however, left with completely new clothes. For people who had lived most of their lives in fear, praying not to fall victim to the brutal reality of a secret-police state, such explosive acts of wanton destructive rage were common. During the civil war, this rage materialized in heinous acts of street justice and cold-blooded killing. On a September night in Benghazi, this rage materialized in the form of an animal-like pillage of a compound that had, for the most part, been burned to the ground.

Some of the looters brought spray paint cans with them so that they could forever leave their mark on the crime scene. Such catchy Benghazi slogans as "Be Fierce" and "Together!" were painted on the main gate, as well as on the DS residence and the ambassador's villa. For effect, those who found weapons on the ground or came with a firearm of their own raised their arms to the sky and fired a few rounds toward the moon. If Arabs could fire into the sky to celebrate a wedding, then they could certainly launch a few rounds to celebrate the destruction of the American presence in their midst.

The ambassador's residence was still on fire when the looters made their way inside. The looters used water from the pool to partially extinguish the flames inside the vast rooms and hallways so that the building could be searched and whatever wasn't smoldering or nailed down could be stolen. The residence was already an absolute mess. Debris was everywhere, the smoke was horrific, and the furniture was charred and eviscerated. The looters used their phones as makeshift flashlights. They examined each room and crevice as they searched for whatever items were abandoned that could be valuable— both on the black market and, perhaps, to the men from Derna who would pay a premium for any raw intelligence that could be exploited operationally or for propaganda purposes on the Web. The looters were confident that whoever had lived inside the building was dead; it was unlikely that anyone could have survived the fiery rampage of the terrorists' initial attack.

The men searching for the rewards of picking through the remains of the dead looked through Ambassador Stevens's clothes, his effects, and his luggage. They ransacked rooms already devastated by rage and fire. Some, eyewitnesses reported, urinated on the floor; others became riot-inspired Cecil B. DeMilles and made home movies of their postattack rampage. It was a despicable sight to behold.

The looters were soon joined by the curious and the concerned. A large segment—believed to be a sheer majority—of Benghazi residents passionately appreciated the efforts invested by the United States and the NATO powers to free Libya from Qaddafi and to create the template for a democratic state to flourish on the ashes of a brutal civil war and an ugly history written by a despot. The Arab Spring, from their perspective, offered hope and change. These native sons and daughters watched the chaos and the "meet the new boss, same as the old boss" hypocrisy that had resulted in elections in Egypt and Tunisia; in Egypt, after all, a brutal dictator was replaced by a brutal Islamist regime. These sons and daughters of the overthrow were all familiar with the nightly reports of maiming and massacres from Syria. These men and women wanted none of it. So when word disseminated that the U.S. mission had been attacked and that the ambassador had been killed, the city's embarrassed and fearful population also made their way to the Special Mission Compound. The residents of Western Fwayhat now came out as well. Most had hunkered down once the first shots and jihadist screams were heard; when the real shooting started, they fell flat on their marble floors hoping that stray ordnance would not strike them down. They had seen the British diplomats flee. They didn't want the Americans to follow suit. Most Libyans feared the Islamists just as they feared Qaddafi. All had known of Chris Stevens. News, emanating through the grapevine of chatter and SMS messages, that Ambassador Stevens had been murdered caused great shame and pain.

The looters made several attempts to break through the metal gate separating the safe haven from the rest of the rooms inside the villa. The fact that this section of the building was separated from the rest heightened their sense of curiosity and determination to make it through. The looters, like the attackers before them, had tried to smash and bang their way through the locked door but were unsuccessful in their attempts. A crowd had gathered outside the egress window and helped to pry it open; another crowd ventured in, seeking whatever prizes they could carry home.

The DS agents, in their search for Ambassador Stevens, were certain that he had succumbed to the debilitating smoke and had collapsed on the ground. The agents scoured the floor, on their hands and knees, in multiple attempts to search for him and bring him out and save his life. The agents—and later the GRS team—went inside the area on numerous occasions, too many to count, in order to locate the ambassador, but their attempts yielded nothing. ▮▮▮▮▮
▮▮▮▮▮▮▮▮▮▮▮▮▮▮▮▮▮▮▮▮▮▮▮▮▮▮▮▮▮▮▮▮▮▮▮▮

▮▮▮▮▮▮▮ The looters were looking for stuff to steal and went straight for the drawers, cupboards, and the closet. ▮▮▮▮▮▮▮
▮▮▮▮▮▮▮▮▮▮▮▮▮▮▮▮▮▮▮▮▮▮▮▮▮▮▮▮▮▮▮▮▮▮▮▮

▮▮▮▮▮▮▮▮▮▮▮▮▮▮▮▮▮▮▮▮▮▮▮▮▮▮▮▮▮▮▮▮▮▮▮▮

▮▮▮▮▮▮▮▮▮▮▮▮ it is believed that during the initial chaos of the attack and horrific blaze that followed the assault on the villa, Ambassador Stevens was separated from A. and Sean Smith and, overcome by smoke, became disoriented; seeking shelter and some air to breathe,
▮▮▮▮▮▮▮▮▮▮▮▮▮▮▮▮▮▮▮▮▮▮▮▮▮▮▮▮▮▮▮▮▮

News of the discovery sparked a mixed reaction from the crowd outside the egress window. One eyewitness, a videographer interviewed by CNN, recalled that at first the men in the crowd believed the body belonged to a Libyan. Then, as the videographer, who identified himself as Fahed al-Bakush, commented, "We thought he was a driver or one of the security people. We didn't know that he was the ambassador." However, in video footage of the men pulling Stevens out of the safe haven, some of the men inexplicably began chanting, *"Allahu akbar,"* or "God is great." The religious connotation of invok-

---

*The exact number of times that the DS agents and the GRS operators entered the smoke-filled safe haven in the desperate search for Ambassador Stevens is unknown, but a *conservative* estimate is that they ventured inside more than twelve times.

ing God's name was all too often irreligious; it was the Middle Eastern version of "U.S.A.!" as was expressed following news of the death of bin Laden. But right after the looters praised God's greatness, some were heard shouting, *"Ho ajnabi,"* or "He's a foreigner," before increasing the ferocity and the frequency of their praise of the Almighty. Once it was established that the lifeless body was that of a dreaded crusader, yells of *"Allahu akbar"* became a hypnotic rave.

The looters—most of them, anyway—were not believed to have been jihadists. But still, several of the men who emerged from the safe haven with Stevens's body were carrying AK-47s (the telltale front sight of the weapon was seen on several video snippets filmed at the villa during the removal of Stevens's body). One of the men, wearing a white T-shirt and a red-and-white checkered keffiyeh headdress as a scarf around his neck, dangled a cigarette in his lips and had an AK-47 clutched in his left hand.

Blood splatters, ██████████████████████████████ ██ ██ ████████████████████ were found on the walls near the window. A bloody palm print was also evident.

One unidentified man, believed to be in his late twenties or early thirties and wearing a white button-down blouse and brown slacks, emerged from the egress window clutching the tan body armor that was issued to ████████████████████ so that he could wear it in case the compound was under attack. ████████████████████████████ ██

When Stevens was brought out, his body was laid out on the bricked walkway in front of the villa and photographed. It is believed that someone in the crowd checked Stevens for a pulse, and when none was found, members of the crowd rolled him to the side; it is doubtful that any of the men in that wave of looters had the medical training to determine a pulse or any other vital signs. A man, wearing a Manchester United training polo and holding his Sony Ericsson smartphone between his teeth, sat him up to be photographed.

There were no apparent marks on his body to indicate trauma, but his eyes, nose, ears, and mouth were all black and blue. Stevens's attire spoke of the sudden surprise of the terrorist attack. He wore blue slacks and a white T-shirt. His black leather belt was unbuckled. It was evident that he had been in his room, kicking back and reviewing work or just relaxing, ████████████████████████████ ███████████████████████ warning came over the public address system, and the agent retrieved him to take him to the safe haven. ██████████ ██ ██ ██ The inhaled combustion gases and ambient heat within the residence replaced oxygen with toxins such as cyanide gas and carbon monoxide, worsening his plight. The irritation of his airway ensued, causing reflex constriction, engorgement of the surrounding tissues, and leakage of fluid and mucus into the airway. Attempts at taking a small breath would have become a monumental task for the ambassador. Delirium would have set in as the blood oxygen content continued to decrease. In moments the ambassador's fight for life would have given to unconsciousness. Finally, functionality of the heart would have been lost as initial tachycardia was replaced with a lethal arrhythmia degrading into a systolic cardiac arrest.[1]

The horrific pictures that the looters shot of a lifeless ambassador were quickly broadcast around the globe, shocking the world.

Some sources have estimated that hundreds of looters swarmed over the Special Mission Compound in their attempt, like vultures, to pick the flesh off the bones of an installation that was left to burn in the Benghazi night; other sources believe that the number was far greater. No fewer than twenty-five men lifted Stevens's lifeless body off the ground and carried him outside the compound to a commandeered car. The men were all wearing Western dress—certainly not the dark shirts and fatigues that were the fashion of the day for the jihadists. Virtually all the men wore blue jeans and T-shirts and soccer jerseys; FC Barcelona was the popular team, and while stars like Lionel Messi and David Villa would have been the players most revered, the men at the compound proclaimed their loyalty to Zlatan Ibrahimović, the Swedish international superstar who was born to a Muslim father (and Catholic mother) and was revered in the Arab world; the jihadists, as a rule, were not big fans of international soccer. Nearly all the men wore sneakers, while a few wore brown leather sandals. Only a handful of the men who rushed Ambassador Stevens to the car that had pulled up to the front of Charlie-1 sported beards that could be construed as "somewhat" Islamic.

According to one international correspondent who witnessed the compound shortly following the terrorist strike, "It is likely the intent of the men who found their way onto the U.S. mission was initially criminal, or less than proper, but once the body was found, they tried to become Good Samaritans."[2] There were a dozen or so all-night medical clinics open throughout Benghazi—many situated near the mosques that were headquarters to local jihadist militias and gangs. These impromptu clinics by day and patch-up centers by night were already filled to capacity tending to the gunshot wounds that were so common once darkness fell in the city. They were now bursting at the seams when the casualties from the battle at the Special Mission Compound were thrown on the examination room tables, chairs, or floors of these human-tissue fix-it shops. The slabs at the nearby mosques were also filled to capacity, preparing the dead from the night's battle for a burial befitting a martyr. If the intent of the Good Samaritans was to kidnap or bargain off the body to the highest bidder, there were countless locations where they could have brought Stevens. They could have buried him altogether in some nondescript grave; both Hamas and Hezbollah, as a macabre game of taunting Israeli governments, held the Jewish state hostage while using corpses as bargaining chips. Instead, the men in the crowd drove the two miles, speeding down the Third Ring Road, to Benghazi Medical Center—the finest hospital in the city.

It was 0145 hours on September 12, 2012.

24.

The Terminal

Benina was a small and poor-looking hamlet nineteen miles east of Benghazi's city center. A backward town with, curiously, an inordinate number of brand-new Mercedes and BMWs in many driveways, Benina had dirt roads, several corner stores, and numerous mosques. Benina boasted a state-of-the-art soccer stadium that could seat 10,550 people and had at first been named after the Venezuelan dictator Hugo Chávez by his close friend Muammar Qaddafi; after the revolution, the pitch was renamed Martyrs of February Stadium. Benina was also the home of an international airport, the second largest in Libya. There was a lot of history surrounding the airport. During World War II, the airfield was home to the U.S. Army Air Force's Ninth Air Force during the eastern desert campaign against the Desert Fox, General Erwin Rommel; B-24 Liberators from the 376th Bombardment Group flew hundreds of sorties against Axis forces from what was then known as Soluch Airfield. It had also been bombed by the U.S. Air Force in 1986 when President Reagan decided to retaliate against Libya for the La Belle discotheque (a nightclub frequented by U.S. service members) bombing in Berlin, which was attributed to Libyan intelligence agents.

Little, though, has changed at the airport in the seventy years since the last B-24 took off from the narrowly paved path of its tarmac, and the patchwork from the 1986 bombing was still evident. The terminal, the grounds, and the pace of activity have all remained provincially backward. The terminal was a run-of-the-mill sand-colored building with the departures and arrivals sharing the same space; the building houses offices and a customs and immigration hall.

Benina International Airport was really two airports—a military airfield and a commercial international port. The military side consisted of a few transport aircraft and logistic supplies. Smuggling was rampant at the military side of the field, and even though the national army was in charge of security, arms, explosives, uniforms, and other tools of war changed hands often and for rock-bottom bribery fees. The volume of ordnance transiting the military field was extraordinary, which in part led to the profound black market, and it was always a buyer's market. The civilian side of the airport supported domestic and international flights from all over North Africa and the Middle East. Libyan-based carriers, such as Libyan Airlines, Buraq Air, and Afriqiyah Airways, called Benina International home, and the airport also handled international flights to Cairo, Alexandria, Amman, Khartoum, Tunis, Dubai, Istanbul, Jeddah, Athens, and Doha.

Four separate militias and security entities controlled the airport, each mapping out its piece of the pie and determined not to surrender one inch: not to the NTC, not to a rival militia, and certainly not to the CIA. The Libyan Preventive Security Services controlled overall security at the airport, but many of the postrevolutionary leaders inside Libya likened this group to nothing more than a "gang of thugs."[1] The Libya Shield Force, too, owned part of the airport grounds and controlled some of its operations, but the brigade's loyalties to law and order were always suspect, as were the worst-kept-secret rumors that it was linked to al-Qaeda. The National Police, the al-Amn al-Watani, were also responsible for policing duties and security operations at the airport; the Libyan immigration services handled all matters of border control.

Many of the militia subunits, especially those that controlled a slice of the lucrative airport, were family-run affairs and, as a result, often fought among themselves. And, of course, the four heavily armed forces that shared jurisdiction—and ongoing criminal enterprises—made it so nothing got done unless all sides were appeased. "There were times that the airport ran very smooth, just like a European airport," a journalist commented. "But if one clerk was bribed and another from a different faction wasn't, the entire infrastructure went into North African shutdown, and it didn't matter who was left stuck in an aircraft or shackled to a bench inside one of the immigration department's holding cells."[2]

One of the local militias operating at the airport should have been attended to in a byzantine sort of way before the unscheduled C-130 touched down at Benghazi at approximately 0115 hours. Tripoli station and the RSO's office at the embassy had arranged a quick turnaround for the Tripoli Task Force to be met at the plane and then rushed to the Annex to rescue the American intelligence and diplomatic staff. But they were stuck in Benghazi purgatory, not allowed to leave the airport.

Suddenly there were logistic details that had to be worked out. Which militia would provide the armored vehicles for the Annex and Special Mission Compound personnel? Which militia would escort the Americans and to where? Which militia would drive lead? Which would take the follow position? How much money would be charged for these services? It was all so very surreal, but it was how things got done and how they didn't get done. The negotiations to solve the inertia on the tarmac were equally surreal. Commanders wearing different uniforms argued vehemently with one another, and they argued with the Tripoli Task Force leader. There is a remarkable and culturally driven pantomime to the art of arguing—hands waving, voices lowered and raised, and the obligatory turning of one's back and the returning to the heated discussions—that Middle Easterners have mastered to a level of expertise that, according to one Lebanese-born journalist, "has become a form of foreplay. The deal will always get done," she remarked, "but unless there is wrangling, insults, apologies, someone walking away, and at the end a reluctant compromise, the deal simply isn't worth making."

This was the case at Benina International Airport. The back-and-forth involving men wearing half a dozen different uniforms representing the same number of divergent interests, all with their hands out, went on for hours. The Task Force leader called the Annex in addition to the embassy in Tripoli. Men desperately pleaded for help on the tarmac, and bosses, inside SCIFs at the embassy, frantically worked their mobile phones to try to resolve the issue. The foreplay and the coordination would last more than three and a half hours. A journey of approximately twelve miles, from the airport gates to the wedge barrier at the Annex, appeared as though it would not begin before it was too late.

The Annex was quiet as 0200 hours approached. Inside the walls of the fortified compound, agency personnel worked feverishly to prepare the facility for departure. A secret intelligence station was not built overnight, nor was it easy to disassemble it in a matter of hours. Records of sources and assets had to be destroyed. Hard drives on laptops were smashed with hammers and paper files shredded in crosscut shredders. The CIA had great resources and efforts invested in the network it had established inside eastern Libya and did not want it compromised or eliminated. Leak of an asset's name could mean certain death for him and his family; the CIA's failure to safeguard the identity of one of its resources in country would make it virtually impossible to convince others to knowingly and willingly assist the United States ever again.

The Annex maintained constant communications with its station in Tripoli, and its personnel were on the phone with the Tripoli team leader stuck in the middle of the byzantine bureaucracy on the tarmac. There was no ETA given.

The GRS operators and DS agents maintained a constant vigilance at their defensive positions, and they continued to scan the outer perimeter of the Annex in search of the expected next wave of the attack. There was little doubt that the position would be hit again, and it was the proverbial question of when rather than if.

As the seconds dragged on, there was true concern that the attacks had been well coordinated and executed in concert with the Islamic militias who ruled the city. There was, in the minds of the Annex defenders, no other explanation behind the delays at Benghazi airport. Benghazi bureaucracy was ball-bearing-in-the-machinery slow, but by now elements throughout the country were aware of the attacks against the American presence in the city. If there was a will to expedite an end to the bloodshed, then certainly there had to be a way.

The attacks so far had been puzzling. There were no IEDs or VBIEDs used. The terrorists had not introduced suicide bombers into the equation yet, nor had they attempted to use the heavy firepower at their disposal, the concrete-chewing cannons mounted on their trucks, in any coordinated manner. Terrorists in Libya fielded impressive combat credentials and enough ordnance and delivery systems to take over any target in the city. The attacks so far had been comparatively small-scale.

A blanket of beguiling silence had overtaken Western Fwayhat. The darkness revealed no signs of movement. The shooters on the rooftops looked at their G-Shock watches and depressed the button revealing the time in a muted greenish light. It was 0215 hours. The quiet gave the CIA staffers and the DS agents time to reflect. The quiet also gave the terrorists time to clean their weapons and reload.

Back in Washington, there would have been a distinct feeling that the worst was over. There was no adverse intelligence to indicate anything more was planned. The drone had also seen nothing of concern on the perimeter. Daylight brought hope and a new beginning to end a night under fire. Those inside the Annex hoped to be out of the kill zone by dawn. The DS agents needed medical treatment.

25.

Benghazi Medical Center

Doctors working the midnight shift at Benghazi Medical Center (BMC) in the early morning hours of September 12 were used to chaos. The resident physicians were primarily junior, and although they had become experts in combat emergency care treating the casualties from the civil war, they were rookies to the routines of hospital administration and emergency room management. The hospital, in fact, was never supposed to have an ER; Muammar Qaddafi wanted the proposed thousand-bed hospital to be a beacon for medical excellence for the entire eastern half of the country, not a trauma care center. Qaddafi ordered the facility built in 1979, but it only opened for business thirty years later, toward the end of his tenure—a typical reality of life in Qaddafi's Libya, where grandiose ambition was often thwarted by the shackles of dystopia. But a city that had suffered enormous violence and collateral damage in the campaign to oust the Libyan dictator had an acute need for a hospital where gunshot wounds and angina attacks could be treated at the same sophisticated location. Twenty minutes after the civil war began in Benghazi, the hospital's emergency room was open for business.

A visit to the ER was just as much a medical emergency as it was a family affair. If a Benghazi resident needed the ER, he usually ventured to the hospital with his family—spouse, children, cousins, and more. The ER was always crowded with children wandering the halls, women crying, and men in need of care. It was a 24/7 sea of pain and healing.

Boston's Massachusetts General Hospital had partnered with BMC to help bring its advanced know-how and experiences to postrevolutionary Benghazi. In September 2012, Dr. Thomas F. Burke, the chief of Massachusetts General's Division of Global Health and Human Rights, at the time of the attack found himself in Benghazi for the second time since the revolution. Dr. Burke was no stranger to conflict and tactics: he spent seven years in the U.S. Army with several overseas deployments, and he served as the doctor for the FBI Hostage Rescue Team, or HRT, at the sieges at Ruby Ridge, Idaho, and Waco, Texas. With many years of medical support work in conflict and post-conflict nations, Dr. Burke found Benghazi an ambitious yet familiar project.

Beyond the covert and the diplomatic American presence in the city, there were American businessmen and even tourists—primarily backpackers—who walked around openly and freely. But the American presence was nomadic—lone souls looking for a business opportunity or the chance to visit rare ruins before they were discovered by scores of tour buses ferrying Euro-pinching holidaymakers from the Continent. "I have traveled to war zones and zones reeling from war all over the world," Dr. Burke would comment, "and the lack of an *official* American presence, government and corporate, in Benghazi was truly stark."[1]

The Americans—and indeed all foreigners—resided in the Tibesty Hotel, the last functioning hotel in the city accepting foreigners. In the afternoon of September 11, Dr. Burke left his hotel room to take a walk with some colleagues in downtown Benghazi and along the corniche. All along his journey, he encountered pedestrians and motorists who, seeing that he was a Westerner, embraced him, wanting to know if he was an American. "It was something like a U.S. soldier walking through Europe after World War II ended," Dr. Burke remembered fondly. "We were almost celebrities. The people in the city were grateful for helping them rid Libya of Qaddafi."[2]

But Dr. Burke was under no illusions that Benghazi was a normal city at a normal time in its history. His counterpart at Benghazi Medical Center, Dr. Fathi al-Jehani, had been shot in the chest in May 2012 after he refused to sign the hospital over to one of the many militias in the city; Dr. Jehani was back at work two days later, walking the halls of the hospital with a tube in his chest. There was no law and order at all in Benghazi. It was a very dangerous place to be, especially because, as Dr. Burke said, "some of the thirty-five militias that ran Benghazi promoting Sharia law ruled by the gun."

Dr. Burke had, in fact, spoken to Ambassador Stevens at 2030 hours on September 11. The ambassador was slated to visit Benghazi Medical Center to express his appreciation and enthusiastic support for six programs that Dr. Burke and Massachusetts General were coordinating with the hospital; the programs covered executive health-care development; health-care management; ER development; ambulatory care management; advanced radiology (the training was being conducted in Boston); and the establishment of a Libyan national poison control center. Ambassador Stevens considered his trip to Benghazi Medical Center an affirmation that engaging the Libyan people with dedication and kindness would produce priceless political and cultural dividends. He considered his visit to Benghazi Medical Center one of the most important stops of his brief visit to the city.

At 2140 hours, Dr. Burke and a colleague were on the phone with one of the DS agents when he heard an explosion in the background, and then gunfire, and then the words "We've got a fucking problem here."[3] The line then went dead. Over the course of the next few hours, while hunkered down in his room at the Tibesty Hotel, Dr. Burke heard gunfire and explosions. Ambassador Stevens would be arriving at the hospital much earlier—and under very different circumstances—than originally planned.

At 0215 hours a phalanx of young men burst through the back door near the emergency room entrance at BMC. They rushed quickly through the corridors and shouted that they needed a doctor. The men took turns carrying Stevens, hauling his body over a shoulder as they negotiated the crowded triage and admitting area. News of the attack had become public knowledge by midnight, and the emergency room physician, Dr. Ziad Abu Zeid, was able to surmise that the man now on his gurney was the missing American ambassador.

Dr. Abu Zeid worked feverishly to resuscitate Ambassador Stevens. He and other doctors worked on Stevens's body for nearly ninety minutes. CPR was applied without letup; Stevens was injected with epinephrine to get his heart going, and a tube was inserted down his throat toward his lungs to generate breathing. According to Dr. T, an emergency room doctor with extensive battlefield experience, "A forty-five-minute code [the EMS/emergency room vernacular for cardiac arrest], much less ninety-minute, feels like hours. It is a literal time warp as you act and react in a code."[4] But Libya's greatest champion for freedom was already dead. Many of the young doctors attending to the U.S. ambassador were Libyans who returned to their native country from lucrative careers in Europe and the United States. They had hoped to become the pillars on which a new and free Libya could be built. At approximately 0200 hours on September 12, 2012, they would declare the death of John Christopher Stevens. He was fifty-two years old.

Knowing what the loss would mean for Libya, some of the doctors wept over Stevens's body. In an adjacent room, approximately twelve men were lying unconscious on gurneys being prepped for surgery. The armed men who had brought them into the hospital an hour earlier would not leave their names at the desk.

As the night dragged on, the mood at the U.S. embassy in Tripoli was "wall punching" frustration. The Annex had just held off a serious attack, the seven JSOC and GRS operators were still stuck in an endless struggle of Middle Eastern "show me yours and I'll show you mine" at the airport, all this while the whereabouts of Ambassador Stevens remained a mystery. At this moment, the President's representative to Libya was presumed a hostage. The embassy even prepared for an evacuation, not knowing if *it* would be hit next. Cable traffic between Tripoli and Washington was frenetic. It was 1900 hours in the U.S. capital, and dinners and drinks were being missed at Foggy Bottom, at the Pentagon, and at the Libya desk at CIA headquarters in Langley.

At approximately 0215 hours, the RSO received a call from A.'s mobile number. Yet instead of talking to the DS agent to receive a situation report from the Annex, the RSO found himself talking to a young Arab male saying that he was with the ambassador at the hospital; the phone had been taken from Stevens's pocket as he lay on the gurney being resuscitated and was the same cell phone Stevens had used to ring the DCM in Tripoli earlier in the night.* The caller was long on emotion and very short on fact and detail. His description of Stevens was skewed by his wounds.

The fear had been that Stevens had been kidnapped and that an image of him would appear shortly on a jihadist chat room confessing to crimes against the Islamic world, shortly before a dagger was to be raised to his throat. American hostages had, after all, been beheaded before for the horrific shock value. A YouTube broadcast of an American ambassador being executed, like the *Wall Street Journal* reporter Daniel Pearl, who was brutally beheaded in Karachi, would have been a horrific event. But the RSO and the chief of station had another concern. Was the call from the hospital indeed genuine? Was it a ruse? Were the terrorists intent on starting the light of a new day with a tandem strike against the Annex and against rescue attempts to come to the hospital to retrieve the ambassador's body? Nothing made sense. Expanding the attack to three locations would have been nightmarish and would require the absolute intervention of the U.S. military, which, as had been seen in Somalia, was a Pandora's box with limitless disaster possibilities.

RSO Tripoli summoned a recently hired Foreign Service National, known as an FSN, a local brought on to help out with logis-

---

*See May 8, 2013, testimony of Gregory Hicks before the House Oversight Committee (*Benghazi: Exposing Failure and Recognizing Courage*).

tic in-town tasks at the Special Mission Compound, to venture to Benghazi Medical Center and see for himself if the man was indeed Ambassador Stevens. The FSN* was new to this game, and he had been hard at work trying to gather local intelligence on what was actually happening in the city, and was attempting to appeal to all the fractious elements at the airport so that the Tripoli team could get on their way. But, reportedly, the hospital was full of Ansar al-Sharia gunmen, who were wandering about the hallways and who had their vehicles parked outside the main entrance. The FSN was quick-witted and feared that he would be recognized as working for the U.S. government and be abducted immediately; when it came to the men with the black flags, it was also likely that his family would have been massacred just to make a point that the penalty for working with the crusaders was death. So the FSN mustered an unidentified friend who also knew Stevens to wander into the hospital and see what he could find out. The identity of the FSN's friend is unknown.

The friend was scared and intimidated by the men in camouflage fatigues and black outfits patrolling the grounds as if they were the rule of law (which in fact was mostly true). Their AK-47s dangled carelessly off shoulder slings. Some barked orders into mobile phones or walkie talkie–like radios that the Gulf states had distributed en masse to the ragtag fighters during the revolution. The friend, however, displayed great courage. He walked past the men with the guns, past unsavory souls who wandered the hallways looking for trouble and opportunity, and past the nurses and doctors rushing to and from the ER triage. There was no notion of hospital security; anybody could walk right in.

The FSN's friend made it to the morgue and to where several doctors were conversing with one another. Some were on their mobile phones; others wept silently. The friend glanced inside the room marked *mashrahah*, or morgue, and saw Stevens's body on a gurney. The friend had met Stevens before, and he immediately recognized the man on the slab as the U.S. ambassador. The friend, startled by

---

*The identity of the FSN is withheld to safeguard his security and the security of his family in Libya.

what he saw, covered his mouth with his hand. He walked out of the hospital to give the news to the FSN in person.

The death of Ambassador Christopher Stevens was a moment of stolen innocence to many in Benghazi. It was hard for a city that had survived forty-two years of Qaddafi and the bloody mess of a brutal civil war to claim innocence, but the Arab Spring brought hope to many who had suffered for years. Libya's petro-wealth, it was thought, could remedy many ills that other Arab nations, like Syria, were suffering through with plague-like lethality. Ambassador Stevens, because he looked at the Arab Spring through that eternally American ailment of passionate optimism, had been Libya's most ambitious advocate in Washington, D.C., and elsewhere around the world. His murder was a fatal sign, perhaps, that Libya was destined to suffer through many more years in hell.

The friend emerged from the hospital with his head held low and his shoulders slumped in anguished defeat. He broke the news to the FSN, who then had to notify the RSO in Tripoli. The FSN hesitated for a few moments before calling the RSO. This was not the sort of news that was transmitted with nonchalance. The FSN took a breath and then dialed the number. It was 0400 hours.

26.

Incoming

0430 hours, September 12, 2012: Benina International Airport. After three hours of intensive negotiations on the tarmac at Benghazi's Benina International Airport, men skilled in the art of Middle Eastern deal making brought an end to the stalemate by achieving points of reason and mutual satisfaction—and paying a king's ransom. It is unknown how many crisp new Benjamin Franklins were promised in order to reengage the services—and guns—of the February 17 Brigade. The amount generously transferred to the militia that was supposed to have protected the Special Mission Compound and the Annex is unknown, but the group assembled a formidable force to escort the seven men and their equipment to the Annex. After all, this was the time for the Middle Eastern absolution that follows a *sulcha,* or agreement on forgiveness; this would be how the February 17 Brigade, realizing it was on the precipice of a "you-are-with-us-or-against-us moment," tardily laid claim to the American partnership.

Nearly a dozen February 17 Brigade vehicles transported the seven Americans who remained stoically silent in several armored SUVs; the seven men were in their battle kit, hands on their weapons. The convoy was considerable in size and in firepower. Half a dozen pickups, each sporting a heavy-caliber machine gun or a large cannon, raced west along one of the airport roads south of the city at speeds that exceeded a hundred miles per hour. There were very few vehicles on the roadways at that hour; even the Mediterranean lifestyle of living at night required a few hours of sleep. And any vehicle unfortunate enough to be near the motorcade would have been run off the road. Once the initial ten-kilometer run from the airport was complete, though, the motorcade had to slow down as it entered the southeast outskirts of the city, but not by much. The closer the armored convoy made it to the Annex, entering the Fwayhat section of the city, the more cautious the Libyan militiamen became. There were several sharp turns that they had to negotiate before they reached the Fourth Ring Road, and each presented its own set of potential choke points that offered a sniper or an RPG team advantageous cover. There were countless spots along the route from the airport where terrorists could have planted a powerful IED. Even with fifty militiamen on their side, and an unarmed Predator drone hovering silently in the dark skies above, the motorcade was never truly safe.

The Tripoli Task Force arrived at the Annex at just after 0500 hours. The gate was lowered seconds before the vehicle darted inside, in a scene of precision that resembled a James Bond film; the February 17 Brigade members positioned their vehicles just outside the main gate on the east-west crossroad. The militiamen stayed in their trucks and on the outside roadway, making sure that no suicide bombers approached, though in the darkness there was little for the men to do and nothing for them to see. Some checked their cell phones. Others grabbed a smoke. Several of the men placed their prayer rugs on the backs of the vehicles, near the cases of 12.7 mm ammunition, awaiting dawn's first light and morning prayers.

The men from Tripoli were there to ensure that the Annex was evacuated quickly, efficiently, and with extra triggermen along to provide security. There was little time for niceties when the seven operators arrived. They exchanged a few greetings with the GRS staffers, and one of the JSOC operators looked over A., who was slowly recovering from his wounds and smoke inhalation. They went to the building on the compound where Sean Smith's remains had been respectfully covered up. The seven men from Tripoli wanted to make certain that no more Americans would die in Benghazi.

The Tripoli team smelled the remnants of the burned villa in the air; the smell off to the distance was unmistakable. The signs of a fierce fight were also evident in the Annex. Spent shell casings were everywhere, as were small craters where RPGs fired from adjacent high ground had impacted. The men defending the Annex looked as if they had been through an ordeal; they looked tired, and their clothes smelled as if they had been burned. The arrival of the seven men had brought a sense of relief and closure to the Annex defenders. The reinforcements were fresh and energetic. Their weapons hadn't been fired all night.

The base chief was busy coordinating the trip to the airport. News of Ambassador Stevens's death had caused a whirlwind of activity in Tripoli, and American officials urged NTC leaders to commit military assets to safeguard the departure of the mini CIA station, the DS agents, and the bodies of IMO Smith and Ambassador Stevens back to Tripoli. The NTC, perhaps realizing that its inaction during the previous seven hours might ultimately place negligent culpability on its doorstep, now committed the most reliable force it had in Benghazi—the *Istikhbarat Askaria*, the soldier-spies of the Military Intelligence Service. As the first blue hint of daylight emerged far in the distance over the eastern horizon, a convoy of trucks and a company of heavily armed and politically reliable Libyan Special Forces soldiers were en route to the Annex. They were expected before sunrise.

The Annex detail was hard at work readying the Annex for a "broom clean" departure when a brief crackle of automatic weapons fire was heard approximately a hundred meters away. The Annex, once again, was under attack. Tyrone Woods, according to the words of one of the CIA staffers at the Annex, rolled his eyes in an expression of absolute frustration over the audacity of the Libyan terrorists and said, "I am going to rain down hate among them."[1] It was 0515 hours.

Woods, along with the rest of the GRS team and the Tripoli operators, ran toward his defensive position. The DS agents grabbed their kit and rushed to assist. The two former SEALs Glen Doherty and Tyrone Woods were relieved to see each other in the wrong place at the wrong time in an upscale neighborhood in Benghazi. Doherty reportedly looked at Woods and said, "Let's go, two is one, one is none."[2] Woods grabbed his Mk 46 light machine gun, while Doherty grabbed his HK416. The two men climbed a ladder to the roof and prepared for battle.

Terrorist fire was coming in from all directions. Heavy bursts of machine gun fire were bounding in from the sky. Each trigger pull propelled a tight group of fire toward the Annex and toward the men on the roofs returning fire; green lines of tracer fire crisscrossed the receding night's sky. The Annex's defenders responded in kind. Return fire was lethal. The ten-man GRS contingent, the five DS agents, and the seven men from Tripoli gave as good as they got from their rooftop positions, unleashing walls of fire at targets they could identify from the muzzle flashes of the terrorist weapons being fired. This was the terrorists' big push, and they weren't pulling their punches. Several RPGs swooshed in toward the rooftops from approximately fifty meters away. The cone-shaped warheads closed in like glowing fists before punching through chunks of the Annex's outer wall.

The battle also widened. Most of the terrorist focus was initially against the western side of the compound, but it soon spread to the northern tier. The defenders had to dilute their positions against the western approach and shift their sights to a 180-degree field of fire. The terrorists moved fluidly and proficiently from cover to cover in their assault; there were no doubts in the minds of the post's defenders that these men had had advanced military training and extensive combat experience. The attackers were not a ragtag assembly of militants looking to throw a few rounds down range. Their advance and assault were methodical.

The chief of base once again relayed back to the chief of station in Tripoli that they were under fire when suddenly the mortar barrage began.

There were tens of thousands of Soviet-produced 82-PM 82 mm mortars throughout the third world; thousands were supplied to Qaddafi's military. The mortar, which saw service with the Red Army during World War II, was a robust and reliable infantry-support weapon that could be transported to a firing position by several men. Although the system consisted of nothing more than a metal tube, a firing plate, and a sight, it did require advanced training in order to operate. A mortar was not an ideal third-world weapon, like the RPG, where if you aimed it in the general direction of a target, odds were likely for a direct hit. Mortar crews required weeks of training and endless hours on the range in order to hone their skills. Unlike the RPG, a mortar also required a crew. The system had to be broken down into pieces and carried into battle. The tube alone weighed 120 pounds; each 82 mm round weighed nearly 7 pounds. Between four and six men were required to operate one mortar. The mortar's maximum range was three thousand yards, though it was incredibly lethal and effective at a range of one thousand yards or less. A good mortar crew could launch twenty rounds in a minute. A good crew could, firing three or four 82 mm rounds to gauge distance and wind, correct itself along the way to drop a round square into the center of the crosshairs.

What made the mortar so feared on the battlefield was its ability to rain fire down on a target, and afterward the crew could pack itself up and move toward a new position. The mortar could be fired just far enough from its destination that it couldn't be engaged and close enough that it could decimate a target with uncanny accuracy.

The first mortar round hit a grassy patch of nothing in the northwestern corner of the compound. However, those at the Annex knew that the introduction of mortars to the battle was a game changer. An 82 mm mortar round could spread neat pockets of devastation to a battlefield, and the next round would more likely strike at or closer to its target. The Annex defenders were trapped inside a square kill zone with nowhere to run and nowhere protected enough to hide.

The second and third mortar rounds hit the northernmost complex in the compound, causing serious damage and a few minor shrapnel wounds. The Annex defenders were no strangers to mortars—they had used them, and come up against them, in Afghanistan—and they tried to gauge the battery's location after each round was launched in order to direct fire against its crew; the terrorist mortar crew relied on a spotter, possibly hiding in the trees, who reported the point of impact of each round fired. Even with the Predator drone flying overhead, its images coming in crystal clear on the ROVER computer terminal that was being monitored by one of the JSOC operators who had come in from Tripoli, pinpointing the exact coordinates of the terrorist mortar crew was difficult. It was assessed that the mortar rounds were fired from between eight hundred and a thousand yards away. The operators also believed that the crew had done this before. The crew members must have been Libyan military veterans or veterans of the jihadist campaigns in Iraq, Afghanistan, Yemen, or Derna.

Without air support, and without artillery of their own, the Annex shooters were limited in what they could do against the mortar team itself; the mortar crew, it was gauged, had nestled itself behind a building south of the Fourth Ring Road, southeast of a large mosque at the roadway's junction, and out of view. The crew's spotter, though, would have to be in a high-ground position and would be easier to pinpoint and terminate. Without the spotter, the mortar crew would be blind, and its effectiveness would be seriously diminished.

Many of the February 17 personnel fled once the shooting started. Those who stayed simply hid under their vehicles, hoping not to become part of the collateral damage of the exchange of gun, rocket, and mortar fire. This should have been their battle. They received U.S. assistance and U.S. money. But when their mettle was tested and their loyalty needed, their true colors were exposed. "It should have come as no surprise to anyone concerning the February 17 Brigade," a Libyan senior intelligence official* commented in confidence. "The militia commander didn't send any reinforcements, because this would have hindered his interests. He [the commander] is widely despised in Libya."[3]

An orange glow began to appear in the east as daylight neared and Benghazi was awakening to the sounds of war. Inside the city's mosques—some quite large, and others spartan and small—muezzins were readying themselves to call the faithful to prayer. The terrorists required darkness to retain their tactical advantage, but the black cover of night was quickly evaporating.

---

*Identity withheld for security considerations.

The third mortar round landed approximately a hundred feet in front of the main building, which Doherty and Woods were using as their firing perch. Seconds later, a fourth round was fired, landing squarely on the roof where Woods was firing his Mk 46. The blast was lethal. Woods was killed instantly by the explosion. His body lay over his weapon, the barrel still red-hot from the course of fire he was throwing to the west. Glen Doherty rushed to reposition himself and tend to his mortally wounded friend, but then the fifth mortar round came crashing to the rooftop. The impact of the explosion shook the building and sent shrapnel into a wide field of destruction. When the smoke cleared, Glen Doherty was dead. He was killed instantly by the direct hit.

One of the agents* was climbing the ladder to the building's rooftop to support Woods and Doherty when the last two rounds hit. The round that killed Glen Doherty showered the DS agent with razor chunks and slivers of flesh-slicing shrapnel. One of the Annex's medics immediately stopped the bleeding from a gaping hole in the agent's thigh and quickly patched up gushing lacerations across his arms and chest. He had multiple fractures as well.

And then, once again, the terrorist fire ended as abruptly as it began. The deafening explosions of mortar fire and full-auto machine gun bursts were muted into a befuddling silence. The defenders looked around and scanned for targets. They looked at the damage, and from their vantage point above the ground they could see a blurred maze of lights marking the outline of a city skyline. The reality of their plight during the night that was surrendering to day was daunting. They should have all been killed. There was trepidation that more would die.

The shooters remained in their positions ready to absorb yet another attack. Images transmitted to ROVER from the Predator flying its invisible patrol indicated that the area around the Annex was still inundated with armed threats. But the sounds of trucks and heavy vehicles barreling toward the Annex were faintly heard coming in from the northeast; the rumbling engines became louder with each

---

*The identity of the agent is being concealed.

passing second. The terrorists sensed who the new reinforcements were, and they wanted nothing to do with the soldiers from Libyan Military Intelligence. The battle for Benghazi had come to an end.

The Libyan intelligence officer ordered to secure the American departure from the city wore neatly pressed camouflage fatigues and carried a sidearm in a leather holster worn on his hip. He didn't wear any rank; the spies never did. The officer saluted the base chief and then spoke to him and the interpreter in order to coordinate the evacuation. The language used was polite, and very respectful, but also very rushed. The Libyan was given explicit orders to safeguard the expeditious and immediate disappearance of the CIA presence from the Annex and to safeguard its passage straight to the tarmac and the awaiting private jet. There were to be no detours and no delays. It was in everyone's national interests to get the Americans out of the city as quickly as possible.

The Annex staff loaded their crates, Pelican cases, cardboard file holders, and technical equipment into the cargo holds and trunks of their vehicles. The Americans could not allow the Libyan personnel to touch the CIA material.

Thirty-two survivors boarded the vehicles for the ride to the airport. Three bodies were very respectfully loaded onto the rear of an SUV, in an emotionally charged moment for the agents involved. As the convoy readied itself to depart for the airport, the new day erupted with the first promises of glowing sunshine as a rhythmic cadence flowed from the distance rather than the rat-a-tat of gunfire that predominated for the past two and a half hours. These were sounds of peace; it was morning call to prayers.

27.

Aftermath

Hoda Abdel-Hamid did not think twice when her mobile phone rang after 2100 hours on September 11. The best calls in the Middle East always happened after dark. She had been sitting at a café in Istanbul, enjoying a dinner of famed Turkish kebabs, when the home office called. Specifically, the Qatari-based Al Jazeera news giant, the 24/7 news source for much of the Arab and, yes, Western worlds; even right-wing stalwarts like Fox TV routinely used Al Jazeera clips in their broadcasts to show their grasp of the Middle East. Though Al Jazeera has grown in recent years to become a global supplier of world-wide news, its strength has remained in its roots: the Middle East. The Egyptian-born Abdel-Hamid was something of an anomaly in the Arab world—a female war correspondent who, more often than not, was in front of a camera wearing body armor and a Fritz helmet while ducking artillery shells, snipers, and RPGs. She had covered conflicts throughout the Middle East and the Global War on Terror (in Iraq, Afghanistan, Kurdistan, Yemen, and the South Sudan, just to name a few) over the last few years, and her travels had taken her from the fighting between the Israel Defense Forces and Hamas, to revolutionary chaos in her native Egypt, and, of course, to the civil war in Libya. She was an award-winning journalist recognized for her reporting, as well as her courage under fire.

When the bullets began flying in Benghazi and the first SMS hints of an attack against the U.S. diplomatic post hit the Al Jazeera news desk in Doha, there was only one person whom producers wanted to send to Libya. Abdel-Hamid had a valid visa for Libya, after all, and having spent too many hours to count under fire in Benghazi alongside rebel forces during the civil war, she knew the lay of the land. As the GRS team began its battle at the Special Mission Compound, Abdel-Hamid was in her hotel room getting her got-to-catch-a-flight bag ready. As the battle came to an end at the Annex, Abdel-Hamid was fast-tracking a path through check-in at Istanbul's Atatürk International Airport so that she could prepare her notes in the business-class lounge. As the *Istikhbarat Askaria* motorcade rushed to Benghazi airport using both lanes of the airport highway, Abdel-Hamid was heading west from the airport on a secondary road, rushing to Western Fwayhat. She was going to be the first correspondent to see the destruction at the Special Mission Compound.

The initial feeds that Abdel-Hamid received from her sources concerning the attack were of murder, assassination, and absolute destruction. As day broke in Western Fwayhat, Abdel-Hamid approached the Special Mission Compound with her film crew. She found an abandoned outpost and an absolutely contaminated crime scene. She expected to find Libyan police swarming all over the location and the entire area cordoned off by militias aligned with the NTC and even military units. But she found local residents wandering curiously through the burned-out shells of the villa and the February 17 command center. She found dismay. Charlie-1 gate was wide open, and no yellow crime scene tape warned people to step back.

"What I found was really strange," Abdel-Hamid recalled. "The grounds, the lawn, the flowers, everything was neat and pristine, and there was only havoc around the four buildings. There wasn't any evidence of a lot of people having been there."[1] The grounds remained an oasis of sorts—a killing ground that did not reveal the signs of bloodshed it had witnessed. The stench of fires that had burned themselves out stifled the sweet perfume from the rows of guava fruit trees behind the villa. The shattered masonry, the bullet holes that punctured the walls around the complex, burned-out vehicles, and the deadly ambience of silence signaled that something quite awful had transpired here.

Considering that an hour-long exchange of gunfire had been waged on the grounds, there were very few shell casings to be found, leaving one to wonder if the perpetrators had tried to collect any evidence that one day could bring them to a federal courtroom inside the Southern District of New York (SDNY). The murder of an American official overseas is a violation of U.S. law, which gives the Department of Justice and the FBI extraterritorial investigative jurisdiction in crimes overseas. FBI New York is the office of origin, called "OO" in the FBI vernacular, for most international terrorism cases, and the SDNY becomes the federal court for prosecution. The FBI works hand in glove with DS and RSOs in most international terrorism cases. Ironically, DS agents or security protective specialists working for DS protect the FBI agents sent to hostile areas to investigate crimes. In most cases, the teams work well together, because DS agents open doors with the foreign police and security services.

One had to search for blood splatters in order to find where someone had been hit. The dead had been removed hours earlier. The looters had left a few hours before daybreak, eager to catch an hour or two of sleep before the sun's heat hit the city. They had taken much of what was of value and not nailed down. They spray-painted innocuous graffiti throughout the yellowish sand walls on all the buildings. Slogans such as "Unity in Numbers" were scrawled over walls pockmarked with 7.62 mm bullet holes and bloodied handprints. Cushions and what were once end tables floated in the pool.

The neighbors came out once morning arrived. They had stayed indoors for much of the night, terrified to be caught in the crossfire and wary of a militia or terrorist group using their homes for cover. Human shields often found themselves killed during the civil war, and hostage taking was common in the city, especially in a neighborhood where ransoms could be paid. Some of the neighborhood residents stood in silence, frozen by what had happened. There was promise in having the Americans in the neighborhood; they provided a sense of hope in a city where hope was becoming a commodity in short supply. And then some treated the attack with absolute insouciance; this was Benghazi after all. The women were out of sight, of course. It was still too dangerous for them to venture out.

Jamal al-Bishari,* who had leased his property to the U.S. State Department, was in a fit of rage. His property had been destroyed, the best tenant in the world—one who always paid on time and didn't make many demands—was gone, no doubt forever, and he—as well as Benghazi—had lost a dear friend.

As Abdel-Hamid and her crew walked the grounds, trying to re-create the night's terror, the absolute devastation to the site became shockingly apparent. The villa looked like the inside of a furnace. It was completely blackened by the fire, and shreds of burned paper, burned fabric, and burned furniture littered the floor. The marble floor was covered by a thick dusting of black. Desk drawers had been ransacked and tossed about. A copy of *New York* magazine, the August edition, was found on the floor, as were books and other personal effects; the dust jacket of Simon Sebag Montefiore's book on the history of Jerusalem was found trashed on the floor.[2] Suits, shirts, and ties were strewn about everywhere. The looters weren't interested in fine men's haberdashery. The destruction was complete and absolute.

Shockingly, and perhaps most tellingly, the attackers—or the looters—left behind a chilling memento in the bathroom of the safe haven where Chris Stevens's body was found. Someone had used his finger to scrawl the words "I AM Chris from The dead."[3]

The smaller villa was spared a fiery destruction, but it had been ransacked. MREs were thrown about everywhere, as were utensils from the kitchen, and drawers from the bedrooms. Official-looking documents were everywhere. Business cards, with golden embossed eagles, were tossed about as well. "I didn't touch anything," Abdel-Hamid remembered. "I didn't want to disrupt anything, even though

---

*Some accounts have identified this man as Ahmed Busheri, as well as Adel Ibrahim.

I knew that there had been a lot of people there before me and there were probably going to be a lot of people after me there as well."[4]

Hoda Abdel-Hamid remained in Benghazi for more than a week, attempting to piece together the true story of what happened on the night of September 11. Libyan militiamen were not eager to share their accounts. The Americans weren't returning.

28.

Home

Dr. Thomas Burke and his colleague from Massachusetts General arrived at Benghazi Medical Center in the morning. It wasn't safe for them to travel at night, and there was little that they could have done in any event. When they arrived, they found the midnight shift at the ER shattered by grief. Intelligence agents had already come and commandeered an ambulance.

It was deemed too dangerous for the Military Intelligence convoy to stop at Benghazi Medical Center to retrieve Ambassador Stevens's body. The officer in charge arranged for an ambulance to transport the remains to the military side of Benghazi airport. The Libyan NTC had urged the one military asset that it could trust to make sure the departure from Benghazi was without incident and with the utmost dignity and respect. The gunfire that followed the American presence throughout the night could not follow it to the tarmac.

Select personnel, and the severely wounded, were loaded onto the C-130. The aircraft took off at 0730 hours. The remaining CIA staffers, the DS agents, and the GRS personnel would head back to Tripoli on board another Libyan Air Force transport that the NTC had made available to the American government. R. was one of those who took the second Libyan Air Force flight; he needed to remain behind in order to positively identify the body of Ambassador Stevens. R.

unzipped the black heavy plastic body bag and identified Stevens, silently weeping, overcome by emotions. The sense of failure for losing his principal was overwhelming. In the world of dignitary protection, the greatest sin, you are taught, is to lose a principal.

At 0845, air traffic around Benghazi came to a halt as the aircraft taxied for takeoff. A dozen or so Americans were on board watching over the bodies of Chris Stevens, Sean Smith, Tyrone Woods, and Glen Doherty. The DS agents on board were numbed by the loss and silent in their sorrow. Their vacant stares were all that was needed to understand the hell they had just been through. The flight to Tripoli took all of an hour. For the men on board with the bodies of the fallen, it seemed to last forever. In addition to their loss, they were now in nothing less than retreat, not a desired end state for any warrior.

The flights from Benghazi were met by many of the staffers—DOD, DS, and CIA—from the Tripoli embassy. The U.S. embassy nurse triaged the arrival and tended to the agent who was blown off the ladder. In a perfect world, he would have been at the Shock Trauma Center at University of Maryland Medical Center. In Tripoli, the nurse *was* the shock trauma center. The injured were rushed to the hospital for emergency care, while the remainder were cared for, fed, and issued new clothes and documentation; many had had to leave their passports behind. It was imperative that the survivors from Benghazi be brought out of the country as soon as possible. Not only did all the personnel need to be debriefed, but there was always the concern that the Libyan government, bowing perhaps to internal pressure, would want to debrief or, possibly, prosecute the DS and CIA contractors for shooting Libyan citizens on Libyan soil. State Department agents involved in shootings are often urged to leave the country immediately after an event in order for the host government not to PNG, or deem them persona non grata, and declare their diplomatic status null and void.

The U.S. Air Force dispatched a behemoth C-17 Globemaster III transport jet to Tripoli to bring the Benghazi survivors, and much of the gear and material from the Annex, out of the country. Material from the U.S. embassy in Tripoli was also boxed and transported out. Nonessential staffers were ordered to leave as well. No one knew if the attack in Benghazi was but a first round in what would become open warfare on American diplomats, soldiers, and spies.

To augment security at the embassy, a fifty-man contingent of Fleet Antiterrorism Security Team (FAST) marines arrived in Tripoli on the morning of September 12. The marines were greeted by a shell-shocked embassy staff on the shores of Tripoli, bringing to full circle the Marine Corps hymn and the words "to the shores of Tripoli." Some cried, and others hugged the nineteen-year-old grunts; help had arrived, in the form of America's finest. Loaded for bear, the marines did what they do best: setting up sandbag emplacements, stringing concertina wire, and tactically positioning .50-caliber machine guns and squad-support M249s on the perimeter of the mission. There would be no Benghazi-like attack on Tripoli. The visual footprint echoed intent and projected American power.

AFRICOM also dispatched a special hospital transport, a modified C-130, to fly the wounded to Ramstein Air Base in Germany for recuperation and debriefing. A small army of specialists would await their arrival. CIA debriefing agents, DS special agents, and various other nameless faces from the intelligence community were eager to pick the brains of men who had fought the battle of their lives in a city and country that were all too familiar with no-holds-barred combat.

For the dead, for the DS agents, and for the CIA staffers, the actual battle for Benghazi was finally and truly over. The real battle about Benghazi, though, had only just begun.

Epilogue

0622 hours, September 14, 2012: Benghazi, Libya.

As daylight broke and the city of over one million inhabitants awoke to the morning calls to prayer, the American presence in their city, both official and otherwise, was gone. Though many Islamists cheered, the vacuum of diplomacy was an ominous sign to the majority of Benghazi's residents, who felt that the attack of September 11 was a shameful indication of the direction where the Arab Spring, for Libya at least, was heading. Christopher Stevens had urged that the United States invest its diplomacy in the eastern portion of the country. The return on the investment had been a bloody one. And on this day, it threatened to be bloodier still.

The citizens of Benghazi were already on edge, and they fully appreciated the bloody implications to their future. Salafist militias, proudly waving their black flags, patrolled portions of Benghazi in their cannon-carrying Toyota Hilux pickups in search of the rumored American Special Forces commandos who the mullahs promised were in the city in order to avenge the attacks. The militants prayed for American intervention. Martyrs and battles fed the jihadist call to arms, as did the idea that North Africa might become a new graveyard for the best of American intentions.

Later that morning, as a harbinger, Libyan authorities were forced to close the airspace over the Benghazi airport. Islamic militias, believing that CIA drones were flying over the city, haphazardly unleashed a furious antiaircraft barrage into the skies above. Tens of thousands of heavy machine gun and cannon rounds were launched at the mere thought that somewhere up above, the CIA had come calling; it is not known how many civilians were wounded or killed when what went up came crashing down to earth. "Two American drones flew over Benghazi last night with knowledge of the Libyan authorities," the deputy interior minister, Wanis al-Sharif, explained to the Reuters news agency.[1] Libyan authorities, of course, did not control Benghazi. They had no control of the city the night that Ambassador Stevens was murdered, and they had no control of Benghazi two days after the attack.

Virtually the entire northern half of the African continent was spiraling out of control. The sophisticated attack in Benghazi was a malignant symptom, following a brief period of remission, of a weakened and crippled al-Qaeda seeking new battlefields, new combatants, and new causes in the hope of remaining relevant at a point in history, eleven years after the September 11 attacks, when the world had grown weary of being at war. Al-Qaeda was reinventing itself. It was moving its base of operations from Afghanistan and Pakistan, and even from Arabia, to the new and fertile grounds of North Africa. All this coincided with the regional power vacuum that opened up as a result of the Arab Spring. It was a perfect storm of rage, violence, and Islamic fervor. With an endless supply of weapons, ammunition, armed militias, fatwas, and hungry stomachs and souls, Benghazi promised to be an opening salvo of a new jihad on the African continent. Two days after the attacks in Libya, another American embassy found itself in the crosshairs.

At noon on September 14, as antiaircraft cannons blasted away at pigeons and other unidentified flying objects in Benghazi, more than two thousand miles away in Khartoum, the capital of Sudan, riot police assembled outside the U.S. embassy bracing for a fiery storm. For days, from the pulpits of the city's mosques, clerics had called for a massive show of force to attack the American devil for the Internet film that had caused such outage and furor. The attack in Benghazi emboldened the furious, and it was a call to arms for the militantly opportunistic. The clerics, and the al-Qaeda emissaries, promised bloodshed.

The U.S. embassy in the Sudanese capital was a large compound that housed five separate buildings, including the chancery. The embassy, reportedly built to the Inman-recommended standards of force protection and setback distance, was in a remote southeast corner of town, west of the East Nile River. Unlike in Benghazi, in Khartoum the local police deployed outside the embassy in a show of force. The riot squad arrived in trucks, grotesquely camouflaged in specks of gray and blue, and police formed a human shield around the embassy's perimeter. By 1500 hours hundreds of protesters had gathered, to the northeast and northwest of the diplomatic compound, and they then converged at the main entrance. Some of the protesters carried placards and signs demanding "death to America"; others carried signs and bedsheet billboards lauding the success of the Benghazi operations. Some of the protesters wore black robes, covered themselves from head to toe, and carried the black flag of al-Qaeda. Others, inexplicably, stripped themselves naked in front of the bemused riot policemen.

Some of the protesters fell to their knees and positioned themselves toward Mecca for afternoon prayers. The riot police feared that this was like the blowing of a trumpet to signal a cavalry charge. They braced for a full-scale assault.

S.,* the RSO, and his staff of ARSOs and Marine Security Guards watched cautiously on surveillance cameras. They had already contacted the DS Command Center to provide it with a tense yet steady stream of situation reports. Incident response teams in Washington were preparing contingency plans just in case. The mood on the Beltway and inside the command center was already somber and very tense: this was the day that the remains of Ambassador Stevens, Sean Smith, Tyrone Woods, and Glen Doherty would be returned to the United States. A mournful event was being readied for later in the day at Andrews Air Force Base. President Barack Obama, Vice President Joe Biden, and Secretary of State Hillary Clinton would all be in

---

*Identity withheld for security concerns.

attendance. The command center agents, many old Middle Eastern hands who had seen the violence before, monitored the intelligence from Khartoum; they hoped that the protests would not escalate into another Benghazi. It was 0900 hours. Marine One, the helicopters flown by the HMX-1 Nighthawk Squadron for use by the president, would soon be en route to Andrews. The VP would arrive in a separate motorcade, for security reasons, under the watchful eyes of the U.S. Secret Service's Vice Presidential Protection Detail. Secretary of State Clinton would motorcade it to Andrews AFB in an armored convoy protected by DS agents from the SD, the Secretary's Detail.

Shortly after 1600 hours, the protesters and the police clashed in Khartoum; it quickly erupted into a free-for-all. The police used truncheons and tear gas. When those measures failed, the police simply used their vehicles as people movers. Two protesters were killed when a police truck ran them over. By 1700 hours, the demonstration had turned into a full-scale riot. The protesters began throwing incendiary devices at police, and they torched police trucks; they overwhelmed the riot police with sticks, gardening tools, and rocks; the policemen, underpaid and outnumbered, simply fled back into the center of town. The embassy was on its own.

There were now more than five hundred protesters surrounding the embassy. They progressed around the embassy grounds with moves choreographed to overwhelm the compound's defenses and the defenders inside the fortified perimeter. In precise military-style probing actions, the protesters scaled a row of outer fences that controlled access to the compound and attempted to breach the embassy's outer defenses. The embassy was now under attack. According to reports, some of the attackers were non-Sudanese—visitors from country's northern neighbor or the Arabian Peninsula—and there was also a "clean skin," a white European or American, mysteriously moving about with parts of his face concealed by a keffiyeh scarf.

Inside the embassy, the duck-and-cover alarm sounded. S., the RSO, and his team of ARSOs donned body armor and grabbed their sidearms; each had a job to do, a responsibility and sector to look after. S. and the MSG Gunny coordinated the tactical placement of security personnel. The RSO was in constant communication with the DS Command Center; the Gunny was on an unbreakable radio loop with his men in the embassy. The RSO ordered Joseph D. Stafford III, the chargé d'affaires, and the deputy chief of mission to hunker down; they were in their offices, along with the political officer, calling contacts inside the Sudanese government to send reinforcements and to end the siege. The RSO was juggling several cell phones, talking to the DS Command Center on one and seeking aid from the head of the Sudanese preventive security intelligence service on his local telephone. It was organized chaos that had been rehearsed to perfection. The embassy had been on heightened alert after Benghazi, bracing for some sort of storm or attack.

As the RSO scrambled to make sure the staffers and inside perimeter of the embassy were secure, S. and the MSGs went into full RESPONSE mode. They donned their combat kits and grabbed their M4s and Remington 870 12-gauge shotguns. Some were sent to tactical positions to provide the RSO with eyes-on intelligence; surveillance cameras at several access points had been knocked out by the protesters.

The mob tried to gain access at two access-control points—entry vestibules that had layers of steel and transparent armor embedded in the architecture to keep threats out, whether it was an explosive parcel or a mob of protesters armed with sledgehammers. FSNs manned these access points. They were the first layer of security that safeguarded the embassy. But they weren't a match for the throng of men pounding the glass until it was compromised. By the time the riot gained strength and speed, like a tornado cutting a path of destruction, the police had fled. The rioters set fire to their vehicles and then used the flaming hunks of steel as battering rams to try to punch a hole in the outer walls. Over the next few hours, several nonessential locations on the outer wall were compromised, and the protesters, now officially deemed attackers, tried to set fire to the compound. According to AFP Khartoum, the MSGs fired warning shots from their rooftop perches once the protesters began to successfully puncture the outer perimeter to the compound.[2]

Some of the protesters had jerry cans filled with gasoline. They poured the gasoline onto the doors and walls and set the highly flammable puddles alight. Eerily, a black Toyota Hilux pickup was set on fire near the front entrance of the embassy, as the attack took on a very Benghazi appearance. But the outer walls of the embassy held. The protesters would be stymied in their attempts to replicate the murderous success of Benghazi two days earlier. Tired, frustrated, and realizing that it was time to call it a day, the protesters simply grabbed their signs, prayer rugs, garden tools, and jerry cans and went home. The outer access-control booths looked as if they had withstood an artillery barrage. The outer walls were aflame, and the police trucks and even a few embassy vehicles burned wildly in the darkening skies. The U.S. embassy in Khartoum had been spared. The upgraded physical security standards kept the mob from taking the embassy.* It was 1900 hours in Khartoum.

The following day, the government in Khartoum rejected a request by the U.S. government to send a platoon of FAST marines to the country in order to bolster security at the embassy.[3] Even inside the smoky choke of terror, the niceties of diplomacy overruled necessity. The embassy's contingent of MSGs would have to suffice for possible future attacks.

As the acrid black smoke from the embassy fire darkened the skies over Khartoum, a blanket of light bathed the gray tarmac at Andrews Air Force Base, located five miles east of the seat of power in Washington, D.C., in the plush expanses of Prince George's County, Maryland; the sunshine falsely presented a hopeful sense of optimism on a day that was purely somber. Andrews Air Force Base—or Joint Base Andrews, as the sprawling facility is known—is home to several U.S. Air Force transport wings and, as headquarters for the Eighty-ninth Airlift Wing and the Air Mobility Command, is the launch for Air Force One, the two highly customized Boeing 747-200Bs that, because of their in-flight refueling capabilities, have unlimited range and take the president wherever he needs to travel. Andrews has been the parade ground

---

*The British and German embassies in Khartoum were also attacked that day. The U.S. embassy sustained the greatest damage and only reopened for full business on March 25, 2013.

for foreign leaders visiting the United States, with all the pomp and ceremony such state visits entail, and it has hosted heartwarming reunions and homecomings, such as the return of POWs from Vietnam and the return of the American hostages from Iran. Andrews has also been the first touch on American soil, on the final journey home, for those American soldiers and diplomats who have been killed on distant shores in some of the most horrific terrorist attacks of modern times. The remains of the American intelligence community killed when the U.S. embassy in Beirut was obliterated by a Hezbollah car bomb in 1983 were first brought to Andrews in a somber ceremony of honor and remembrance. The ten Americans killed in August 1998 in the simultaneous truck bombings of the U.S. embassies in Nairobi, Kenya, and Dar es Salaam, Tanzania, were respectfully brought back to American shores by way of Andrews. And on September 14, 2012, the four Americans killed in Benghazi, Libya, arrived at Joint Base Andrews for what the air force calls the dignified transfer of remains.

The next of kin had been told of the deaths of their loved ones by phone. Charles Woods, Tyrone Woods's father, received the call early in the morning the day before at his home in Hawaii. "It was real early in the morning," Mr. Woods remembered, "and a female voice said that she was calling from the government and that she was calling to inform me that Ty had been killed." There was little explanation offered as to the details of Ty's death, just straightforward information of what, when, and where. "I knew never to pry into Ty's work," his father recalled. "I knew better than to ask him where he was going or what he was doing. I used to worry about Ty a lot when he was on active duty, but I never prayed. When he took this job and went to the Middle East, I prayed for him." The Woods family, especially his sister, prayed regularly for him. They would now watch a U.S. military honor guard, their brass polished and their uniforms pressed perfectly, carry his flag-draped coffin to the vast expanses of a hangar where the dignitaries would speak.

The families were flown to Washington, D.C., and sheltered in a hotel in Georgetown, far from prying eyes or outside threats. "We were told that this hotel was the safest place to be in Washington, D.C.," Mr. Woods stated.[4] The following day, the families were ushered on an air force bus to Joint Base Andrews and directed to a large room, plain and isolated, that was well lit and contained several banks of sofas, each separate from the other, where families could assemble and meet the president and the nation's leaders. Each of the officials would have private time with each of the bereaved families to pay his or her respects. The notes played in one last rehearsal by the USAF band were muffled by the earth-rumbling roars fired from Pratt and Whitney F117-PW-100 turbofan engines lifting the gargantuan C-17 Globemasters to the skies.

Vice President Joe Biden was the first person to greet the families. Undeterred by the solemn mood of the event, the vice president, Charles Woods recalled, lived up to his folksy blue-collar image, talking of Woods's heroism and amazing courage.

Secretary of State Hillary Clinton was next to meet with the Woods family. The events of the previous forty-eight hours had physically drained the sixty-four-year-old secretary of state. "She looked tired," Mr. Woods said. "The events had apparently taken their toll on her."[5]

President Barack Obama, in addressing the solemn crowd at the hangar, offered his sorrow-filled gratitude to each of the men who perished that fateful night in Benghazi. He said:

> Scripture teaches us "Greater love hath no man than this, that a man lay down his life for his friends." Glen Doherty never shied from adventure. He believed that, in his life, he could make a difference—a calling he fulfilled as a Navy SEAL. He served with distinction in Iraq and worked in Afghanistan. And there, in Benghazi, as he tended to others, he laid down his life, loyal as always, protecting his friends. Today, Glen is home.
>
> Tyrone Woods devoted twenty years of his life to the SEALs—the consummate "quiet professional." At the Salty Frog Bar, they might not have known, but "Rone" also served in Iraq and Afghanistan. And there, in Benghazi, he was far from Dorothy and Tyrone Jr., Hunter and little Kai. And he laid down his life, as he would have for them, protecting his friends. And today, Rone is home.
>
> Sean Smith, it seems, lived to serve—first in the Air Force, then, with you at the State Department. He knew the perils of this calling

from his time in Baghdad. And there, in Benghazi, far from home, he surely thought of Heather and Samantha and Nathan. And he laid down his life in service to us all. Today, Sean is home.

Chris Stevens was everything America could want in an ambassador, as the whole country has come to see—how he first went to the region as a young man in the Peace Corps, how during the revolution, he arrived in Libya on that cargo ship, how he believed in Libya and its people and how they loved him back. And there, in Benghazi, he laid down his life for his friends—Libyan and American—and for us all. Today, Chris is home.

Four Americans, four patriots—they loved this country and they chose to serve it, and served it well. They had a mission and they believed in it. They knew the danger and they accepted it. They didn't simply embrace the American ideal, they lived it. They embodied it— the courage, the hope and, yes, the idealism, that fundamental American belief that we can leave this world a little better than before. That's who they were and that's who we are. And if we want to truly honor their memory, that's who we must always be.[6]

In closing his remarks, knowing full well that the event was coordinated by the U.S. Department of State *for* the Department of State, President Obama made it clear that the United States would not be deterred from its global mission as a result of Benghazi. He stated, "That's the message these four patriots sent. That's the message that each of you sends every day—civilians, military—to people in every corner of the world, that America is a friend, and that we care not just about our own country, not just about our own interests, but about theirs; that even as voices of suspicion and mistrust seek to divide countries and cultures from one another, the United States of America will never retreat from the world. We will never stop working for the dignity and freedom that every person deserves, whatever their creed, whatever their faith." President Obama continued, "To you— their families and colleagues—to all Americans, know this: Their sacrifice will never be forgotten. We will bring to justice those who took them from us. We will stand fast against the violence on our diplomatic missions. We will continue to do everything in our power to protect

Americans serving overseas, whether that means increasing security at our diplomatic posts, working with host countries, which have an obligation to provide security, and making it clear that justice will come to those who harm Americans."[7]

Following the solemn movement of remains and the eulogies rendered, the bodies of the four Americans killed that night in Benghazi were quietly taken by the FBI for forensic autopsies.[8] The tedious and procedural work of a criminal death had just begun. The bodies were evidence of a crime. There was every intention to bring the perpetrators—somehow and someday—to justice.

The remains were later released to their families for burial.

Lost in the political eye gouging that would eventually erupt over Benghazi was something that Secretary of State Clinton said in her remarks at the dignified transfer of remains. "There will be more difficult days ahead," the secretary stated, "but it is important that we don't lose sight of the fundamental fact that America must keep leading the world."

The linchpin of America's ability to lead the world, *from* around the world, even in locations and war zones where the intelligence community drives the diplomatic engine, is the courage, dedication, and sacrifice of the men and women of the Diplomatic Security Service who find themselves in harm's way, driving a follow car or maintaining security programs at fortresslike embassies, and those that are not fortresses, in locations that few Americans would be able to locate on a map. American diplomatic interests—and the realities of day-to-day expeditionary diplomacy—could never be protected if this intrepid force of federal agents were not on post and on guard. The true story of the Benghazi attack is not one of failure or cover-up. The true story of Benghazi is that men and women volunteer to place themselves between a bullet or a bomb and America's diplomats and interests inside the crosshairs, inside the most dangerous and volatile locations in the world. In that sense the story of the attack was nothing new at all.

On the morning of Thursday, January 31, 2013, on her last day in office, Secretary of State Clinton summoned four of the five DS agents who were in Benghazi that night to her office. The seventh floor at Main State, the bastion of decision making, was quiet and empty; it was a far cry from the usual high-octane activity that followed such an energetic secretary of state. Mainly, staffers who weren't remaining behind at Foggy Bottom were in their offices and cubicles, loading personal items into Staples storage boxes. The four agents were called to Foggy Bottom for a low-key presentation of the U.S. Department of State's Award for Heroism. The award is presented to State Department and USAID personnel, as well as Marine Security guards, assigned to diplomatic and consular posts in recognition of acts of courage and outstanding performance while under the threat of physical attack and at a risk to one's personal safety. Each of the four men was being decorated for his acts of heroism and self-sacrifice in Benghazi that fateful night. One of the agents had already returned to the Middle East following the attack to continue his assignment, not wanting the attack to be something that scarred his career as well as his mind. He traveled from the Middle East to receive his commendation. He returned to his post after the ceremony to face his demons. Only the agents and senior DS leadership attended the presentation.

The press was often invited to cover these types of award ceremonies, though DS agents being decorated for valor was not usually the breaking-news item that an editor or a program director felt was worth the time and cost of a reporter's carfare and the parking fees for a camera crew. DS wasn't news that Main State often promoted. In any event, it didn't matter as far as this incident was concerned. The press was never informed about this ceremony, though the room wouldn't have been large enough to accommodate all the journalists and cameras that would have rushed to cover the event or any event concerning Benghazi. They wouldn't have been allowed in the building, regardless. In keeping with the agents' adamant requests to remain anonymous, the press was never invited.

The following day, in perhaps his first official act as the new secretary of state, John Kerry traveled to the Walter Reed Army Medical

Center in Washington, D.C. In a display of great reverence and respect to a combatant wounded in action, Kerry presented the agent severely injured in the attacks on the Special Mission Compound and the Annex with his Award for Heroism. The ceremony was low-key and personal. His visit resonated loudly through the rank and file; the agents were grateful for his show of compassion and kindness. It was unprecedented for the secretary of state to make such a gesture, and it was important for DS agents everywhere to see. His visit was without fanfare and without any leak to the media. The new man on deck realized that the world was only going to get more dangerous and that a lot would be asked of them. It was important that the agents in the field, and those at the far-flung outposts, see that their boss had their backs.

As the special agents on the Secretary's Detail stood outside their fellow agent's hospital room, Secretary Kerry, who himself was no stranger to combat, talked face-to-face with the wounded hero, to hear for himself the story of death and determination under fire that night in Benghazi.

Glossary

AFRICOM:	U.S. Military's Africa Command
AK-47:	Soviet-produced select-fire gas-operated 7.62×39 mm assault rifle developed by Mikhail Kalashnikov in 1947. Robust, easy to operate, and ever reliable, the AK-47 is one of the most widely proliferated weapons in history and is the favorite of terrorists and third-world armies.
ARSO:	Assistant Regional Security Officer
ATA:	Antiterrorism Assistance
CIA:	Central Intelligence Agency
DCM:	Deputy Chief of Mission
DOD:	Department of Defense
DS:	Bureau of Diplomatic Security and term for Diplomatic Security Service
DS/CC:	DS Command Center
DSS:	Diplomatic Security Service
EAC:	Benghazi Emergency Action Committee (U.S. State Department)
FAST:	U.S. Marine Corps Fleet Antiterrorism Security Team
FAV:	fully armored vehicle
FBI:	Federal Bureau of Investigation
FEBRUARY 17:	February 17 Martyrs Brigade (a local Benghazi militia)

FE/BR:	Forced-entry/blast-resistant
FSN:	Foreign Service national
FSNI:	Foreign Service National Investigator
GRS:	CIA's Global Response Staff; contracted dignitary protection operators
ICRC:	International Committee of the Red Cross
IED:	Improvised Explosive Device
IMO:	Information Management Officer
JSOC:	U.S. DOD Joint Special Operations Command
MANPAD:	Man-Portable Air-Defense Systems (shoulder-fired antiaircraft missiles)
M4:	the ruggedized and tactically modular shorter and lighter version of the U.S. M16A2 5.56 mm assault rifle
MSD:	Diplomatic Security Service Mobile Security Deployment global tactical team
MSG:	Marine Security Guard
NGO:	nongovernment organization
NTC:	National Transitional Council
PKM:	Soviet- (and Russian-) produced 7.62 × 54 mm squad-support light machine gun
QRF:	Quick Reaction Force
RPG:	Soviet- (and Russian-) produced shoulder-fired antitank grenade
RSO:	Regional Security Officer
SCIF:	Sensitive Compartmented Information Facility
SCORPION:	the most skilled and veteran CIA GRS contractors*
SEO:	security engineering officer
SSC:	Supreme Security Committee (a coalition of individual and divergently minded Libyan militias)

---

*The true acronym is protected for operational security purposes.

SST:	Site Security Team
SY:	Office of Security
TCCC:	Tactical Combat Casualty Care training
TDY:	Temporary Duty assignment
TOC:	Tactical Operations Center
USSOCOM:	U.S. Special Operations Command
VBIED:	Vehicle-Borne Improvised Explosive Device

Acknowledgments

They didn't know it at the time, but the paths of Fred Burton and Samuel M. Katz would begin to intersect in February 1995.

Burton, deputy chief of the Counterterrorism Division at the Diplomatic Security Service, had just bucked State Department protocol in facilitating the arrest of Ramzi Yousef, the mastermind of the 1993 World Trade Center bombing and a terrorist genius who was in the execution stage of one of the most grandiose terrorist plots in history—the destruction of a dozen airliners over the Pacific, killing four thousand people in the process, and the assassinations of both Pope John Paul II and President Bill Clinton in the Philippines. Burton had learned from the two ARSOs in Islamabad that Yousef was in town finalizing details of his heinous plot, and the DS agents assigned to the embassy were poised to seize him; the U.S. State Department Rewards for Justice Program had issued a $2 million reward for Yousef, and he topped the FBI's Most Wanted list. Previously, when the DS agents in country were close to capturing Yousef, State Department protocol of notifying the Pakistani government led to Yousef's being mysteriously tipped off; he subsequently escaped. Burton was not going to let that happen. A lucky blizzard crippled the D.C. area, and Burton found himself the only person able to get to work the morning the agents sent a cable regarding Yousef's whereabouts. It happened to be a fateful storm. All the agents needed was a green light from HQ to proceed, along with Pakistani internal security forces, and snatch Yousef. Burton thought of the higher purpose over the niceties of bureaucracy and gave them the authorization to move.

The two DS agents in Islamabad spearheaded the arrest, and Yousef was brought to justice. Burton's DS career, though, was over.

Katz was writing a book about the NYPD's Emergency Service Unit (ESU) in February 1995, when on a serendipitous four-to-twelve shift he found himself witnessing history while riding along with a unit lieutenant who had been summoned to respond—along with a force of some twelve ESU cops—to the South Street heliport to pick up a package from Pakistan. That package was Ramzi Yousef, being returned to the United States, to be arraigned at 26 Federal Plaza. A few months later, a member of the NYPD Emergency Service Unit whom Katz had befriended while researching his book called him to say, "Your next book should be on DS." When Katz asked why anyone would want to write a book about the Department of Sanitation, the police officer used some colorful language and then said, "Diplomatic Security!" The ESU officer went on to tell Katz that it was DS that had captured Ramzi Yousef in Pakistan and that no one knew its story. After a few meetings with some of the more colorful DS agents of that period, Katz began looking at how he could tell that story. The DS story would soon be told in articles, books, and documentaries. That journey, though, began in June 1996 when Katz met Burton at a mini UN General Assembly in New York City before spending time with the first of the many DS protective details he would have the chance to experience. Burton and Katz spoke at length when they first met and became instant friends.

There are a few people whom Fred Burton and Samuel M. Katz would like to thank collectively. We would like to offer our most sincere gratitude to our agent, James D. Hornfischer, for his vision, guidance, and support in realizing this project with us. Jim has been a good friend during this process and a good teacher. We are both grateful to him. We would also like to thank our editor at St. Martin's Press, Marc Resnick. It has been an honor and a privilege to work with Marc, and we are both incredibly fortunate to have had such a unique and enjoyable experience.

We both owe a tremendous amount of thanks to Rami El Obeidi, a heroic and patriotic Libyan. We would like to thank Dan Meehan, and Al Golacinski, two very unique and talented SY and DS agents, and Greg Bujac, former DS director. We would also like to thank Charles Woods, father of Tyrone Woods, for giving of himself, and we would like to thank the former comrade of Glen Doherty's in the U.S. Navy SEALs Clint Bruce. Bruce founded Carry the Load (www.carrytheload.org), which is a nonprofit organization helping people celebrate a meaningful Memorial Day by partnering with communities to hold local events and hosting a cross-country relay to honor veterans and active-duty service members, law enforcement officers, firefighters, and their families.

We would also like to thank Steve Bray, retired RSO/DS agent, for his firsthand insight on the attack of the U.S. embassy in Saigon, and the family of the SY agent Jack Herse, murdered in Rosslyn, Virginia. A special note of thanks, as well, to former RSO/DS SAIC Pat O'Hanlon for shedding light on the Herse murder. We'd also like to thank former CIA and State Department officer Larry Johnson.

The authors would like to thank Dr. Dustin Tauferner, an American hero, for his life-saving efforts on the battlefield. We would also like to thank Mike Janke, former U.S. Navy SEAL, bestselling author, and CEO and cofounder of Silent Circle (www .silentcircle.com). We would like to thank Jamie Smith, a true American patriot and hero, who provided incredible assistance for the book. His forthcoming book about the gray world of counter-terrorism missions will be an exciting and eye-opening read. We would also like to offer our heartfelt thanks to the Glen Doherty Memorial Foundation, a charitable organization that honors Glen's life by helping others by paying it forward, for their support and assistance; the foundation's Web site is http://www.glendohertyfoun dation.org.

We would like to offer our special thanks to Congressman Michael McCaul (R-Texas).

Of course a book of this nature—especially one concerning sensitive information and about what has become so controversial and polarizing a topic—would not have been possible were it not for some amazing contacts and some very close friends in government and in the security and intelligence communities. These men and women gave us their confidence, their insight, a recollection of events, and their stewardship. They asked very little of us other than that we keep their identities a secret. Some are still working in their capacities, and being quoted in a book does not coexist with the pursuit of their long-term career aspirations and covert existences. It is important, though, that they know how grateful we both are.

And, of course, there are individual thanks to be made by each of us.

I would like to thank Stratfor's Dr. George and Meredith Friedman, Shea Morenz, Tom Prate, Aaron Kozmetsky, Scott Stewart, Kyle Rhodes and the multimedia department, Anya Alfano, Korena Zucha, Ben Sledge, for his wonderful graphics, and Stratfor's research department.

I would also like to thank my children, Jimmy, Katie, and Maddie, for their unwavering love and support. Finally, to my wife, Sharon, I've been truly blessed to have you beside me and thank you for your endless support and love.

—Fred Burton

I would like to thank Tommy Gallagher and Vincent O. Martinez III, the two men who introduced me to DS and two of the best and most loyal friends anywhere. I would like to thank the real-life DS "Dirty Harry" Scot "Doc" Folensbee, a man whose life reads more like James Bond's than a federal agent's and someone who has taught me an awful lot about personal courage.

I would like to thank Dr. Thomas Burke of Massachusetts General for his time and generous insight, as well as for his service; one's life seems "light" when it is compared with that of someone who has traveled to the most dangerous spots on the planet to render aid and medical assistance to the most needy. I would like to thank Al Jazeera's Hoda Abdel-Hamid for her friendship, kindness, and undeserved generosity. I would also like to thank my good friend Mohammed Najib for his invaluable Arabic assistance.

I would like to thank my three children for the inspiration, joy, and pride they give me. Last, but certainly not least, I wish to thank my wife, Sigi—a woman who has given me the gift of love and who has made my life truly worth living.

—Samuel M. Katz

We are big supporters of the DSS and its agents and the families they sometimes leave behind. The Diplomatic Security Foundation (DSF.) is a 501c(3) charitable nonprofit, that provides timely financial support and charitable contributions to members of the U.S. Department of State's Diplomatic Security Service, security professionals, and other colleagues in the law enforcement and foreign affairs communities. For more information on how to support this wonderful organization, please visit : http://www.dsfoundation.org/.

Notes

PROLOGUE: THE ONCOMING STORM

1. Interview, January 30, 2013.
2. As per the U.K. Foreign Office, March 15, 2013.
3. Lieutenant Colonel (U.S. Army) Andrew Wood, in testimony before the U.S. Congressional Oversight Committee, Washington, D.C., October 10, 2012.
4. Huma Khan, "Benghazi Doctor: Gadhafi Using Foreign Mercenaries to Quell Protests," ABC News, February 22, 2011.
5. Interview, August 6, 2012, posted on UN Web site (UNSMIL).
6. Michel Cousins, "Tunisian Consulate in Benghazi Attacked," *Libya Herald*, June 18, 2012.
7. Michel Cousins, "Terrorists Strike in Misrata," *Libya Herald*, August 5, 2012.
8. James Risen, Mark Mazzetti, and Michael S. Schmidt, "U.S.-Approved Arms for Libyan Rebels Fell into Jihadis' Hands," *The New York Times*, December 5, 2012.
9. Interview, March 3, 2013.

1: THE LIBYAN

1. Sami Yousafzai and Ron Moreau, "Killed by a Drone Strike, Top al Qaeda Recruiter Abu Yahya al-Libi Will Be Hard to Replace," *The Daily Beast*, June 6, 2012.
2. Michael Moss and Souad Mekhennet, "Rising Leader for Next Phase of Al Qaeda's War," *The New York Times*, April 4, 2008.

2: THE GLOBAL PROTECTORS IN A WORLD AT WAR

1. John Pimlott, "The Tet Offensive," in *Vietnam: The Decisive Battles* (New York: Macmillan, 1990), 128.
2. June 2012 e-mail exchanges with retired SY/DS agent Steve Bray.
3. June 16, 2012, e-mail from retired SY/DS agent Steve Bray.
4. Interview, February 17, 2013.
5. http://www.state.gov/m/ds/terrorism/c8583.htm.

3: 9.11.12: A FIERY MORNING IN THE ARAB SPRING

1. Billy Hallowell, "What Does the Film Show? This Is the Anti-Muhammed Movie That Sparked Deadly Islamist Protests in Egypt and Libya Yesterday," *The Blaze*, September 12, 2012.
2. Roee Nahmias, "Egypt to Try Embassy Rioters," *Jerusalem Post*, September 10, 2011.
3. Cameron W. Barr, "A Day of Terror Recalled: 1979 Embassy Siege in Islamabad Still Haunts Survivors," *The Washington Post*, November 27, 2004.
4. http://www.state.gov/m/ds/rls/50458.htm.

4: LIBYA

1. Fred Burton, *Ghost: Confessions of a Counterterrorist Agent* (New York: Random House, 2008).
2. http://www.odmp.org/officer/10093-special-agent-daniel-emmett-ocon nor; and http://www.odmp.org/officer/7906-special-agent-ronald -albert-lariviere.
3. Steven Erlanger, "A U.S. Envoy Who Plunged into Arab Life," *The New York Times*, September 15, 2012.
4. Ibid.
5. Mario Montoya, "Mission to a Revolution," U.S. Department of State, December 2011, 20.

5: SPECIAL MISSION BENGHAZI

1. http://www.aljazeera.com/news/africa/2011/06/201161214758950926 .html.
2. See Montoya, "Mission to a Revolution," 20.

3. http://www.state.gov/m/ds/rls/c31108.htm (photo 232) and interview with local sources in Benghazi.
4. Confidential source contact with authors, February 6, 2013.
5. Interview, February 17, 2013.
6. Garance Franke-Ruta, "The Welsh Security Contractor Behind America's Benghazi Consulate Guards," *Atlantic*, October 18, 2012.
7. Damien McElroy, Richard Spencer, and Raf Sanchez, "British Firm Secured Benghazi Consulate Contract with Little Experience," *Telegraph*, October 14, 2012.

6: THE SPECIAL AGENTS

1. Tabassum Zakaria, "Former Envoy Pickering on Problems at Benghazi Mission," Reuters, February 24, 2013.
2. Interview, March 6, 2013.
3. Ibid.
4. Ibid.
5. http://oversight.house.gov/wp-content/uploads/2012/10/DEI-to-BHO-10-19-2012-attachments.pdf.
6. Accountability Review Board into the Benghazi Terrorist Attacks of September 11, 2012.
7. Interview, February 8, 2013, Virginia.
8. Ibid.

7: LIFE IN CRITICAL THREAT

1. U.S. Accountability Office, *Diplomatic Security's Recent Growth Warrants Strategic Review*, GAO-10-156, November 2009, 53.
2. Hind Turki, "Accidental Death of Libyan at US Embassy in Tripoli," *The Tripoli Post*, September 8, 2012.
3. For the discussion of physical security arrangements, protocols, and shortcomings, see United States Senate Committee on Homeland Security And Governmental Affairs, *Flashing Red: A Special Report On The Terrorist Attack At Benghazi* by Senator Joseph I. Lieberman (chairman) and Senator Susan M. Collins (ranking member), December 30, 2012, pg 14–18.

4. Interview, February 1, 2013.
5. Alyssa Raymond, "Diplomatic Security Training Center," Winchester 3 News, February 27, 2013.
6. Interview, February 22, 2013.
7. Joseph Lieberman and Susan Collins, *Flashing Red: A Special Report on the Terrorist Attack at Benghazi*, U.S. Senate Committee on Homeland Security and Government Affairs, December 30, 2012.

8: FROM WHEELS DOWN TO LIGHTS-OUT

1. Interview, February 17, 2013. The identity of the intelligence official is concealed for the protection of himself and his family.

9: THE COOL OF NIGHT

1. Interview, February 17, 2013, Washington State.
2. Steven Sotloff, "The Other 9/11: Libyan Guards Recount What Happened in Benghazi," *Time*, October 21, 2012.
3. Interview, January 30, 2013.

10: ATTACK! ATTACK!

1. Jamie Doward, "How Cigarette Smuggling Fuels Africa's Islamic Violence," *Observer*, January 26, 2013.

11: THE ANNEX

1. Interview, March 1, 2013.
2. Interview, February 15, 2013.
3. Interview, February 13, 2013.
4. Greg Miller and Julie Tate, "CIA's Global Response Staff Emerging from Shadows After Incidents in Libya and Pakistan," *The Washington Post*, December 26, 2012.
5. Ibid.
6. Ibid.
7. Interview, January 15, 2013, Honolulu.

8. Ibid.
9. See Interview, Charles Woods, January 15, 2013.

12: OVERRUN

1. Interview, February 18, 2013.
2. May 8, 2013, testimony of Gregory Hicks before the House Oversight Committee (Benghazi: Exposing Failure and Recognizing Courage).
3. Jason Chaffetz, "Ambassador Stevens Called for Help During Benghazi Attack," *The Blaze*, November 1, 2012.
4. Interview, February 28, 2013.
5. Eli Lake, "Exclusive: Libya Cable Detailed Threats," *The Daily Beast*, October 8, 2012.
6. McElroy, Spencer, and Sanchez, "British Firm Secured Benghazi Consulate Contract with Little Experience."
7. Paul Schemm and Maggie Michael, "Libyan Witnesses Recount Organized Benghazi Attack," Associated Press, October 27, 2012.
8. Shashank Bengali, "Libyan Guards Speak Out on Attack That Killed U.S. Ambassador," *Los Angeles Times*, October 13, 2012.
9. Kevin Peraina, "Destination Martyrdom," *The Daily Beast/Newsweek*, April 19, 2008.
10. As per a broadcast (November 1, 2012) from the newswoman Jenan Moussa, on Al-Aan TV (Dubai, United Arab Emirates).
11. Interview, January 31, 2013.
12. Interview, February 27, 2013.
13. See Raymond, "Diplomatic Security Training Center."
14. Interview, February 28, 2013.

13: NOTIFICATIONS

1. Interview, February 27, 2013.
2. See Senator Joseph I. Lieberman (chairman) and Senator Susan M. Collins (ranking member), *Flashing Red: A Special Report On The Terrorist Attack At Benghazi*, United States Senate Committee On Homeland Security And Governmental Affairs, December 30, 2012, p. 4.

3. Jim Garamone, "Little Describes Pentagon's Benghazi Decision Process," U.S. Department of Defense American Forces Press Service, November 12, 2012.
4. Michael Wood, "Spy Fiction, Spy Fact," *The New York Times*, January 6, 1980.

14: THE FIRES OF THE MARTYRS

1. Interview, January 31, 2013.
2. Interview, February 28, 2013.
3. First-person account of the June 5, 1967, mob siege of the then U.S. consulate in Benghazi, as published in the findings of the Accountability Review Board report that was convened concerning the September 11, 2012, attacks against U.S. facilities and diplomatic personnel in Benghazi.

15: END OF SIEGE

1. Confidential interview, March 15, 2013.

16: DIPLOMATIC POUCH

1. Tabassum Zakaria and Susan Cornwell, "Washington Rejected U.S. Embassy Request for Plane in Libya," Reuters, October 5, 2012.
2. Eric Schmidt, "C.I.A. Played Major Role Fighting Militants in Libya Attack," *The New York Times*, November 1, 2012.
3. Interview, January 30, 2013.
4. As per www.glendohertyfoundation.org, a charity set up in memory of the former U.S. Navy SEAL Glen Doherty.
5. Interview, January 16, 2013.

19: CONTACT

1. Glen Doherty and Brandon Webb, *Navy SEAL Sniper: An Intimate Look at the Sniper of the 21st Century* (New York: Skyhorse, 2013).

20: BREAKOUT

1. Chris Stephen, "The U.S. Consulate Attack: The Facts, the Questions," *Libya Herald*, October 7, 2012.

22: THE ANONYMOUS TARGET

1. Interview, March 13, 2013.
2. ROVERS had been used in Benghazi before, as per Giles Ebbutt, in his article "JTAC ROVER," RUSI Defense Systems, Summer 2012, 53, and indication that the system was used by the GRS operators in Benghazi was referenced in Brandon Webb and Jack Murphy, *Benghazi: The Definitive Report* (New York: HarperCollins, 2013).
3. Harald Doornbos and Jenan Moussa, "Troubling Surveillance Before Benghazi Attack," *Foreign Policy*, November 1, 2012.

23: THE LOOTERS

1. Interview, Dr. T., March 23, 2013.
2. Interview, February 28, 2013.

24: THE TERMINAL

1. Interview, March 16, 2013.
2. Interview, February 28, 2013.

25: BENGHAZI MEDICAL CENTER

1. Interview, March 18, 2013.
2. Ibid.
3. Ibid.; and Ethan Chorin, "What Libya Lost," *The New York Times*, September 13, 2012.
4. Interview, March 23, 2013.

26: INCOMING

1. Charles Woods, interview, January 15, 2013.
2. Clint Bruce, interview, January 16, 2013.
3. Interview, March 30, 2013.

27: AFTERMATH

1. Interview, March 28, 2013.
2. Chris Stephens, "Inside the US Consulate in Benghazi: Material and Human Damage Laid Bare," *Guardian*, September 13, 2012.
3. From "What We Found in Benghazi," photographs were taken by Jenan Moussa of Dubai's Al-Aan TV and the freelance journalist Harald Doornbos at the U.S. consulate in Benghazi, Libya, for their article "Troubling Surveillance Before Benghazi Attack."
4. Hoda Abdel-Hamid, interview, February 28, 2013.

EPILOGUE

1. "Libya Closes Benghazi Air Space Temporarily," *Anti-Islam Video Protests Live Blog*, Al Jazeera, September 14, 2012.
2. AFP Khartoum, "U.S. Embassy in Khartoum to Re-open After Six-Month Closure," March 24, 2013.
3. "U.S. Embassy Attack in Khartoum: Sudan Rejects Marine Deployment Request," *The Huffington Post*, September 15, 2012.
4. Charles Woods, interview, January 15, 2013.
5. Ibid.
6. White House release, September 14, 2012.
7. Ibid.
8. Woods interview.

Index